ABOUT THE

Debbie Seunarayan is the founder of Gallus C̲ _ _ng Ltd, a socially minded enterprise committed to helping organisations take strategy to reality. Building on 20 years of experience in industry across a variety of sectors, Debbie has spent the last decade consulting with organisations across the world facing disruptive change or fast growth. Her most recent work has focused on helping organisations and their leaders to navigate a volatile present while preparing for an unpredictable future.

Debbie has long held a deep interest in how the past, present and future collide. She is a vociferous reader and meditates upon how concepts from ancient spiritual schools of thought and discoveries of modern science contradict and confirm one another's hypotheses and combine and interact to bring about new insights. A hunger for learning, a great love of books and an insatiable curiosity about the future has led her to writing speculative fiction in her spare time.

Debbie's Mum has vascular dementia. Her Mum's experiences throughout the diagnostic process and beyond (along with the experiences of her Dad as main carer) have driven her to focus on this condition and the medical and social support systems that surround it. Debbie considers this to be one of the wicked problems of our time and it's a cause she cares deeply about. She is in the process of setting up a wicked tribe – *The Big D* – in an effort to raise awareness and understanding. The idea is to work towards providing people diagnosed with dementia, their carers and their families with clearer pathways, guidance and support as they navigate through a complex and largely underfunded system. Her aim is to 'connect the dots' that are presently scattered far and wide.

Debbie lives in the Midlands, England, with her husband, daughter and two dogs.

Some play the game while others change the game

SHAPESHIFTER

HOW TO MASTER THE ART OF WORKING WITH
THE FUTURE AND MAKE YOUR STRATEGY
REALITY IN A CHAOTIC WORLD

DEBBIE SEUNARAYAN

ISBN 978-1-9161190-1-7

British Library Cataloguing in Publication Data.
A catalogue record for this book is available from the British Library.

Typeset in the United Kingdom by Indie-Go
https://www.indie-go.co.uk

CONTENTS

PART 1
MOVE ONE: SUPPLE STRATEGY

PART 2
MOVE TWO: BUILD A META-TRIBE

THE POST-TRUTH FAST SHOW

No, you're not imagining it. The world has changed, and it's changed fast. Moreover, it's still changing, faster than ever. A lot has happened in just one generation…

We only have to look back across the last 30 years to find a number of seismic shifts to the world order that created risk and provided opportunity in equal measure. Shifts of this magnitude create chain reactions of volatile and unpredictable change. For example, the fall of the Berlin Wall in November 1989 led to the reunification of Germany. The chaotic transition that ensued significantly altered the rules of the game across much of Europe. The wall falling played no small part in the subsequent dissolution of the Soviet Union in December 1991, the end of the Cold War and the opening of Eastern European markets. Chinese economic reform had already started but it accelerated in the nineties with the privatisation of state-owned industry and exponential growth of the private sector. China now boasts a fast-growing middle class, a lofty rate of consumption and is predicted to dethrone the US as the world's largest retail market imminently. Now, it seems that the East is where it's at for business – could this reasonably have been perceived in 1990? We'll never know, of course, but with hindsight the patterns are clear to see – it looks like an obvious progression.

In 1990, upon leaving school you either went to university or, more likely, you joined a trade as an apprentice alongside a college education, or you entered an organisation with a well-structured career path. The probability was that you would remain in your chosen trade or career (and probably the same organisation) for most of your life. National Insurance contributions went towards the provision of a pension in later years. And, in more established organisations, you were automatically enrolled into a final salary pension scheme. This guaranteed you a lump sum and a regular income based on your salary level at retirement, typically following 40 years of service. The expectation and promise of a 'job for life' was alive and kicking. In theory, many people were confident of receiving some form of regular income for the majority of their time on this planet.

Economies and markets, while connected, were nothing like as intertwined as they are today. Supply chains obviously existed but were slower and simpler. There were, of course, always cycles of economic growth and recession – boom and bust still existed – but the speed of oscillation between highs and lows was slower and more predictable (or at least that's how it seemed). And politicians, in the most part, at least appeared to be capable and fully committed to serving their constituents and country.

People worked fewer hours, jobs were more defined, commutes were shorter, relationships were deeper and… everything took longer. There was no email, no Internet, no smartphones. It was a time when the landline phone was the only means of remote contact, physical books were the main source of reference and you would need to visit a library to perform research of any depth.

The world we now live in is fast, connected and dynamic. Complexity, information and speed are the order of the day. There are few 'jobs for life' and the frazzled masses crave income stability and growth while navigating their portfolio careers. We're in the age of the smartphone, live news and reality TV. Social media has turned the world on its head. Key 'influencers' (a recent concept) now have the platform through which they can reach millions at the push of a button (or two). They have a mouthpiece to change the world for bad or good – a powerful mechanism to promote ideas, drive behaviour, spark sensations and facilitate fads at the speed of light. Ideas ignite or fade into obscurity faster than they ever did before.

We are in the information age for sure – there is lots of it and no reliable means to check its validity. Opinions and speculation are now often presented as fact by well-established and once respected news outlets. Story hijacking, news spinning and alternative facts are firmly in the driving seat.

Supply chains are complex and global, and economies are interconnected and reactive. Economies swirl and veer and dip and climb like vertiginous rollercoasters. Boom-and-bust cycles are ever faster and omnipresent. Currency fluctuations no longer seem to follow the rules of old – currencies dip or rise without obvious major cause and yet seem unruffled by the frequent harbingers of imminent economic collapse.

Technology advances at a blistering rate and what was 'the new thing' only yesterday, is suddenly obsolete today. Artificial intelligence, augmented reality and digitalisation are already upon us while our economic models, legal frameworks and political structures seem stuck in a twentieth century time warp. Politics is now a career rather than a calling. Short-termism trumps long-term thinking and the rules-based world order seems to be facing its shakiest decade in recent living memory.

People are constantly connected to more information than they could ever sensibly consume, let alone interpret. Caffeine and adrenaline power the decisions of boardrooms as they engage in the daily 'tough mother' event that is running an organisation today. Apparently innocuous actions and decisions set off chain reactions that change the course of history across the globe, causing major ramifications from tiny seeds at significant distances in space and time.

There's much talk of clean energy, calls to 'save the bees!', encouragement of recycling and yet no genuine global engagement with the issue beyond slogans, unenforceable emissions targets and uncoordinated subsidies. Despite indisputable evidence of man-made climate change, we collectively bury our heads in the sand and continue to burn fossil fuels like there's no tomorrow – if we carry on there might not be!

We're avoiding our biggest and most complex problems, paying them lip service and hoping they'll quietly and miraculously go away or at least won't cause a catastrophe on our watch.

We immortalise the status quo, but one look at the past tells us that the world can and has changed on a sixpence on many occasions, and with little clear advance warning (though with the benefit of hindsight the warnings are always pretty clear to see). Countries that were enemies are now allies and vice versa. Once 'developing' economies are thriving and previously world-leading economies are floundering. And there's more to come.

We live in a 'VUCA' world – a world of volatility, uncertainty, complexity and ambiguity.[1] A turbulent, unpredictable world where established models fail fast and novel ideas emerge victorious. We have entered a post-truth era of alternative facts, unreliable data and unpredictable futures.

The process of making meaningful strategic choices and creating a new reality over time has changed. If it hasn't changed it needs to, and fast!

It's tempting to look back with rose-tinted glasses to a simpler less chaotic time. But the truth is, it's always been like this. The truth is, change has always been the way. The truth is, we can't uninvent what's been invented, and nor should we want to. The truth is, we need to embrace the madness, become a match for the era and create our own truth! And to do that we need to change the way we consume, analyse and utilise information. We need to change our individual and organisational thought patterns. We need to focus on the future and prioritise the critical. We need to devote proper space and time to strategic problem-solving. We must create space for serendipity.

Unless we ask the right searching questions 20 to 30 years ahead of time, we're unlikely to spot the next potentially seismic shifts in the world order and therefore global markets.

ASK YOURSELF...

- What external changes are causing problems for or providing obvious opportunities for your organisation right now?
- Which big and/or complex problems is your organisation confronting?
- Which big and/or complex problems is your organisation avoiding?
- How is the post-truth fast show affecting your organisation and the world around it?

WHY I WROTE THIS BOOK

The future has always fascinated me. For as long as I can remember I've wondered what might be heading towards us on the superhighway of future time. I've daydreamed about what might suddenly join or leave the carriageway, or what might unexpectedly enter the lane ahead. And I've marvelled at how we unsuspectingly career towards the unknown, every single day of our lives. It's a constant gnawing disappointment to me that we haven't yet mastered time travel!

It won't therefore surprise you to find that I'm a bit of a sci-fi geek. Given that we can't yet physically visit the future, I like to give my imagination a good long stretch, a bit of a workout, and jump inside the minds of others to do the next best thing. I devour films and literature where future worlds or alternative timelines are the central themes and I relish any opportunity to imagine how things might be or might have been.

One of my favourite sci-fi romps is *The Futurological Congress* written by Stanislaw Lem in 1971 (the year I was born incidentally).[2] In Lem's book, a cosmonaut, Ijon Tichy, has been sent back to earth to attend the Eighth World Futurological Congress. The event is a gathering of scientists all focused on finding solutions to the world's overpopulation crisis. The congress turns out to be quite an experience; its absurdity only amplified by the consumption of hallucinogenic contaminated tap water. It transpires that the government of the time has used the water supply to deliver 'benignimizers' to its people – a drug that makes people helplessly benign and benevolent. Events spiral out of control and, after a time, our hero suspects he may be 'no longer safely inside the illusion but shipwrecked in reality'. This phrase and the concept of benignimizers haunt me every time I enter into dialogue with a leadership team.

For more years than I care to remember I've been privileged to work with many organisations (large and small, new and established, global and local) and their leadership teams in an effort to take their strategy to reality. We've 'consciously coupled' and collaborated hard to enhance strategic dialogue, identify strategic options and map paths towards successful future realities. Every one of these organisations has something in common – disruptive change. They are either experiencing it or causing it, and they are striving for survival or growth to create a brave new world. Every time (no matter how it's first described), when the gloves are off, it's a need or want for serious change that gets us talking.

Some of these organisations have struggled. The ones that suffer most are riddled with assumptions – the biggest being the perceived desired destination. There's an embedded reticence to unearth truths and examine beliefs, coupled with a bad case of inertia. They've succumbed to the beguiling benignimizers. Others have been wildly successful in their quest – unicorn[3] births, successful IPOs[4] and saved giants are amongst them (more about that later). Over time I've learned that there are patterns of thinking and behaviour that determine success or failure at a very early stage. Noticing and analysing these patterns has led me to change the way I work and to develop an approach that can guide more organisations towards a successful future. There's a pattern to everything – you've just got to work out what it is.

Nowadays, when working with organisations, I focus on four moves that I've learned make *the* difference to organisational success in such a complex, unpredictable and ever-changing world:

1   I use scenario planning to help organisations see around corners to spot emerging opportunities and dodge potential meteors (Part 1).
2   I work with organisations to build a meta-tribe that will enable them to transcend existing historic tribes (Part 2).
3   I partner with organisations to identify, demystify and make progress on the wicked problems that seem too big or too difficult to solve (Part 3).
4   And I help organisations to better align and amplify the power of collective intelligence in support of a cause through the creation and animation of a magical movement (Part 4).

Working directly with organisations and leadership teams is great, but not all organisations can afford support of that kind and there are only so many people I can work directly with at any one time. I've written this book so that many more people and organisations can have the best chance of making the right journey, at the right time, with the right people, in the right way.

HOW TO USE THIS BOOK

This book isn't about disaster planning (although the ideas within may help you to do that more effectively). This book is about noticing patterns and seeing around corners. It's about making plans to be in the right place at the right time and, perhaps more importantly, to have some idea of what the hell to do if you happen to get there. This book will help you to work out if it might be prudent to change direction, why you may benefit from having a broader range of options at your disposal, where it might be good to head for, how to potentially get there, and how to get a whole load of people to jump on board to help you with whatever journey you decide to make.

Lao Tzu (the great Chinese philosopher and author of the *Tao Te Ching*) said, 'if you do not change direction, you may end up where you are heading'.[5] It's worth thinking about that for a moment. Most organisations spend quite a lot of time and effort working out how to get where they want to go, but only a few consider if they actually still want to go there.

Do you know where you are heading? And, if you do, are you sure it's the best option? Is it an option that will even exist in an unpredictable future? To significantly up our odds of success we must quit the benignimizers cold turkey! We must open minds, challenge assumptions, deal with obstacles and galvanise people in numbers. Dare I say it – we must politely revolt, with a purpose and lots of good questions.

Let's face it, the world is chaotic. We like to think there's an order to things, and for a time sometimes there is, but largely it's chaos. Success may be down to luck, but our ability to take advantage of any luck is predominantly determined by our approach towards the chaos we experience around us. The choices we make and the behaviours we demonstrate play a major part in our success or otherwise. Chaos can generate unprecedented risk but it can also present us with immeasurable opportunities, should we choose to engage with them.

This book will provide you with alternative ways to engage with the future, navigate the post-truth fast show, and tackle the problems that you encounter on your journey. The questions dotted throughout the text are there to get you thinking about how your organisation might benefit from some of the ideas within.

The majority of the book is devoted to the four moves that shapeshifter organisations use to take their strategy to reality. For each of these moves I outline how shapeshifter organisations do things differently and the steps your organisation can take, right now, to improve its odds of remaining successful and relevant. These sections are written in such a way that you can choose to read them in order or you can immediately dip into the move that seems to be highest priority for your organisation right now.

Each of the moves contains a maturity model. You can use the maturity models as a map for your journey should you wish to travel the path of a shapeshifter. When setting out on a journey it always pays to know where our starting point is, where we're heading and whether there may be some places to rest along the way. Moving towards becoming a shapeshifter organisation and embedding the required new habits and behaviours is no exception. Organisations have identities and personalities that have built up over time and around the heroes that walk their corridors and the legends that dominate water cooler conversations. While you may wish to reinvent yourself, it's clearly better (and safer) to do so in a sustainable way that allows you to carry on with the important business of the present as you adjust and evolve. Revolution may seem exciting (and sometimes may be called for), but typically a process of evolution accelerated by targeted shifts in organisational perception and behaviour is more rewarding and fruitful.

For each of the four moves I have found that organisations generally evolve along a spectrum of approaches that can be organised into five broad stages. While the typical gradual direction of travel is towards Stage 5 (Shapeshifter), many organisations never reach this level of complex networked thinking. A sudden change in the fortunes of an organisation may cause it to evolve suddenly or to slip back to an earlier, more primitive form. Indeed, in some circumstances it may be prudent to do so for a while.

The spectrum and stages used within the maturity models are a simplification of a complex subject; in reality, organisations rarely neatly fit into one stage across all elements and may have one foot in a previous stage and another foot in a more evolved stage while straddling another. The maturity models are purely a tool through which we can take a shared view of the organisation and start a genuinely open conversation about the quality and impact of current approaches. The stages provide milestones for development that can underpin a progressive evolution.

The five evolutionary stages within each maturity model are:

1 Reactive
2 Focused
3 Structured
4 Integrated
5 Shapeshifter

Each stage has a range of markers that signal a certain level of sophistication has been habitually achieved. To work out whereabouts an organisation spends most of its time (within which stage it generally resides) we focus on 10 elements (which are different for each of the four moves). Use these maturity models to reflect upon where your organisation has developed good and bad habits and how you might create greatest value through subtle changes in approach.

Sometimes it can be helpful to learn from those who have trodden a path ahead of you. Each move therefore also contains an examination of a shapeshifter in action – a case study of an organisation that is already exploring and demonstrating many elements of what it takes to be a shapeshifter. These organisations are not perfect (none are), but they are committed to their journey. Crucially, they are brutally honest with themselves and open to learning and adjusting as they travel. They are consciously altering the way they engage with the future and as such have already enjoyed greater alignment, innovation and success.

Whether you're the CEO of a large global organisation, the founder of a new venture seeking funding, a functional leader who wants to make the most of potential development in their field, a specialist in Organisational Development tasked with the cultural evolution of your organisation, a strategy consultant facilitating your organisation's annual planning cycle, a member of the executive leadership team or an aspiring leader, or simply someone with a great idea that might change the world or a powerful cause that you care deeply about, this book is for you – all of you!

My aim is to help you and your organisation think, debate, influence and collaborate differently to make for a better future. A better future for you, your organisation and the world in general (yes, I know that's a big ask). Let's go on a journey from strategy to reality together. Are you ready? Buckle up – the world needs you and so does your organisation!

CHAPTER 1

THE STRATEGY APOCALYPSE

When I started writing this book I wanted to make sure that I focused on the issues as they exist, not purely as I perceive them. From my experience working with organisations and leaders over the years, it would be easy to assume that I have a relatively good idea of their typical major challenges and how existing practice might amplify them rather than diffuse them. I wanted to be absolutely sure that my experiences were not just an anomaly, and also unearth any further valuable insights. To test my hypotheses, I contacted a whole range of people, in various roles, at differing levels of seniority, in a wide variety of organisations, to ask them what they consider to be the biggest strategic challenges they face and how their existing strategic planning processes help or hinder them in dealing with these effectively.

Their feedback was affirming and illuminating. There were obvious similarities in experience which demonstrated clear trends in the challenges faced, regardless of industry or life cycle stage of the organisation in question. And there was clear evidence of shared frustration regarding existing practice and its ability to respond to the demands of the 21st century. Here are the 10 strategic challenges that were mentioned the most:

1   Maintaining financial performance and delivery of value to shareholders, demonstrated by the unrelenting consistent achievement of short- to medium-term financial objectives.

2   Achieving growth and entering new markets organically or via acquisition.
3   Divesting unprofitable or unpopular elements of the portfolio and those that are not in line with future strategy.
4   Responding to advances in technology and delivering technological transformation at a pace to ensure future competitiveness within agreed budget parameters.
5   Reacting to changes in geopolitical and regulatory environments relevant to the organisation appropriately and in good time, and adequately preparing for potential future changes.
6   Prioritising effectively and efficiently, making courageous decisions to explore new ideas, develop new products and services, and stop activities that are superfluous or that dilute effort.
7   Developing capability and finding the right people and technologies to enable the organisation to deliver.
8   Embedding autonomous decision-making capabilities throughout the organisation by establishing devolved leadership and activating informal networks.
9   Cascading strategic ambitions and choices – getting people to believe in, engage with and deliver upon the strategic plan.
10 Examining the fundamental business model to ensure it is fit for the future and can continue to deliver results.

These are 10 big asks; big responsibilities to deliver and big questions to ponder. And, without exception, everyone I spoke to felt that their existing strategic planning process was, at least in part, failing them in this endeavour. In fact, the final strategic challenge – the examination of the fundamental business model – was rarely, if ever, seriously embarked upon.

This is no real surprise when we take a long hard look at typical strategic planning processes in the cold light of day. If we detach ourselves from the allure of 'best practice' and interrogate genuine impact, we find that organisations are relying on strategic planning processes that are better suited to (and probably first designed for) a twentieth-century (slower) change cycle as opposed to the post-truth fast show in which we now find ourselves.

So, how are we inadvertently shooting ourselves in the foot? What is it that we unconsciously do or neglect to cause ourselves future pain?

What unhealthy habits and associations have we formed? Let's meet the 12 horsemen of the strategic apocalypse...

RIDER 1: BUDGET EATS STRATEGY FOR BREAKFAST

There's a great deal of truth in the phrase 'culture eats strategy for breakfast'. Unfortunately, many organisations never truly get to find out as their budget has already dined out on strategy and cannibalised it from the inside out – like an Ichneumon wasp devours its caterpillar host (who is initially blissfully unaware of its inevitable future demise) – long before culture has a chance to do so.[6]

Organisations tend to run their strategic planning process alongside and intertwined with their annual budgetary process. On the face of it, this makes perfect sense – there's a clear logical fit, and a combined process demands less management resource. The coupling of strategy and budget into a step-by-step process demands an outline of strategy by each function or business unit and the objective identification of outcomes and decisions deemed to be strategically significant to each. Key performance indicators (KPIs) are identified to demonstrate the success, or otherwise, of the organisation in pursuit of its accepted strategic agenda. This process is complex, convoluted and takes hideous amounts of time.

Despite being the prevalent model of the day, this lockstep arrangement has significant downsides. The timeline is usually tightly controlled (by shareholder demands and market sensitivities), the process has regulatory implications (and financial reporting requirements) and, as a result, any form of lengthy dialogue that unearths assumptions beyond the immediately obvious tends to falter. In this typical scenario, it becomes inevitable that the agreement of an annual budget takes priority.

Let's take a moment to make sure we understand what a budget is. The Oxford English Dictionary defines budget as: 'the amount of money needed or available', and budgeting as 'allowing for or arranging for in a budget'. In both of these definitions there's an elusive entity – the actual thing the budget or budgeting is in service of. We've got it the wrong way around! The elusive entity should be guiding the budget, not vice versa (although, granted, there may be occasions where the elusive entity is constrained by the budget available, but that's a slightly different matter). At the very least they should be equal partners. A budgeting exercise should be focused on how to best make use of resources in service of the chosen strategy.

A budget is typically discussed and analysed using historical data, statistical modelling and projections based on numerous assumptions. The resulting budget is often heavily steered by the proclivities of the most senior person in the room. While this approach may be appropriate for the agreement of an annual budget, it has the effect of stifling curiosity, challenge and the genuine examination of future direction to any useful depth. Strategic discussion is limited to a cursory examination of the ability of the organisation to deliver the required numbers while travelling in the general direction established by the strategic plan as previously set. While initially this has a limited negative effect, over time the strategic plan becomes dated, diluted by a bevy of small alterations (each on their own potentially insignificant but, once combined, creating tendrils of distraction and confusion).

Antidote: strategy must be front and centre!

RIDER 2: EVER-DECREASING CIRCLES

In his bestselling book *Intuition Pumps and Other Tools for Thinking* Daniel C Dennett reminds us that thinking is hard.[7] He introduces us to a range of approaches to support independent thinking and creativity. When we're fully conscious of our role in collaborative thinking we reach out for tools and techniques that help us to think more clearly, evaluate information more effectively and arrive at sounder decisions. However, when we're overwhelmed by deliverables and short on time we tend to seek out our typical data sources, exercise habitual thinking patterns and rely on unsound heuristics (decision-making mental shortcuts) when making decisions.[8]

The decisions of boards and senior leadership teams are only as good as the quality of their thinking and the robustness of the information that forms its foundation. Ultimately, garbage in equals garbage out. Information required may relate to financial results, market analysis, client experience, employee opinion and many other areas. When appropriately used, it can amplify the ability of an organisation to effectively consider the options available to it and arrive at a plan for the future. However, there's a huge amount of data out there and not all data is useful or data sources reliable.

Many organisations use the services of analysts (market analysts, portfolio analysts, investment analysts) to support their thinking and planning endeavours. While this is helpful, it's easy to forget that these too are faced with an overwhelming volume of information and have probably also developed habitual routes to simplify their data feeds. So how do we know that the data and information we're relying on is genuine, accurate, representative and up to date? How can we tell if the analyst in question is at the top of their game and competently across the entirety of their specialism? How do we ensure that where specialisms collide, data is re-evaluated in light of the impact of the holistic context? How do we make sure we're not running in ever-decreasing circles towards the centre of an echo chamber that largely supports our initial assumptions (as psychological research suggests we might)?

The problem with data is that it's historic. Where data is analysed and manipulated to represent the future, it is purely an extrapolation of existing information. Modelling historic data to represent the future is inevitably based on existing paradigms and cannot typically conceive or adequately represent any potential seismic shift therein. Where such a shift is evident it is due to the interpretation of patterns based on the modeller's own perception of reality or statistical manipulation – the modeller could be very right or very wrong, and we all know what's said about statistics.

Cries of 'show me the evidence to support your thinking' fall on deaf ears or produce meaningless data manipulations that cannot reliably predict a future outcome. Data is flawed, but we use it to assuage our fear of gut reaction and impulse-driven decision-making. In many cases intuition drives the selection of data used and therefore has a greater ultimate impact on the choices we make than we might at first realise.

There's reassurance in logical data, but also potential treachery. If we want to think about the far-future this approach is woefully inadequate – we cannot predict the future (and neither can the data). Let's face it, if we could, you wouldn't be reading this book!

Antidote: consciously seek diverse data and information that challenges embedded assumptions and ingrained thinking patterns!

RIDER 3: LIFE'S TOO SHORT TO THINK ABOUT THE FUTURE

We've already established that life is fast and is getting faster. Constantly connected, it's increasingly difficult to prioritise the genuinely urgent and give proper focus to critically important activities, decisions and conversations. As a result, looming deadlines harry us into dealing with the immediately urgent more often that we care to admit (and, more often than not, we react to what others consider to be urgent rather than performing our own informed appraisal). The critically important gets placed on a mental shelf – out of sight out of mind – until it too becomes an imminent crisis that requires our urgent attention.

Business advisors of all persuasions always promote the importance of 'working on the business' rather than 'working in the business', but when you're busy fighting fires this gets difficult. Getting things done, winning new clients, delivering results, making more, and doing things faster, all seem more important. But what if we're getting the wrong things done, trying to win the wrong type of clients and missing the right ones, delivering unimportant or, worse, damaging results, or making the wrong things? What if we're following the wrong strategy?

Taking time out to think deeply, challenge assumptions and connect with those around us is considered a luxury. Luring a team of leaders away from a complex organisation operating in a challenging trading environment to decompress from the present and immerse themselves in a future they can only imagine is hard! I've lost count of the number of times I've been asked to facilitate a scenarios exercise in a day, or worse half a day (I won't do it – it cannot be done – don't believe anyone that says it can!).

The time to talk about the future never comes until the future is upon us as the present. Its inherent opportunities and threats are not examined until their potential implications are already taking hold. Again, we end up in a state of urgency – responding to events, if we still can. The self-sustaining short-term cycle starts again… until the future delivers a devastating blow that is beyond survival.

Antidote: thinking beyond a current crisis is a core survival skill!

RIDER 4: IS THAT YOUR EGO TALKING?

Strategy has developed a pompous aura. It is high-status, high-brow thinking and it's reserved for the few who are considered truly deserving of partaking in it – the 'landed gentry', the 'old money', of the corporate world. Those historically involved in strategy development are held in awe, and the manufactured barriers to entry are many and grand. Strategy is hallowed ground. It is the established domain of the board, the executive leadership team and perhaps a small number of venerable senior advisors. Others have but a supporting role, if they're lucky. To be invited to contribute to strategic dialogue is to have 'arrived'. High-potential future leaders are enticed on to leadership development pathways with the promise of board exposure and inclusion in strategic activities.

Where an analysis of existing operations is required, it is very rare that those who are involved in the everyday running of the organisation are asked for their informed opinion. More often, a team of tight-lipped external experts are ushered in to observe, investigate and unsettle!

Choices are made behind closed doors and any suggestions from 'the floor' face burdensome layers of analysis and approval. Strategic dialogue and related decisions are the domain of the board – those in the broader organisation are deemed to be beneath it and only able to cope with the operational. This approach only serves to entrench the typical inability of an organisation to make decisions quickly, where and when they need to be made, and by a person best placed to make them. Decentralised decision-making is a major casualty of ego-driven strategy formulation.

Consideration of the deep future, where it happens, is limited to a smaller group still – a gathering of the most senior people and their most trusted advisors, typically a very experienced group of people with limited diversity in age, background, values or perspective. The underlying human need to be right drives two extremes: hesitation and the avoidance of doubt and risk, or impulsivity, complacency and arrogance. Diversity of thinking has the power to generate strategies that are more likely to be successful over time. Neurodiversity, and differences in cultural and generational mindset, are powerful catalysts for change, challenging assumptions, identifying repeating patterns and seeking potential disruptive moves.[9]

The Oxford English Dictionary defines strategy as 'a plan of action or policy in business or politics' – don't we all engage in this kind of activity at some level every day? Granted, there is some clever stuff in strategy and some complex analysis required, but facilitated in an inclusive manner and given the right data sources, surely a broader church can be mustered to good effect. Strategic thinking suffers from closed loops, closed minds, and closed shops.

Antidote: diverse thinking, inclusive dialogue and open minds!

RIDER 5: NEED-TO-KNOW BASIS

Typical planning processes deprioritise the far-future, and elevate true blue-sky thinking and strategic dialogue to be the concerns of a chosen few. The masses, if they can still be bothered or have the time to spare, watch from a distance piecing together what they think they know. Speculation mounts as clandestine meetings, 'war rooms' and bizarre requests for copious data provide fuel for the fire. Leaks confirm or deny circulating hypotheses and seed new predictions and conspiracy theories. People are distracted from their day-to-day activity and start to catastrophise, dramatise or trivialise. Cynicism or anxiety set in and impatience grows with a leadership that seems wholly disconnected from reality.

Humans are natural storytellers and use stories to make sense of situations, events and people. We don't take well to operating in a vacuum of information – our natural reaction is to fill it. Where communication is scant, we will collectively craft a story – the story that allows us to make sense of the world, take action and make decisions.

Once the secretive activities have been concluded by the shadowy figures behind a curtain of intrigue, strategic proclamations are made from on high. The people at the back of the room (at the end of the communication chain) can't hear due to the vociferous whispering amongst their colleagues. The vacuum has already been filled with a story – perhaps the right story, perhaps the wrong story, possibly somewhere in between, but most certainly not the story that will drive the movement you are hoping for or told in a way that will galvanise a tribe. The damage is already done, but that won't be obvious until it's far too late.

There are, of course, times when an organisation needs to be discreet. An acquisition or merger is a complex negotiation and may be subject to market regulations. A groundbreaking new product may be embargoed until launch day. High-profile joiners and leavers may be kept under wraps. Organisations sometimes have to keep things quiet, but this is less often than we care to admit – sometimes the 'need-to-know' approach is an echo of earlier times, where hierarchy and seniority held the authority on thinking.

Antidote: authentic storytelling is good; transparency is even better!

RIDER 6: WE DON'T DO THAT HERE

I can distinctly remember the gradual feeling of despondency I would experience every time I spoke with one of my senior managers way back in the mists of my early career. The disillusionment grew deeper and stronger roots over time and gnawed away at my creativity. Every posited idea was met with 'We don't do it like that' or 'We've tried that before.' Every challenge voiced received an equally banal 'That's just the way it is' or 'This organisation is special/different', or something just as disheartening. Believe me when I say I was behaving well – it was early days and I had yet to find my internal agitator. I raised ideas and challenges politely in one-to-one conversation and, given the consistent reaction over time, eventually I just stopped. I wonder how many others also stopped, how many others also felt disheartened and surrendered their creative energies on the altar of the status quo. How many succumbed to good behaviour over creativity and impact. My ideas may have turned out to be impractical, impossible to implement or counterproductive, but theirs may not have.

Recent years have seen a positive movement to embrace diversity, challenge exclusion and encourage inclusion, but it is yet to genuinely reach the strategic planning processes in many organisations. Mavericks and rebels are generally frowned upon unless and until their results elevate them to hero status, at which point they can do no wrong; that, or they are discredited and removed – there is little middle ground.

It's true that there are some troublemakers out there who just want to cause some excitement and rabble-rouse in opposition to any 'powers that be', but often voices of dissent or revolutionary ideas have a kernel of truth in them – a kernel of truth that a leadership team is foolish not to listen to or examine in greater depth. Not doing so causes innovative ideas, new paradigms and avoidable risks to be ignored, dismissed or concealed within a thin skin of hierarchical order. Creativity becomes overwhelmed by the unconscious enforcement of the status quo and rigorous application of bureaucratic constraints.

Wisdom often lies within an organisation in the most unexpected places. Radical reform can be hidden just out of sight around an unforeseen corner. Change catalysts may be waiting patiently to find their moment and a deserving cause. In the main, organisations do their utmost to suppress, constrain and counter-attack any signs of deviance, even when it may be entirely positive.

Kodak is a perfect example of just how badly this approach can work out. Steven Sasson was a Kodak engineer who invented the technology required for digital photography in 1975. He was what we might call a pioneer, an innovator, a positive deviant. At first, Kodak didn't consider the technology to be a potential disrupter. Digital photography was not something it expected to become reality any time soon, let alone normality. 'That's cute, but don't tell anyone about it' is how Sasson once described the reaction he received from management. Even once Kodak had woken up to the realisation that digital photography had the potential to fundamentally change the market within which they operated, they woefully underestimated how quickly this could happen and did little to prepare for the seismic shift. Kodak failed to adapt due to a lack of holistic vision and the assumption that the future would remain largely like the present. The result: Kodak started to experience financial difficulties in the nineties and eventually filed for bankruptcy in 2012. They had the answer in their hands all along, but didn't expect the question to be asked. The moral – ignore creative ideas and positive deviance at your own risk!

Antidote: think beyond the here and now and search out positive deviance (or at least avoid stamping on it!).

RIDER 7: INDIGESTION

As organisations grow it's not unusual for the culture within to change and for values to evolve. Anything that grows and matures doesn't remain the same – that's the very nature of growth. Cultural change happens even when an organisation grows organically. This comes about through an increase in the number of people, the shifting demographics represented throughout its ranks, any expansion into new markets, the influence of the clients it serves and the evolving drivers and demands of its investors.

Growth is not always achieved through purely organic means and this further complicates the picture. To reach a new market or to acquire extended capabilities often requires a strategic acquisition or merger to take place. Despite targeted acquisitions and potential mergers often being cited in strategic documentation as a likely future route to success, often the activation of such deals is quite opportunistic. Timing is determined by the availability of funds, resources and a likely suitable prospect. It's rare that a regimented programme of integrations happens as stated in a strategic plan. It's even rarer that, when they do happen, they go to plan.

Time stands still for no one. Despite the distraction and additional workload caused by any acquisition, life goes on: products are manufactured, clients served, financial objectives strived for – the ship must be kept afloat while it is rebuilt. The impact, complexity and effort involved are usually grossly underestimated and a substantial period of navel-gazing, empire building, process re-engineering and technological integration typically ensues.

In the most ambitious of organisations all this is taking place while another acquisition is being eyed up, perhaps bigger than the first (this one will be 'make or break'). But the organisation still has indigestion from the first. While heads on the bridge are turned to thoughts of their next conquest, world domination and shiny new things, deep below in the engine rooms the furnaces are running too hot, maintenance is deprioritised, machinery is in danger of failing and people are arguing about how best to keep the ship afloat. They don't yet understand one another's languages and customs, have little awareness of true engine capacity at full throttle or what fuel is left in the tank, let alone which direction they should all be heading in. The ability of the ship to reach its destination is in their hands and yet they are at odds with one another, each believing their way is the right way – the true path to success.

Quickly the organisation loses focus on the outside world and the acquisition that was supposed to herald a golden age is the beginning of the end. Two tribes are not yet aligned and, in worse-case scenarios, are firmly at war. Making time for proper cultural integration and the development of shared values feels like a luxury when handling such pressures but, when neglected, warring factions become agents of ruin.

**Antidote: collectively look up and look out,
and be sure not to look down for too long!**

RIDER 8: YERTLE THE TURTLE SYNDROME

When my daughter was little she was an avid fan of Dr Seuss (and so was I).[10] We chuckled and giggled as I read *Fox in Socks* as fast as I possibly could, and she would then try to do the same – it became quite a competitive bedtime routine for a while. Reading was great fun with Dr Seuss, but there was some serious learning too. Every book was a powerful metaphor for an important life lesson or moral value. *Green Eggs and Ham* encouraged us to try new things and not to prejudge them until we had done so; *The Sneetches* taught us to be happy and confident with who we are, to be inclusive regardless of our differences and not to fall prey to the latest fad; and *The Zax* demonstrated how intransigence and inertia take us nowhere very fast.

One of my favourites was (and still is) *Yertle the Turtle*. It's the tale of an ambitious king (Yertle) who sits atop an ever-growing tower of turtles. Yertle declares he is king of all that he can see and so he keeps adding turtles to the bottom of the tower so that he can survey and rule an ever-greater patch. Yertle is eventually toppled by the burp of a small turtle at the very bottom of the stack (Mack) who had been holding the weight of the entire tower and supporting everybody else above him with little acknowledgement, recognition or attention. Mack had been signalling his discomfort for some time, but nobody had listened to him and more turtles kept getting added on top of him regardless.

Organisations are complex creatures, but their interconnectedness results in a few Macks around the place. From their view at the top, leaders have the destination in sight but just out of reach. Just a bit further and they can grab it – it's that close. And so, a rallying cry is issued – greater output, higher quality, faster change… more, more, more! Meanwhile one or more of the organisation's Macks are fast crumbling under the pressure. If they have time to spare and the energy remaining they may well voice their concerns, but too often they're ignored or, worse, made out to be negative detractors – until, of course, it's too late. This is how cynicism sets in across organisations – it becomes more entrenched with every Mack that gets ignored or slandered.

The trouble is, from the view at the top, it's all too easy to forget the impact of decisions and actions upon those at the bottom – the people actually making things happen. Impatience, greed and speed gain traction and those who can't cope or won't oblige are considered inadequate or troublesome. The temptation is too great, and it becomes impossible for the leadership to choose between the possible trophies and treasures ahead of them. They prioritise everything and pursue them all, resulting in an ever-increasing burden of technical debt, change fatigue and faltering client and employee relations. A lack of robust prioritisation is the enemy of strategic success!

**Antidote: robust prioritisation and listening
hard to those who speak truth to power.**

RIDER 9: JUST DO IT!

Of course, there comes a point in any strategy where other people must become involved. You can't build Rome in a day – or alone! While those 'in the know' have had the benefit of an ongoing conversation that makes sense of the chosen direction and path selected, and various opportunities to scrutinise plans, many across the organisation have had nothing of the sort. They have not been invited to the strategic off-sites, haven't been party to the high-level programme planning and have contributed sporadically, when asked to, with disassociated budget projections, people plans and data reporting.

When you have been part of a process from the start and understand its intricate mechanisms, vague associations and interconnected outputs, it's easy to forget that others have not had the same experience and are not privy to the inbuilt understanding you have developed over time. Standing at the mouth of (what seems to them) an unlit tunnel receiving unintelligible instructions from a disassociated voice some miles down the track is not particularly enticing. All manner of perils may be waiting to greet them the moment they enter, and they have no comprehension of the wonderful future that you promise awaits them. You could be a fraud. You could be mistaken. Why on earth should they take the risk without a reason to enter, a picture of the promised land, a map of how to get there and some advice about how best to do so and the potential traps en route?

Impatience builds at the far end of the tunnel, while avoidance and regression are the response. Ambivalence towards the very people who will carry the change results in no change at all or, worse still, the wrong change. Telling people to 'just do it' is not a great approach!

Antidote: explain your thinking, share your why and co-create the how.

RIDER 10: SO WHAT?

This brings us to an important conclusion – if you allow strategic dialogue to remain the privilege of an elite group behind closed doors it just gets far harder to take strategy to reality. The 'So what?' question is very difficult to answer when most of the organisation have not been involved in the conversation.

Motivational speaker and author, Simon Sinek, encourages us to 'start with why', and it is good advice.[11] The often vapid statements of 'our mission' and 'our values' are heckled and ridiculed because they are vague and hold little depth or meaning to most of the people they are there to inspire. Collectively arriving at a clear vision – a mission if you like – and agreeing how you would like to behave and approach the achievement of that vision – perhaps the values you aspire to – is a worthwhile and potentially powerful exercise. But it's only worthwhile if you really mean it and believe in what it embodies. And it takes time and energy – well-spent time and energy I might add.

Without a reason 'why', the strategy is rudderless; it has no guiding principles that can steer it through choppy waters and may become stranded on the rocks with the destination just out of reach. 'Why' can't be an afterthought – it's often rather obvious when it has been. 'Why' mustn't be everything to everyone – that's pointless. 'Why' needs to be capable of framing strategy within the future identity and personality of the organisation. A strong and meaningful answer to the inevitable 'So what?'

A lack of time on meaning and little attention to how that meaning relates to available strategic choices might seem like something that can be corrected retrospectively. In reality, it dilutes belief, limits engagement and stifles energy. It stalls a movement.

Antidote: why comes first and it has to be real!

RIDER 11: NOTHING HAS CHANGED!

Watch a news channel for a short while on any given day and you'll probably see a politician be publicly vilified for a 'U-turn'. Any change of direction signals a lack of commitment or a deep camouflage for irresponsibility or dishonesty. So abhorrent is the U-turn that politicians and organisations alike will go to desperate lengths to deny they have performed one or are about to do so. Alternative facts are mustered to give the impression that this was the direction all along. Looking back at the campaign trail for the 2017 snap general election, many of us in the UK will remember the moment Theresa May awkwardly ingeminated 'nothing has changed' to throngs of baying reporters – it was not a particularly good look and was in all likelihood the moment her parliamentary majority was forfeited.[12]

While it's important to stick to your convictions and follow things through, there are times when a U-turn may not be such a poor idea. Sticking with something when you clearly should not is not only a recipe for eventual disaster, but will also cause you to lose credibility in the eyes of those observing. Performing a U-turn and then denying that it is one is equally nonsensical and embarrassing to watch.

Starting a difficult change journey takes courage, commitment and resilience. It's unhelpful to suggest that it may be the wrong path at the outset – that just encourages detractors to up their game early to cause a derailment. But a journey takes time and, over time, contexts change. How do you know that the path you originally plotted is in fact the right path, and that the destination you thought would be nirvana is not hell in disguise instead?

There are two perfectly valid situations where a U-turn (or a change in course) is not only understandable but is in fact the most sensible option:

1   The change journey you are undertaking is not delivering the outcomes you expected (after a suitable amount of time has passed).
2   The environment in which you operate has fundamentally changed and your strategic context has (or will) shift significantly as a result.

In each of these situations, to continue as before would be reckless. After adequate examination, you should be seriously considering a U-turn or at least some level of readjustment as an effective and sensible response.

We need reliable data and trusted feedback to reach a sound judgement. If we identify 'metrics that matter' at the very start of the change journey, we can continually examine the impact of our actions and decisions. 'Metrics that matter' should give us a constant view of the health of the organisation, our progress towards its goals and the state of our strategic environment. Internal metrics regarding performance, quality, engagement and client satisfaction can provide us with insight as to whether our strategy is taking us to where we want to be or moving us in the wrong direction. External data points and horizon scanning can provide us with leading indicators that may suggest our strategy is no longer appropriate. If we have engaged in scenario planning, we will also have 'path indicators' – a valuable reference point for the anticipation of the future context and the strategic choices it may call for so that we can switch paths with relative ease ('Paths? We only have one path!' I hear you cry).

Unfortunately, most organisations use their existing (often overcomplicated and inaccurate) system for managing that was perhaps developed a decade ago, never overhauled and only repeatedly added to since. Others have no feedback to speak of and rely on gut feel and intuition alone. Neither of these approaches is satisfactory. The preparatory work of identifying a dashboard of metrics and indicators that tells you something genuinely useful and relevant – that really matters and clearly links to the outcomes you seek – is critical.

A set of well-defined metrics and regular interpretation of these by a broad group will provide you with an ongoing satnav for strategic success. It also provides you with the rationale should you ever need to perform a route correction or the abhorrent U-turn.

Antidote: metrics that matter provide confidence and justification for mission-critical lane changes and U-turns.

RIDER 12: WHO AM I?

Perhaps the most pervasive of damaging organisational issues is that of identity; the attachment we form with who we are, what we're capable of, where we've come from, where we fit and how we operate. On a human level our ego takes care of this side of things and usually performs a valuable role, but sometimes it can get a little stuck in a rut. Reinventing ourselves at various points throughout life can be a risk worth taking to release us from the shackles of limiting beliefs and outdated concepts.

Reinvention is equally powerful for organisations. Organisations that out-survive their original peer group typically have a historical pattern of reinvention; reinvention in terms of the markets they serve, the products they offer, their very reason for being. IBM abandoned PC manufacturing to instead provide IT services to corporate clients;[13] Nokia moved from rubber and paper to phones;[14] *National Geographic* extended its reach from magazines to broadcast media;[15] and there are many more examples. If these organisations hadn't questioned and shifted their business model would they be here now? Reinvention isn't a one-off – organisations need to reinvent themselves again and again.

Many leadership teams I've worked with have a fixed view of what it is their organisation does – that is, what it's here to provide, the clients it serves, the markets it operates in and the value it generates. The identity has built over time and experience and is embedded in culture, entrenched in processes and, in the main, remains unquestioned. Beliefs and values lie hidden under multiple layers of habitual thinking.

The responses I received about key strategic challenges and the ways in which existing strategic planning processes help or hinder organisations cited this as the most damaging issue of all. A fixed mindset regarding the business model and limited examination of its congruence with the current, let alone future, strategic context was all too prevalent.

If we can't or won't re-examine the fundamental beliefs that we hold about ourselves, those very beliefs will limit us. If we don't question the strength of our value chain and how it can provide longevity of success, it will snap when we least expect it and can perhaps ill afford it. If we don't have a clear understanding of how our organisation continues to provide value for its shareholders or generate funds and resources for reinvestment, we cannot expect future investors to take the risk and we're unlikely to be the next disruptor (or even survive the next disruption).

Painful as they are, tough questions must be asked. Better to realise now that the business model is flawed and lacks longevity. Better to notice that barriers to entry are low and competing on price is no longer a viable long-term option. Better to accept that our identity, and all that goes with it, might need reinvention than suffer the slow death of irrelevance.

Antidote: operating models can and must be reinvented from time to time.

THE THIRTEENTH HORSEMAN: THE BENIGNIMIZERS

The 12 horsemen of the strategic apocalypse I've outlined lead to one thing – a bad case of the benignimizers. With our blinkers on and our mindsets rigid we can only lead our organisations to achieve more of the same. More of the same can only be successful if the world remains the same, and we know for sure that that won't happen in the post-truth fast show.

No one has had to put anything in our water, we've sedated ourselves. Unconsciously we've unhooked from our antennae, we've fixed up a closed feedback loop that tells us what we want to hear, and we've shut out the very voices that may just save the day.

It's time to wake up. It's time for new habits. It's time we reinvented the way we take strategy to reality. It's time to become a shapeshifter!

ASK YOURSELF...

- What are your organisation's biggest or most pressing strategic challenges?
- Which horsemen of the strategy apocalypse can you recognise from within your own organisation?
- Are there other horsemen of the apocalypse that I haven't mentioned?
- Which antidotes is your organisation presently using?
- Which antidotes does your organisation need to deploy?
- Is your organisation succumbing to the benignimizers?

CHAPTER 2

MAGICAL BEASTS AND HOW TO BE THEM

As the curtain came down on the Cretaceous period, around 65 million years ago, the dinosaurs took their final bow following a 165-million-year reign. A small number of species remained, but the likes of diplodocus, tyrannosaurus rex, pterodactyl, triceratops and stegosaurus met their demise. The remaining living specimens, who were typically small in size, went on to battle mammals and insects for their place in the world. They were the ancestors of the crocodiles, alligators and birds of today. No one really knows for sure what caused the mass extinction; a sudden ice age, global disease epidemic, competition with other more adaptable animals, but one theory is considered most likely – a massive meteor strike from the skies above.

Even if the dinosaurs did in some small way ponder their futures, it's unlikely they would have foreseen such an event let alone had the capacity or capability to do something about it. Contingency planning, sabotage analysis, risk mitigation and disaster recovery were probably somewhat beyond their collective cognitive faculty. Looking further than the next meal and beyond their immediate territory was likely alien to them – a field of potential that never crossed their satsuma-sized brains. Survival in the present moment stretching to predictable events of the immediate future was the extent of their range of perception.

Humans, on the other hand, are set up for change. Adaptable as a species, we survive and thrive in the harshest of environments. Our opposable thumbs, use of tools and general inventiveness see us well placed to master the world around us. We can imagine potential outcomes, plan sequences of activities, devise machinery and tools, and communicate effectively – or at least we like to think we can. Groups of humans congregate and collaborate to find solutions to complex problems. Our capacity for thinking and innovation is of the order dinosaurs couldn't have even dreamed of (if they did indeed dream).

We humans flock to cinemas and eagerly consume dystopian dramas or tales of global disaster where human ingenuity and integrity gallop to the rescue at the very final moment. In our imaginations we've destroyed asteroids, travelled the universe, overcome alien invasions and revolted against tyranny in post-apocalyptic worlds. In reality we've split the atom, mapped the genome and landed on the moon. Our minds are amazing – we have limitless imaginations – and those creative tendencies are probably there for a reason. By visualising these events and outcomes in advance we can devise strategies, plan experiments and plot routes that protect us from harm and secure the future of our genes, and therefore our species. As a by-product we also propagate the belief that we can and will surmount our challenges, however great.

As individuals we're strong, as organised groups that communicate and collaborate we can achieve most anything. Why then do we leave these fundamental skills at home? The corporate world is littered with organisations that didn't imagine, failed to collaborate and neglected to look up. Organisations that, as a result, took a direct hit from a meteor hurtling towards them at speed. A meteor visible from some distance for some time, that could have been managed – disaster averted – if spotted in time.

There are dinosaurs still amongst us. They're large and unwieldy, slow to respond, seduced by the here and now, eyes down and seeing only as far as what's for dinner.

Dinosaurs seem 'too big to fail' but fail they do. They're the kind of organisations that we think will still be there when we're long gone. Sometimes they get help just before they fall. Governments may step in to bail out the beast before it falls and takes many smaller ones with it. If a huge meteor hits, like the financial crisis of 2008, governments are faced with an unenviable choice: use taxpayers' funds to prevent a further deepening of the crisis (much like the Federal Reserve did in its support for the giants of the American automotive industry such as General Motors and Chrysler or the UK government saving major banks such as RBS and HBOS) or allow events to run their course and leave any casualties in collapse (such as Enron and Lehman Brothers), with potentially catastrophic impacts upon connected markets and economies. When a meteor hits sometimes there's nowhere to run or hide.

In the aftermath of a metaphorical meteor strike the small and nimble are often the only survivors. As in a forest fire, the ground has been emptied of dead wood and waste – a clearing is made for new shoots to rise. These agile shoots need less sustenance to survive and can turn fast towards the light to avoid catastrophe and make the most of opportunities as they emerge (remember those U-turns – they come in handy here!). The next big thing is born and the trick is for it to avoid becoming a dinosaur and the inevitable fate that befalls them.

As you already know, I find a little well-aimed fantasy does the mind good – gives it a healthy stretch of its legs and gently takes it by the hand to beyond its normal walls of limitation. I like to think of organisations in terms of their force of personality – the attributes that allow them to operate successfully, the curses they are afflicted by and the magical powers they have at their disposal to help them on their way. We could end up with a cast of a thousand monsters, demons and fairy godmothers but, in my experience, organisations can be boiled down to five main archetypes:

1   Dinosaurs
2   Giants
3   Imps
4   Unicorns
5   Shapeshifters (the most magical of all)

We've already established that to be a dinosaur isn't a fruitful ambition, so let's spend some time on the remaining four.

GIANTS

Giants are big; they wield huge power and take up lots of space in the market. Their supply chains are often made up of a cacophony of smaller organisations that respond to their every whim should they wish to remain alive. If giants move, everyone feels it and they can cause major landslides and paradigm shifts in markets should they fall. Their sheer size and weight give them reach and strength others can only dream of. Highly visible and with roaring voices they can be heard and seen over great distances. When they move people watch and when they speak people listen. Markets respond with delight or panic – slowing the giant's climb or hastening a fall.

Be giants a force for evil or a force for good, a staggering force they are. If a giant decides to fatally injure a smaller rival they can do so with one well-aimed smite. If a giant wishes to protect and promote fledgling ideas, they can grow unhindered in an environment of safety and adequate resources. Intelligent and friendly, or stupid and violent, the underlying character of a giant is augmented and amplified by its every thought and move.

A giant's colossal size means, whether clumsy or precise, movement is slow. It takes time for a message from the brain to get to their little toe and from their little toe back to their brain. In times of difficulty (if, for instance, the giant stubs its toe) this distance can be a blessing at first, shielding the mind from any pain that may emanate and diluting its impact on the rest of the beast. But if the injury should worsen, only limited signals pass through, greatly diluted by their long journey. What starts out as a sore toe, becomes a virulent infection and, without fast treatment, eventually causes the giant to succumb to what could be described as organisational sepsis.

Creatures of habit, their lives are a patchwork of many well-oiled routines and ancient rituals, both of which are resistant to sudden change. Their stories are of ancient battles with mighty foes in foregone eras. Heroes and villains from the distant past form the foundations of their civilisation. Looking backwards to better times can distract them from the here and now and can leave little room for the future. Visualisation can strengthen their mind, exercise will reconnect their gargantuan body, and collective preparation allows them to get through tight spots intact. Arrogant, ignorant or nostalgic giants are the ones that fail hard and sometimes fall astonishingly fast.

Giants are human in form. They have complex brains that can imagine the future, and their well-developed bodies allow them to look up and around them; to horizon scan over great distances, should they choose to do so. They can avoid the fate of a dinosaur and they can prevent sepsis setting in. Used effectively, their size and form is a gift. It bestows credibility, influence and ultimately the power to change, not only themselves, but everything around them. If they 'wake up and smell the coffee' in time, and commit to the Herculean effort potentially involved, they can change the world – many do.

IMPS

Imps are small and nimble, mischievous and lively. They can move fast and like to cause disruption to the status quo. Their size and energy make it easy to turn on a sixpence, to ably respond to events as they happen and, with foresight, to prepare for potential future market developments. The masters of the U-turn, imps don't allow history or precedent to hold them back. Internal synapses and neurons are ablaze. Connections are abundant and ever-forming, delivering lightning-speed communication and swift course correction.

Intelligent and curious, imps consume data and create technical solutions to problems we didn't yet even realise we had. Quirky, fun and cheeky, they unpick the past, ask questions of the present and ignite the future.

Their heroes are in the building, right here right now, living legends and making myths real-time every day. And there's room for more – new heroes are born with every major step taken forward. Their story is just beginning and that's a fascinating place to be.

Some go pop early with all the excitement, unable to maintain focus, set a direction and forge a safe path past the giants. Others shimmer and sparkle for a while and then fade into a cloud of insignificance as they struggle to find food for a growing tribe of mouths or lose interest in the endeavour – perhaps chasing the next shiny new thing instead. Some attract the interest or wrath of the giants and are eaten whole or added to the giants' portfolios as play things (to become a favourite toy or to be discarded into oblivion – who knows). The lucky ones forge a path and steel the limelight as they tiptoe in front of the resident giants with apparent ease.

Imps invent markets and give birth to new products and solutions. Their fate is determined by their ability and willingness to take a break from the hyperactive dynamo and wild roller coaster ride that is their lot, to think and learn and play. Did I say play? Yes, playing future-paced games with translatable metaphors is the way of the successful imp. Those that make it can make it **BIG**, but don't be fooled, the journey is hard and fraught with danger. Remaining alert and primed every step of the way and for many steps ahead is the trick. It takes time, attention and experimentation to be a successful imp.

UNICORNS

Unicorns are such elusive mythical creatures they are rare even in legends and fairy tales. Beautiful and graceful, they are believed to possess potent magical powers, which are at once seductive, addictive and spellbinding.

In business, a unicorn is considered to be a privately held start-up with a valuation in excess of $1 billion – a rare thing indeed. Venture capitalist Aileen Lee was the first to use the term 'unicorn' in this context, choosing the mythical creature as an apt metaphor to represent the rarity of such ventures.[16] In folklore and the corporate markets of modern times alike, unicorns are highly desirable but difficult to find, obtain or create.

When asked to think of a unicorn most of us picture an elegant white horse with a flowing white mane and a single horn emanating from the middle of its forehead. This is the image portrayed in fairy tales and folklore of old, but unicorns can take many forms and have done so throughout history and across cultures. In the corporate world, unicorns come in many shapes and sizes. Many imps want to grow up to be unicorns – this is a massive undertaking, but it's not impossible. The statistics suggest that at least some will make the journey, but it's improbable at best.

SHAPESHIFTERS

So, you're an imp that wants to grow up to become a unicorn, or a giant that wants to survive the inevitable meteor strike and not go the way of the dinosaurs. The route for both is that of the shapeshifter. Shapeshifter DNA is the key to success, and it seems that surviving giants, the most successful imps and long-lived unicorns have some shapeshifter DNA in their midst.

Shapeshifters can transform their physical form, change inherent properties and capabilities, evolve the way they behave and engage with the world. Shapeshifters are masters of change; inward change of the type that transforms an entity into something unlimited by history, entirely different to its prior form, and greater than the sum of its pre-existing parts.

Shapeshifting is an ancient art. It's the province of shamans, deities, warlocks and witches. Nowadays it's anyone's game – yes, even you and your organisation. Whether you're an imp, a unicorn or a giant, and regardless of whether you're currently thriving, striving or just about surviving, if you want to be a shapeshifter the same basic rules apply.

Let's take a deeper look at what it takes!

CHAPTER 3

SHAPESHIFTER DNA

Deoxyribonucleic acid (DNA) is the master molecule of every cell in a living body. It's the base code that determines how our bodies are built and maintained, the route map for cellular structures and the roles they go on to perform. Four key nucleotides form a genetic alphabet that combines to create sentences of instructions (genes) that control the creation and action of proteins throughout the body. Each species has a unique DNA blueprint and (with the exception of identical twins) each individual within a species has entirely unique DNA.

In our bodies this DNA foundation is what controls how we look, how we work and, to some extent, what we might achieve. It provides us with the baseline for a well-functioning organism and continues to inform how that organism develops and operates over time.

DNA is a metaphor that works well in the analysis of organisations. If we are attempting to isolate what makes organisations fail or succeed, we can typically identify factors shared amongst each species. Failing organisations demonstrate shared attributes that successful organisations don't seem to replicate and vice versa.

The most successful organisations are shapeshifters. To create a shapeshifter organisation, we need to understand the DNA of a shapeshifter and how that DNA differs from other organisations. We need to know the shapeshifter base code and how to apply it in the real world.

SHAPESHIFTER BASE CODE

The shapeshifter base code is made up of four key building blocks that are fundamental to an organisation's success. They are the keys that enable the organisation to learn from its environment, adapt to a changing environment and evolve in a way that allows it to be successful in any number of future environments. The four building blocks are:

1   Thinking
2   Conversation
3   Experimentation
4   Progress

THINKING

Shapeshifters think differently. The thinking in shapeshifter organisations is tremendously deep and broad. When shapeshifters think they engage and investigate multiple perspectives, interrogate conflicting data and explore ways to move beyond current constraints and existing paradigms. They think about the past to identify patterns, they think about the present to isolate wicked problems (more about these in Chapter 11) and they think about the future to generate multiple future worlds in which the organisation might be asked to operate.[17] Their thinking is collaborative; a shared process that at once forges deep understanding and challenges unhelpful patterns of 'groupthink'.[18]

CONVERSATION

Conversation is how this thinking comes alive and shapeshifters make sure they have critical conversations. Constructive dialogue is the conduit to a shared understanding of the strengths, opportunities, threats, risks, obstacles and inherent problems that face the organisation. Shapeshifter conversations are courageous and challenging. They remove taboos, unearth assumptions, reconcile misunderstandings and lay a solid foundation of deep connections, simultaneously held multiple perspectives and heightened awareness.

EXPERIMENTATION

Shapeshifters play to learn. Shapeshifter organisations consciously and continuously experiment to test their hypotheses and drive systemic innovation. Practical experiments are designed to test ideas and innovations in small-scale reconstructions of the real world and the results are evaluated objectively against predetermined metrics. Shapeshifters encourage risk-taking within defined parameters and expect to fail fast – learning from every slip. Alternative future worlds form the backdrop for their war games and simulations, and gamification (see page 189) is employed extensively to embed new ways of thinking and enhance capability.[19]

PROGRESS

Shapeshifters work together to seek progress over solution. Shapeshifter organisations have courageous leaders everywhere who are willing to take accountability and make decisions. People are empowered through engaged networks focused on real issues and the recognised ability and authority to make principle-led decisions. Wicked problems are accepted as real and dealt with constructively. The elusive elixir of a problem 'completely solved' is replaced by a drive for 'real progress'. Shapeshifters work hard and fast to align people, resources, decisions and activity to best effect. Priorities are recognised, and complex issues are treated with respect. Shapeshifters move mountains and bring new worlds into being on their journey to co-create the next big thing.

Where most organisations merely play the game, shapeshifters change the game.

SHAPESHIFTER GENES: BELIEFS THAT CHANGE THE FUTURE

The fundamental difference between shapeshifter organisations and their contemporaries is that shapeshifters create the future. They go beyond planning for the future and mitigating the risks it may present. Shapeshifters have a deep and lasting impact on the very fabric of the future, and they do this very consciously. Ten powerful, enabling beliefs allow shapeshifters to do this:

BELIEF 1: IT'S ALL CONNECTED

The ancient mystics of most world cultures prophesised that the fundamental building blocks of the universe were all connected, regardless of the space or time between them. This idea has stood the test of time, despite much scepticism, and is now the focus of physicists worldwide. It transpires that the discipline of quantum mechanics provides us with evidence (if not yet reasons as to why) that proves this is indeed the case.[20] Entangled particles can be connected in such a way that changes to one particle result in changes to the connected particle, regardless of their separation across great distances.

The same can be said of the individual parts that make up a complex organisation. If we think about this principle more practically it leads us to consider which levers we might leverage to bring about a change, and how these levers may act on elements we hadn't first acknowledged and in ways not anticipated. Within a complex system, elements have relationships that we are potentially unaware of. Forces exerted on one element can generate interesting (and perhaps undesirable) effects on another. By keeping this in mind, shapeshifters are more able to generate the change they want to see within and without their borders.

BELIEF 2: THERE'S A PATTERN TO EVERYTHING

In his book *Outliers*, Malcolm Gladwell suggests that it takes somewhere in the region of 10,000 hours of dedicated practice to become a world master at anything.[21] To become generally rather good at something (enough to be considered an 'expert') requires rather less than that. The truth is that for most skills, even the most complex, there is an underlying pattern that can be identified, learned and replicated, for example, the rules of grammar underlying a language, the order of notes in a complex piece of music, the order of movement in a dance routine or the set of actions required to competently drive a car. Once expert, we perform these routines effortlessly and mostly automatically (how many times have you arrived home following a long drive and struggled to remember most of the journey?).

We are surrounded by systems, complex and simple. If we closely observe what is going on around us we can isolate the patterns that drive the outcomes we do and do not want. If we go a step further we can examine the past for patterns, we can spot patterns in action right now in the present and we can extrapolate patterns we have identified into the future (perhaps with some modifications) to predict potential outcomes, test our ability to respond and develop the patterns of capability that will serve us.

Shapeshifters make it their business to find patterns and work out how they can exploit them to their advantage.

BELIEF 3: IT'S THERE FOR EVERYONE

This one is a particularly powerful belief in the armoury of a shapeshifter. Shapeshifter organisations are meritocracies where value and impact leave status and nepotism at the door. Everyone can contribute, learn and share in its success – the concept of talent is truly inclusive. Opportunity knocks at everyone's door and there's no viable reason not to grab it with both hands.

A shapeshifter organisation engenders a collective belief in itself as an entity and in its people as individuals; a belief system which is highly attractive and engaging. Whether an organisation thinks it can or an organisation thinks it can't, it's probably right. Thoughts bring about reality and beliefs power thoughts. Shapeshifters believe they can (in fact they know they can), and nobody gets left behind.

BELIEF 4: THE TRUTH IS TYPICALLY SOMEWHERE IN THE MIDDLE

As we travel through life we form opinions on a wide range of subjects. We may like to think our opinions are based on the facts of a situation, but we're all observing from a different vantage point. Our individual distorted view of reality is based on the facts as we understand them, influenced amongst other things by the experiences we have had, and perhaps the respected voice of a recognised expert or two. We're all a little bit right and a little bit wrong. What we consider to be truths are an automated over-reliance on perception.

There aren't many large groups of individuals that agree on everything – apart from perhaps cults (shapeshifters are not cults, and cults are not shapeshifters). Shapeshifters know that it's healthy to disagree and encourage healthy debate amongst their people. They consciously shape an environment where disagreement is welcome and constructive challenge is the norm.

The 'negative' tag is not deployed as a counterstrike. Instead, when someone disagrees with a course of action, shapeshifters get to work to genuinely understand the frustrations and concerns that might drive dissent.

A shapeshifter organisation understands that it's important to be heard and, more important still, to hear.

Open minds and curiosity drive a search for a truth – a truth that can foster collaboration, alignment and progress. In a shapeshifter organisation opinions and ideas are expressed without fear of retribution and myriad shades of grey are explored to move the conversation forward. Enlightenment, awareness and meaning are the aims.

BELIEF 5: START WHERE YOU ARE

It's easy to kid ourselves about who we really are, how we might behave and what we have achieved – let's face it, most of us have at some point in our lives. We might have an overinflated view of ourselves or we may seriously lack self-esteem – neither of these starting points are great launch pads. We need to get into a state of mind where we believe (without doubt) that we can reach our goals, and to do that demands a level of visualisation beyond the here and now. But, if we ignore, spin or airbrush current reality as we embark on route planning, we're going to get into trouble – big trouble.

To plot a sound route, you need to know where you're heading and where you're leaving from. A different starting point demands an alternative route. Pretending to be somewhere you're not (for better or worse) does not a great route make. To give ourselves the best chance of fulfilling our potential and reaching a challenging goal demands a big dose of reality!

Yes, we've all made mistakes and organisations are no different. Maybe we've polished our brand, as organisations are prone to do all the time. But, at the starting point of what may be our most important journey, the veil must be lifted, the filter removed, and we must face our successes, failures, lapses and detours with honesty and humility.

Shapeshifter organisations do this without fail. Their navel-gazing is truthful and sets them on the right foot along the best path towards the future they want to create.

BELIEF 6: NOTHING IS TABOO

Taboos are emotionally charged, and their like must not be discussed, cannot be aired, due to social custom and likely moral outrage. They are unthinkable acts, terrible happenings, dastardly deeds and villainous anti-heroes. Their very mention triggers hysteria and their enactment brings about punishment, banishment or worse. Taboos are dangerous, they taint the sacred. Taboos are objectionable in the extreme.

Of course, in everyday life there are clearly some things that *are* taboo. The boundaries differ from culture to culture and century to century, and I'm not suggesting you break every social convention and societal norm with abandon. But in the corporate world taboos can be born of the most mundane proclivities of the powerful personalities within.

In a shapeshifter organisation the shackles are off and it's okay to shine a light on the difficult subjects; the product that failed, the leader that derailed, the merger that went wrong or the technology that didn't deliver can all teach us so much. Shapeshifters highlight issues and discuss situations – so long as the focus is on positively changing the world (or the organisation). In shapeshifter organisations courageous conversations that break the mould happen every day.

BELIEF 7: RITUAL MAKES HABIT, MAKES REALITY

The use of ritual in any culture signifies belonging. Rituals are customs and conventions that we perform to fit in, often without a second thought. Confucius, the ancient Chinese philosopher, suggested that rituals can be employed as a lever for change.[22] Becoming conscious of the rituals we automatically perform and adopting rituals now that emulate the state of our being in the future, once at our desired destination, take us further faster on our path. Rituals act as the triggers for habit, and habit makes small adjustments to our identity day by day.

The trick is to be mindful and present in the moment so that a ritual takes on meaning and purpose. The ritual serves as a reminder of our goal and a trigger for the behaviours that will help us on our journey. Using ritual in a mindful, purposeful way allows us to become a different person in that moment – to experience our lives in a slightly different alternative reality.

Humans are creatures of habit and our achievements and failures are greatly informed by the habits we allow to take control. The same can be said for organisations. Organisations have many rituals that drive habitual ways of working and set a tempo for regular activity. Some are formal, for example an annual performance appraisal, a weekly all-hands meeting or an annual leadership conference, while others are less so, such as a habitual workaround to circumvent a protracted process, a recurring conversation that echoes throughout the organisation or the way people typically engage with each other. Shapeshifter organisations understand their historic rituals and the outcomes they have given life to. Shapeshifters consciously go about introducing new rituals to focus, broaden and reshape the collective mind. Learning new rituals and performing them diligently and consistently gives rise to new habitual behaviours and the gradual reinvention of identity. Rituals allow shapeshifters to play in the sandpits of the future and to understand its patterns ahead of time.

BELIEF 8: BEST FIT TRUMPS BEST PRACTICE

Best practice is already out of date – relying on its virtues is like taking an eraser to innovation and placing creativity into a veritable straitjacket. By the time 'best practice' gets accepted and shared as 'best practice', real practice is some substantial way down the track and looking back furtively to see what all the fuss is about. Organisations that become obsessed with and consumed by best practice are already going in the wrong direction. Organisations that base their innovations on established best practice instantly limit the scope of their imagination and ingenuity.

Shapeshifters are different – they aren't bound by best practice. They're independent thinkers and unique in the expression of their gifts. Best practice can only serve to make them the same as many others, crafted in the image of slower organisations still rushing to catch a bus that has already left. Shapeshifters want bespoke solutions, inventive ideas and novel approaches that best fit their reality and future aspirations.

Shapeshifters look forward not backwards.

BELIEF 9: TO FLIT IS TO BE AGILE

Stuck in a rut isn't a great place to be, particularly in the post-truth fast show, where the world is fast-changing around you. It can be difficult to work out which way to jump and we all know organisations that spent way too long playing in their own sandpit while all their contemporaries grew up and moved on to high school.

Shapeshifters consciously create a balance between two time zones and modes of activity. They spend a significant proportion of their time in the here and now, being present and remaining mindful. They make things happen, conquer markets, release and produce products, deliver great experiences, all the time remaining alert and keeping a watchful eye on proceedings as they unfold around them.

On a parallel track they spend an equally significant amount of time dreaming about the future, playing with potential, experimenting with ideas and influencing events through their creative theatre. Shapeshifters do this deliberately – they employ a twin-track focus rather than a one-track mind. The habit of constantly and consciously flitting between present reality and potential futures helps them to be the organisation they need to become ahead of time. They have already seen multiple futures and rehearsed their role within each of them. They have navigated ambiguity before it is upon them. They have ditched myopic thinking for a range of suitably supple strategies, and they understand the indicators of a potential future that they must be noticing regardless of the noise around them.

Shapeshifters think hard, do good and be themselves while imagining the future, playing with its potential and becoming a better version of themselves. Time travel makes agility the shapeshifter's secret weapon.

BELIEF 10: BE A FORCE FOR GOOD

Shapeshifters have a purpose and an ambition that is beyond their own success. They care about the impact they have upon their communities and the people within them. In fact, many of them aspire to have an impact well beyond their immediately obvious reach. They are fastidious about their reason why and inculcate an environment in which people are inspired and enabled to do the right thing and make the right choice, even when the right thing is a tough thing to do or the right choice is a difficult one to reach. Of course, they want to be successful and do well, but they realise that for this to come about the broader environment must be successful too. They are the ones who amplify the unrepresented voices, bring life-changing (and sometimes life-saving) technology to the masses and lobby for positive change and social progress. In short, shapeshifters do and choose what is ethical and work hard to create the greatest good – they do their level best to make a positive contribution to the world.

SHAPESHIFTER HABITS

Shapeshifters demonstrate a set of instinctive behaviours that become habitual life-changing practices for the organisation and its people.

Urban myth suggests that it takes 21 days of focused attention and repeated behaviour to make or break a personal habit. In the real world, we all know how hard this can be and how much longer than 21 days it can take! Time to success (if indeed you get there) is probably quite variable; complexity, motivation and experience all play a part.

Changing the habits of an organisation is hard – really hard; that's why 'change management' is such a 'thing'. Complexity is typically high, motivation patchy and driven by all manner of personal agendas, and the ability to leverage past experience is dependent upon capability and culture (and a willingness to confront the difficult truth). The myths and legends of any organisation pack a powerful punch when it comes to strategic inertia, while processes and structure can add a very effective straitjacket.

Those involved in established strategic planning cycles can be overwhelmed with the level of information that needs to be processed and the demands for detailed analysis from senior management. The plans look great, but when they come up against real life they can quickly be found wanting. The reaction? More structured planning of course…

Planning is a fabulous exercise, but it is only as good as the assumptions upon which it is based. If assumptions are wrong, the plan is redundant. How often do we give proper thought to the assumptions underpinning strategy and how can we ensure we keep an eye on said assumptions to make sure they remain valid throughout the plan's life? What quantity and, more importantly, quality of strategic dialogue is really taking place?

Yes, it's hard to change the lifetime habits of an organisation – but change them we must! Sophisticated planning process or not, there are three fundamental habits worth catching – habits that will create more abundant dialogue, generate creative ideas and sense-check strategic plans as time marches on. Refraction, reflection and rehearsal are the three 'R's that organisations must become well versed in if they want to become a shapeshifter.

REFRACTION

We all accept that light changes direction as it travels through a prism or enters a different substance. In the same way, strategic choices and best-laid plans behave differently in alternative realities or tangled timelines. The fascinating world of quantum physics is already grappling with the likelihood that there are multiple universes like our own, and that a new one pops, sparkles or perhaps flickers into existence every time we make a decision. Each time we choose to take the stairs another version of us picked the lift and a new universe comes into existence at that point to travel the alternative timeline (think *Sliding Doors!*).[23]

We tend to have a mental picture of the likely future but, if we're honest, it rarely unfolds exactly as we expect. We only need consider the current state of global geopolitics to see this in action. Creating space and time to refract strategic plans through a prism of potential, plausible and challenging futures and figuratively travelling a decade or so down their particular timelines can help us test assumptions and generate a range of alternative future strategies that would make sense in alternative worlds should they come to be.

REFLECTION

I'm a firm believer that there's a pattern to everything and that, if you look hard enough, you can see patterns emerging even in the most mundane. With hindsight it's often quite easy to be able to isolate critical decisions or events that precipitated a major change. In the moment it's far more difficult to do so. Journaling at an individual level and periodic reviews at a team or organisational level deliver huge value. Encouraging a truthful look-back at history (near and far) can unveil patterns that may well be replicating themselves right now or evolving into a range of alternative patterns with shared roots. This is systems thinking in action – catching the system mid-flow and noticing what drives what and why. The habit of reflection can provide some protection against myopia, signal risks way ahead of time and has been known to shine a light on valuable opportunities that remain well hidden to most.

REHEARSAL

Most strategies live in a two-dimensional world. Captured on paper they describe a chosen approach and assume a level of engagement, capacity and capability that may or may not be available in reality. Rehearsal brings strategy to life by working through situations as a group against the backdrop of a range of potential futures. It's a means to find pitfalls, unearth assumptions and isolate critical prerequisites for success. Wind-tunnelling strategies and rehearsing moves that are most likely to create the reality you really want to see (or at least be successful in whatever future emerges) generates process learning and future memory, if that's possible.

And our 'prospective memory' does indeed make future memory possible. Our prospective memory is responsible for recalling a planned intention and performing a planned action at some future point in time. We do this all the time – our early morning routine is a great example. We each have a programme of a series of actions that we 'remember' take place at a certain point in time (for example early morning) or are triggered by a specific event (like getting out of bed). We remember that when we get out of bed we should visit the bathroom and once in the bathroom we remember that we need to clean our teeth, shower and do a host of other things. We (hopefully) remember that it might be a good idea to don some clothes prior to leaving the house and we remember that at a certain time we need to leave to travel to our place of work. Prospective memory collaborates with our retrospective memory of intentions, decisions or actions in that it calls upon events we have previously experienced and people we have met in the past to inform what to do at a future time or trigger point. The foundation can be actual experiences or mental rehearsals of potential experiences – these are made stronger still through shared experience. Therefore, if we have engaged with these experiences and ideas ahead of time and consciously linked them to a time or event trigger, we are far more alert for said trigger and equipped to respond in the moment. Giving our future memory a workout is a great habit…

CHAPTER 4

STRATEGY TO REALITY
IN FOUR MOVES

My experience of working with organisations has taught me that overcomplication is the supervillain of change and the enemy of progress. Where organisations have concentrated their focus and directed their efforts in a small number of critical areas, they appear to have greater success sooner. I've often been asked to work with leadership teams to clarify their strategy and ascertain their priorities as a collective, so that they can align around a shared vision. In the early days, all too often these sessions degenerated into a volatile free-for-all eruption of personal agendas, misplaced loyalties and a smorgasbord of unrelated priorities.

In these discussions the loudest voice wins, disagreement is castigated and proper investigation and debate is stifled – creativity and imagination are not even let out of the traps. Groupthink is firmly in charge and woe betide anyone who may voice a counterargument or hold a niggling doubt.

Over the years, and with many a bruise, I learned that those teams that focused on the fewest things, and took their time to think about them deeply and collectively, experienced the greatest successes. That's quite counter-intuitive initially. We are programmed to assume activity is productivity and speed is critical. But, all activity is not equal and (as I fondly remember my sixth form maths tutor explaining to a class of eager new drivers) speed and distraction can lead to sudden catastrophic deceleration if confronted with an unyielding obstacle. In my experience, need, greed and speed are the three spears that critically injure a young unicorn or mortally wound an already suffering giant.

A complex, cross-border transformation programme with multiple conflicting priorities does not make for a particularly productive organisation, let alone provide a framework through which people can move the organisation forward in the desired direction through principle-led decisions and aligned action. Successful change is typically focused change that is interconnected across all known fronts (coupled with the agility and space to manoeuvre should unknown fronts present themselves). A leadership team that can effectively and ruthlessly prioritise is a far better bet than a leadership team that tries to do everything simultaneously by yesterday – they might still end up successful, but it will hurt way more than it needs to.

Whatever priorities remain, and regardless of how many, there are four fundamental moves that must be navigated for strategy to become reality. These four moves are at the root of every organisation that becomes and remains successful. I call them 'moves' because they demand direction, they incorporate motion and they deliver progress. They are not static milestones, tick-box exercises or trophies to be collected. They are shared experiences, collective heroes' journeys and organisational quests. They are not solely captured on paper as a two-dimensional snapshot of a point in time that becomes mostly irrelevant as soon as it is recorded. The moves are four-dimensional, incorporating a place in space and a track in time. Unicorn, imp, giant or twinkle in the eye – if you want to be a shapeshifter the same rules apply!

The four moves, put simply, are:

1   Strategy: develop a supple strategy
2   Culture: build a meta-tribe
3   Innovation: engage in wicked thinking
4   Change: build a magical movement

Straightforward right? Well there's a bit more to it than those phrases might suggest.

These four moves are the final pieces that make up the shapeshifter DNA jigsaw. They fast track a shapeshifter's journey from strategy to reality, whatever their sector, location, challenge or opportunity. For DNA to do its job it must undergo transcription, translation, mutation and replication.

DNA is a readable, transcribed map that is translated into amino acids that, in turn, form proteins. DNA mutates to evolve, and it replicates to grow. Organisations must, in essence, do the same. An organisation requires a destination, a plan and a map. It needs to be able to translate these into a culture and its associated values and behaviours. It must innovate to create new products, services and indeed markets. And it must also gather followers in order to grow and drive change.

A shapeshifter organisation does all of these things and more. Shapeshifters craft a strategy that is supple and that can navigate the toughest terrains and weather powerful storms. They take time to see around corners into the future and use their imagination to understand future worlds and how they might contribute effectively. They come together to co-create a range of possible, plausible and challenging futures that take their strategic dialogue to another level. Shapeshifters identify indicators that will herald a potential future and watch patiently and attentively to see which of these emerge. They develop a range of strategic options and influence the future strategic context towards the one they want to see.

Shapeshifters develop a culture that transcends tribes. Shapeshifters understand what makes a powerful culture and what shapes, aligns and mobilises a great tribe – a meta-tribe. They break down typical barriers to form a meta-tribe that is aligned, driven and progressive. They celebrate myths and legends and think nothing of making new ones every day. They galvanise around powerful causes with great meaning, applaud positive deviance, and they draw upon hive mind and swarm intelligence to harness the power of everyone towards a shared goal.[24]

Shapeshifters collectively think beyond current paradigms. They tackle the problems that are too complex or entrenched to be solved and they systemically innovate and co-create to make real progress on thorny wicked problems. They fall in love with the problem not the solution, and get right into the complexity and chaos of the problems that will make the difference. Meta-tribes think, play and experiment to invent the future.

And finally, shapeshifters create a movement than can move mountains. A movement that aligns and amplifies the collective strength of their meta-tribe in support of their cause and in pursuit of a brighter future. A movement with energy, agility and momentum that is connected and courageous at its core. Devolved leadership, strategic alignment and individual agency render it capable, empowered and ready and willing to navigate through a changing landscape to change the world.

Shapeshifters want to positively change the world. Using these four moves, they can, they will and they do!

These four moves are the difference between success and failure, survival or extinction. They are interconnected and interdependent but, for the sake of simplicity, let's take a closer look at the mechanics of each one in turn.

PART 1

MOVE ONE:

SUPPLE STRATEGY

In most organisations, the way strategy is currently organised and the manner in which strategic dialogue takes place (if it takes place at all) is broken. It harks back to a more predictable world and relies upon hierarchical power to get things done. The world has changed; we now live in a fast-moving, chaotically unpredictable world. The world we live in is connected and dynamic. It's a world of complexity, information and speed. Lumbering, over-bureaucratic processes with multiple checkpoints may result in exemplar budgets, but cannot hope to deliver strategy at a pace or of a quality that can meet the challenges and opportunities we may be presented with. Amongst volatility, uncertainty, complexity and ambiguity it's the organisations with options that are best able to navigate a path to success. These organisations constantly watch the horizon, quickly test novel ideas and are willing to learn and turn fast, to shape the future. We need to think about strategy differently, and we need to do it fast!

Strategic plans in many organisations assume a relatively stable status quo. Analysis captures known regulatory changes, potential risks and opportunities already apparent in the market, and likely competitor reactions. Plans detail acquisition aspirations and alternatives alongside divestment opportunities to better focus the portfolio. Some assumptions are identified and mitigated, but the predominant focus is survival, growth, differentiation and perhaps diversification in a 'known' future. But the future by its very nature cannot be 'known'. The only thing we can really be sure of is that any predicted future will not be the future that comes about. We've succumbed to the benignimizers – we've confined ourselves within the boundaries of 'what is' rather than the expansive realms of 'what if'. It's clearly still crucial to place importance on plans for the near and mid-term (organisations that succumb to navel-gazing with little focus on revenue generation don't tend to last too long), but it is now becoming increasingly important to engage more readily and effectively with the far-future too.

So, how can organisations balance the near-term fight to survive and to deliver acceptable returns to shareholders, with the very real need to engage with the far-future (or, better still, a range of potential far-futures)? This is where shapeshifter organisations differ from most. Shapeshifters are comfortable confronting and creating shifting paradigms. Shapeshifters place as much value on the far-future as they do on the here and now.

Wouldn't it be great to be able to see around corners, to view the future with the benefit of hindsight and to anticipate the next big thing? Of course, we can't physically see into the future, but we can be absolutely sure that it will be different to the present and almost certainly not as we would automatically presume it to be or perhaps even want it to be. Unfortunately, time travel is yet to be invented. In the meantime, we have to make do with our own imagination, creativity and intuition to create future landscapes worthy of becoming the foundations to works of fiction.

In our spare time, many of us devour the creations of such literary geniuses as Douglas Adams, Margaret Atwood, George Orwell, Ursula K Le Guin and Stanislaw Lem (to name but a few) and marvel in hindsight at their, sometimes chilling, predictive accuracy.[25] And then we go to work… our creativity shrivels, our imagination stays at home for a duvet day and our intuition is placed through a self-inflicted polygraph at every turn. Our organisational planning processes march on in a predictable battle formation of objective, sequenced activity regardless of events. Evidence-based analysis, limited quality dialogue and future outcomes based on historic benchmarking, hold our gaze permanently in the rear-view mirror. We produce an extended and augmented view of the 'as is' and we all know that stability is an illusion – don't we?!

When we do genuinely consider the future, we typically take a narrow slice of it (around an emerging issue that we are already aware of) and attempt to predict outcomes, forecast impact and mitigate risks. All being well, our prediction turns out to be 'nearly right' although typically we've focused on the wrong narrow slice in the first place! To add insult to injury, our strategic response to the prediction is often fear-driven – let's not lose sight of the fact that the creator of the first digital camera was told by his employers to keep the technology under wraps for fear others may use it to compete. Kodak had its own 'Kodak moment' and missed it!

A major proportion of the time I spend with leadership teams is time engaged in scenario planning. Scenario planning is an exercise through which people and organisations can consider strategic options in the light of a variety of possible, and potentially challenging, futures. It's an exercise that demands some time and can feel rather daunting for a team more used to operating with data, evidence and performance indicators on a daily basis. Instead, they are asked to voyage boldly into the unknown, to create possible futures, and to use these futures as canvases upon which to formulate new strategic pathways and as lenses through which to view their current strategic plans.

Participants are encouraged (sometimes dragged kicking and screaming) to step away from the current data and evidence for a short time. The trick is to embrace imagination and let the creative juices flow. Deeply embedded assumptions are identified and suspended. Expectations of what the future may hold are placed out of reach, on a shelf, so that alternative worlds can be developed without restraint. (In truth, some restraint is allowed – there's likely to be limited benefit to be gained from considering the strategy to be adopted in the event of all-out nuclear war, alien invasion or zombie apocalypse. These scenarios would most likely remove rather than reshape any viable market for a considerable time. But people tend to limit themselves way before we ever get in sight of scenarios that may interest Steven Spielberg.) The creative juices start to run low as soon as we turn the corner into anything that feels remotely unlikely or (dare I say it) potentially uncomfortable, for example, a paradigm shift to the predominant economic model, a destabilisation of local political structures or a giant technological leap. I'm sure we can all agree that all of these have happened many times in human history, any one of them would present major issues for any organisation and they are all very likely to happen again – we just don't know when, or where, or how.

Many of us become entirely seduced by the world we inhabit. We see the current status quo as 'the ways things work', 'the way things are meant to work' and 'the way things will probably work for the foreseeable future'. But we're often very wrong! A quick glance back over relatively recent history shows massive changes to country borders, international alliances, the structure of families, predominant working patterns, pension arrangements and adequacy, levels of home ownership, employment rights, medical interventions and technological capability. But if that exercise doesn't convince you, let me tell you a story…

In 2016 I asked a diverse group of leaders (from all over the world) what they thought would happen in the Brexit referendum. The consensus in the room was that the vote would be close but that the United Kingdom would decide to remain in the EU – we all know what happened there.

Later that same year I asked another similar group to predict who would win the American presidential election. I received a similar response – that it would be close, but that Hillary Clinton would emerge victorious. Very few people in the room were even prepared to consider that Trump might win, but win he did.

In 2017 I supported a number of UK organisations in their early planning for Brexit. In each case we generated a variety of scenarios of what 'Brexit' might mean in practice and how this may impact the strategic context. Only one of the teams involved was initially willing to consider a 'no deal' Brexit. This outcome seemed utterly implausible to virtually everyone despite the fact that the legal default position was to leave the EU on World Trade Organization terms.

I also suggested that it may be worth considering a range of political scenarios. For example, what would be the impact upon the UK and European strategic context should Jeremy Corbyn lead the Labour Party to general election victory and become Prime Minister? At the time, this outcome seemed highly unlikely, but we all know how dangerous it can be to dismiss and fail to consider the impact of highly unlikely potential outcomes.

There are patterns to our thinking. We expect the current status quo to continue to be the future status quo. And yet, when we seek to actively improve our situation, we do so because we instinctively know that we can alter the environment around us. We must know this or why would we bother trying? Why the disconnect? These deeply ingrained habits reassure us on a day-to-day basis; they allow us to live our lives from moment to moment without undue anxiety, and to strive to achieve our goals. History tells us that we are wrong – many times have the hands of fate intervened, in a manner unforeseen (or foreseen and ignored) to deliver a totally unexpected outcome.

We also tend to expect any given future to be wholly good or entirely bad, favourable or unfavourable to the extreme (the notorious 'halo and horns effect'). But it's rarely all bad news. The truth is that most situations present a mixture of threats, risks and opportunities. Until we entertain alternative timelines, altered futures and the odd paradigm shift, it's quite impossible to examine the potential within.

And so I implore you to approach the world with an open-minded sense of wonder and curiosity, and to explore the future. What are you assuming won't happen that just might and (after the shock has subsided) what impact might it have if it did? Who knows, you might just stumble across a paradigm-shifting insight – a 'Kodak moment' – with the courage and foresight to see it through and create the future!

In scenario planning we get to play with time a lot. We want to visit different points in space time, travel alternative timelines and visit other universes. This all sounds rather fantastical until you read about recent advances in the physical sciences where multiverses, quantum entanglement and mysterious dark matter are no longer the machinations of an overactive imagination and confined to the realms of fiction.

Suspend reality, imagine the future and play in its sandpit. Move away from predicting and forecasting (for a while at least) to ponder plausible, challenging futures and perceive the array of strategic choices potentially available to you. Collectively explore and interrogate the future for the opportunities it presents.

Time travel is critical to supple strategy development!

CHAPTER 5

HOW SHAPESHIFTERS DO STRATEGY

Shapeshifters approach strategy formulation with a very different mindset and from multiple angles. Their aim is to create a supple strategy that is, much like bamboo, stronger than steel but can be flexible enough to flourish in severe weather. A rigid structure becomes brittle over time and that is also true of rigid strategy. Supple strategy delivers longevity beyond current markets and their participants. Shapeshifters create a networked strategy that involves and engages the community that will bring it about and the communities that will benefit from its successful execution. Their strategy is dynamic and alive; it continuously evolves through ongoing dialogue and broad inclusion. Shapeshifters look to go beyond competition and seek ways they can work collaboratively to form new markets and drive novel solutions. In summary, the strategy of a shapeshifter is supple, networked and collaborative.

To do this effectively, shapeshifters move from the world 'that is' to focus on the worlds that 'might be'. They carefully examine the 'what is' world for clues and then explore the 'what-if' world, in multiple forms, for potential risks and opportunities. Their existing strategy is wind-tunnelled against these 'what-if' scenarios and a strategy supple enough to anticipate, navigate and create the future is then developed. Through the co-creation of a range of possible, plausible and challenging futures, the shapeshifter's collective dialogue is taken to another level.

The co-creation process unearths assumptions, identifies emerging indicators of the future, develops a range of strategic options and enables the shapeshifter to influence the future strategic context towards the one they want through active lobbying and engagement. The scenarios process provides an opportunity for reflection, refraction and rehearsal and creates new patterns of thinking. It fosters collaboration, hones judgement, accelerates decision-making and creates a stronger team. In short, scenarios are a great antidote, even better a vaccination, against an attack of the benignimizers.

If you want to see around corners and co-create a supple, networked and collaborative strategy you're going to need to carve some quality time out from busy schedules and allow people the luxury of thinking space and time. With so much to do and so little time, I know it feels counterproductive initially, but humour me. What could possibly be worse than working day and night to make strategy reality, only to find some years down the line that it was in fact the wrong strategy all along? You really can't afford to be a dinosaur. The meteor with your organisation's name on it may already be in sight. It's time to look up! Let me take you on a guided tour of the supple strategy system.

THE SUPPLE STRATEGY SYSTEM

The system is made up of 15 steps plus a feedback loop and, if required, a turnaround. Initially it helps to work through the steps in order but once you and your organisation become more accustomed to far-future thinking and supple strategy generation you'll be able to mix it up a little and be less constrained as your shapeshifter tendencies grow.

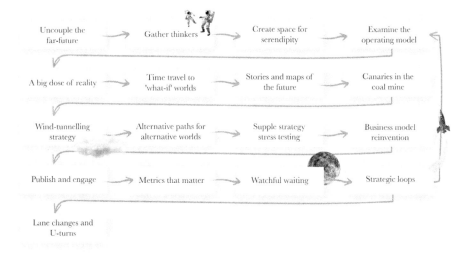

STEP 1: CONSCIOUS UNCOUPLING

It's important to take a moment here to consider the increasing complexity and ambiguity that's inherent in far-future thinking. People are naturally drawn to the unknown out of curiosity and excitement, but they typically feel safer and secure within the relative comfort of what is known and predictable. Therefore, any venture into the unknown is usually short-lived – it's constrained by restrictions and caveats and is ultimately derailed by a quest for evidence. We delude ourselves that we know what comes next and that our well-trodden paths will continue to serve us well. Where it seems that a new path might be required, we seek the advice of renowned experts. Such experts have a fabulous command of the past. They understand its patterns and provide forecasts based on the predictable extrapolation of these patterns. But who can truly be an expert on the future, and how do we know that past patterns will replicate as expected?

The further into the future we travel, the greater the level of complexity and ambiguity. Outcomes are unpredictable, and answers are emergent rather than finite. Myriad interdependencies and ideas criss-cross the timeline and could at any point cause it to veer off in an unexpected direction. The deeper we venture into the future, the greater turbulence we experience. The patterns here are new to us all and are of such complexity they seem random in nature. It feels like we're facing chaos.

Chaos is unintelligible and unmanageable – it all seems too hard to grasp and grapple with – and so we collapse in a heap, exhausted amongst our defined and orderly budgetary planning process having never truly left the confines of rigid strategy long enough to acclimatise. Far-future thinking is different; it is perspective-altering and mind-changing, and it demands time, focus and commitment both to learn how to do it and to get the most benefit from it.

The first step towards a supple strategy system is to consciously uncouple far-future thinking and strategic dialogue from budget and workforce planning processes and conversations. Interlink them at pertinent points and ensure that each can inform the other for sure, but do not, under any circumstances, let existing budget and workforce planning processes and related discussions derail or devour fledgling far-future thinking before it has even had an opportunity to consider life beyond the nest. Given time, space and support, far-future thinking can become embedded into everybody's mindset, enabling a supple, networked and collaborative strategy while still leaving quite enough capacity and capability to deftly handle the here and now.

STEP 2: GATHER THINKERS

The next step is to consider who will become your thinkers. Thinkers are those invited into the room for the fun-packed time-travelling adventure and focused far-future thinking exercises. They will be the souls who perform a deep examination of the business model, capture the detailed business context (now and future) and develop a range of alternative potential futures. Some may also be front and central in the execution of strategy as it emerges – the leaders within your organisation but not necessarily of it.

When dinosaur organisations get to thinking strategically an imaginary line gets drawn, across which only a select few can pass. Most strategic off-sites involve those at the very top of the organisation along with a few well-connected advisors. Diversity of thinking is often far from evident. A supple strategy demands a supple approach to strategic thinking and this in turn demands a broader church of thinkers. It's no good to limit inclusion to senior leaders in the hierarchy. Remember, you cannot afford to be a dinosaur. Thinkers need to be an eclectic bunch. They need to be drawn from every level, every location, every business unit and every function. Age and length of service should not be limiting factors; you want representation across all age groups and your future success depends upon an understanding of how future generations may live and how your proposition will need to evolve. Consciously invite those who can add something different to the thinking mix, for example:

- People who are relatively new to the organisation but perhaps have interesting experience within other markets.
- Innovative thinkers who have already voiced novel ideas or concepts.
- People who volunteer outside of work or who have carer responsibilities who are likely to already have developed an intuitive understanding of the needs of different groups and are able to hold a range of perspectives at any given time.
- Challengers who voice disagreement and do things differently with positive results.
- Creative types who have hobbies that call on artistic talents – the amateur photographers, painters and writers in your midst.
- Consumers of your products and services or, even better, consumers of your competitors' products and services (if they dare to admit it).
- People with large informal networks across the organisation who seem to lead with no formal mandate to do so.

And when I say invite them, I mean authentically invite them to be a part of the genuine strategic dialogue – not a sideshow put on in the name of engagement that runs parallel to the real event while the actual thinking is done by the usual suspects behind closed doors. If you're feeling brave and ready to listen, you could invite real clients and representatives of the communities and populations you affect to some elements of the discussion.

Approach with caution a list of thinkers neatly drawn from your senior leader, functional head, recognised expert and high-potential populations. Participants should, of course, include all of these people, but the group must also extend way beyond. Shapeshifters know that hierarchical leadership is delusional (misleading at best). Tribes and movements are led by game-changers – the believable leaders who are not limited or enabled by their position within an organisation. Game-changers are enablers rather than enforcers. Game-changers are people who gain prodigious followership through being an authentic human and by leading with their soul. Game-changers are:

- **Learners**. Game-changers know that learning agility must come first, it's the enabler that allows them to develop the remaining game-changing dimensions effectively. They are constantly open and curious to learning opportunities where others might least expect them.
- **Connected**. Game-changers value people and relationships and move from small talk to deep talk to get the best results from any team, in any situation, anywhere.
- **Informed**. Game-changers look for emerging themes and are amongst the first to recognise their significance.
- **Insightful**. Innovation and creativity are natural extensions of intellect and intuition for game-changers at the cutting edge.
- **Focused**. Game-changers cut through complexity and do the right things well; always with their eyes on the final outcomes.
- **Valuable**. Game-changers commit to making a difference and creating long-term, sustainable value in everything they do.
- **Inclusive**. Game-changers have a global mindset that enables them to connect, influence and deliver across organisational, geographical, historical, political and cultural boundaries.
- **Believable**. Ultimately game-changers are authentic and credible. People choose to follow them regardless of authority.

Believable game-changers shape the future. If you're lucky enough to have some emerging game-changers in your midst, my advice is to bring them into the thinker tent early!

Actually, there's a step beyond the game-changer; an evolutionary leap that devolves leadership accountability and allows principle-based decision-making regardless of status, a network of actors that brings the future into being through innovation and collaboration. The next stage in the evolutionary development of leadership is the rise of the game-makers. Game-makers design worlds and invent the future. Hungry, playful, courageous and self-aware they aspire to make the world a better place and they are willing to be novices time and time again to learn fast as contexts change. More about game-makers later (see page 191)!

I'm certain you can already see the implications for leadership development and talent identification. In the future (in fact now – right now) we need to include everyone and focus on unleashing the game-changers (and perhaps game-makers) amongst us!

STEP 3: SPACE FOR SERENDIPITY

You've identified your team of thinkers – now what? The next step is to create mental space and a physical place for these thinkers to hang out and think. Some of the 'space' and 'place' will be formal, some will be informal, and if you're inventive some can be virtual. Your very own Futurological Congress can take many forms and have multiple inputs.

It takes time for cohesion to form in any group. Explicit permission and strong facilitation are required for people to dare to think in unfamiliar ways. In the first instance a formal retreat is probably a good idea. One day (or, worse still, half a day) is not sufficient thinking space for an inaugural event. Habits will be broken, assumptions will be unearthed, perspectives will be broadened and intransigence countered through robust dialogue where everyone is genuinely heard, and everyone listens to learn. This can't be done in half a day! Having the space to engage in informal conversation around the edges of a more structured dialogue over a number of days can lead to far-reaching, far-sighted ideas and a shared, deep understanding that will not come about in a more rushed and rigid environment.

Remember, for maximum effect your team of thinkers needs to include a diverse range of people who represent various career stages, generations, functions, business units and backgrounds. Emerging experts in new technologies, people who have already demonstrated they think differently from the organisational norm and creative spirits who are recognised by their colleagues as ideas factories are all great contributors to the process. It is critical that senior leaders are not only present but are fully immersed into exactly the same experience as everyone else and alongside everyone else – this is not a situation where it is appropriate for the thinkers to 'go away and think' with a view to presenting back to senior management later. For paradigm-shifting outcomes, the thinking needs to be done together and that may well take a bit of adjustment for all involved. It may be that your thinker numbers exceed 15, in which case you may need to consider setting up more than one thinking team (the way you organise the membership of these teams is entirely dependent on the situation, organisation and leadership capability).

I find that by labelling these events as exercises in 'what if', there is less temptation for those with more experience, greater seniority or longer service to hold court. Nobody is an authority regarding the future and so no one view is more likely to be correct than another. We're not attempting to predict the future; instead we want to play with it. The most powerful scenarios come from dialogue which properly examines all interpretations of existing reality and visions of the future. Disagreement is good; afford the team time, permission and adequate guidance to use disagreement as it emerges as a powerful lever to challenge assumptions, shift perceptions and multiply lenses. Nobody knows the future, nobody can know who's right – the future is often a hybrid of the many futures discussed. The more each member genuinely understands the experiences, beliefs and opinions of other members of the team, the greater its collective thought power. Disagreeing without investigation is an opportunity wasted. Authentically seeking to understand what leads someone to see a situation in a particular way (that is perhaps different to your own view) or the disparate rationales for conflicting views of the future, recollections of the past and experiences of the present, allows a greater number of plausible alternative futures and their timelines to be considered.

To get thinkers thinking beyond the formal events it pays to set up a virtual platform where ideas can be exchanged, arguments challenged and scenarios developed into fully researched storyboards of potential futures. If you want to create engagement beyond the initial 'thinker' group you can also use the platform to invite a wider audience to review, critique and add to the scenarios as they develop. This works particularly well if your organisation is relatively small or needs to create a significant strategic shift fast. We all know that people are far more likely to buy into a plan if they have played a part in its creation.

STEP 4: EXAMINE THE OPERATING MODEL

Every organisation, successful or otherwise, has an operating model that is the basis for its activities. Before we gallop with abandon into the unknowable future, it's important we have a firm grip on what makes the organisation successful or otherwise right now. There probably isn't one version of that truth and the very act of unpacking this model and spending some time underneath the bonnet checking its mechanical integrity is time well spent. By walking through the operating model as a group of thinkers we often find that there isn't just one model at all (or at least there's precious little alignment around it). Perspectives and priorities differ depending on your vantage point and it's not at all unusual to find that the model actually in operation is not that which is captured in organisational literature or the minds of its leaders.

It helps to capture the operating model visually as a value chain or a cycle of activity. Plotting the organisation's activities and attributes in this way often highlights gaping holes or fundamental faults in the depths of its foundations that may cause disaster should its context shift suddenly.

This is true whether you are a profit-making business, a social enterprise, a charity or a public sector organisation. Regardless of sector and organisational type, a financial surplus is required for ongoing operations, regulatory adherence and investment into even minimal levels of innovation. Income may come from all manner of sources (sales, grants, fundraising) but the requirement remains to deliver products and services within budget and to satisfy stakeholders regardless of whether profit is a key deliverable. What is your success formula and how sustainable is it over time in a fast-changing environment like the post-truth fast show?

When examining the operating model it can be helpful to ask:

- Why do we do what we do?
- What needs, wants or scarcities are we aiming to fulfil?
- Why do clients/customers/end users want our products and services? What value do we create for them?
- What insights, innovations or differentiating capabilities do we have that allow us to create or respond to a viable market?
- What can/do we do better than anybody else and why? What is our competitive advantage?
- How do we create a financial surplus? How do we tend to use this financial surplus?
- What are our investment priorities?

- How do we ensure that we stay ahead of the game and continue to develop our capabilities?
- Which products, services, competencies and capabilities belong to us? What is our intellectual property?
- Are we generating the results we want?
- From the vantage point we currently have (i.e. the present), where do we think we want to go?
- What conditions, situations, events, markets, organisations and/ or people are we expecting to be there for the plan to work? What assumptions underpin our predictions for future success? Where and how are we relying on the status quo being preserved?

Often this exercise highlights a couple of fundamental problems that make ongoing future success challenging or even unlikely. At best you may discover a lack of alignment which, while damaging, is salvageable. At worst it may suddenly become clear that the existing operating model has a fundamental fault that could eventually and suddenly lead to catastrophic failure. For example, reliance on the intellectual property of others rather than the development of house products and solutions, or making a limited margin in a way that is too easy to replicate and with limited barriers to entry, or creating products and services that people 'put up with' until something better comes along (and it will).

This exercise, while illuminating, can be painful and unnerving. The precipice of potential failure comes into sharp focus right before your eyes and it can be tempting to turn away from the issues and act as if nothing is amiss. Old habits die hard and it's a tough moment when you realise that the organisation is heading for a fall without a fully functioning steering wheel, adequate brakes or a map of potentially viable alternative routes.

It may be that the existing model is performing as you believe it should. It might be delivering success for the organisation, its people and its customers or end users. In this case it's time to interrogate whether this is sustainable over the longer term, even in the face of limited change or disruption. Can the existing operating model drive future success even in a relatively benign environment?

An old-fashioned SWOT analysis is a useful tool for capturing the outputs of the conversation.[26] What are the inherent strengths and weaknesses of the existing operating model and how do they measure up to the demands of the present? What threats and risks can you perceive and how might they be mitigated? Are opportunities in the present already becoming apparent and are there obvious opportunities to explore for the future?

At this stage of the process it isn't uncommon to have an alarming collective realisation that the existing operating model is far from fit for purpose and instead already presents some real and present dangers to success or even survival. But worry not, as most of the competition is most likely suffering a similar predicament!

STEP 5: A BIG DOSE OF REALITY

You're probably thinking that you've already had quite enough of reality for one day, but this is where it starts to get interesting. That's quite enough navel-gazing – having cornered and quarantined the existing operating model and drowned any resulting sorrows with copious tea and biscuits, it's time to look outside. Our task at this stage is to capture the external environment within which the organisation operates – from all angles, warts and all.

The strategic context is made up of factors, actors, players and drivers and we need to have a detailed picture of each as they are, right now, in the present.

Factors include such elements as:

- geo-political trends
- international finance and access to adequate funding
- macroeconomics
- energy and commodity prices
- social values
- available and emerging technology
- foreign exchange rates
- demographics
- ecological and safety issues
- regulatory constraints and requirements
- relevant legislation

The acronym PESTLE (political, economic, social, technological, legal, environmental) is a useful reminder of the major classes from which factors might be drawn.[27] It's likely that while some factors are common to all organisations, others are only relevant to your organisation and the operating model you choose to pursue. Capturing these now is a great way to understand the threats and opportunities already present in the operating environment and will be enormously helpful in the later stages of the supple strategy system.

Actors are those groups and individuals who have an influence or can impact upon your success. They may include regulators, government departments and regional councils, NGOs and lobbying organisations, investors, charities, suppliers, clients or end users, and, perhaps most important of all, employees. A list of all actors, with details of their attention focus and extent of involvement, provides a clear view of the influencers, enablers and potential detractors who have a vested interest and some level of power over your success.

You'll notice that competitors haven't yet featured, but they can of course have a significant impact upon the success of your organisation. I find it helpful to create a separate picture of players who may compete, collaborate or make markets with you. Understanding the competitor landscape in the here and now involves looking further than the usual suspects. We want to identify all existing competitors, not only those that compete directly or that offer perhaps a slight variation on your products or services into a similar geographical and sector footprint. We want to notice those that already compete on other terms right now, in the present. We need to recognise those that are busy creating new markets that may be reducing yours or fundamentally changing it. For example, if you are a high-street music retailer selling CDs, not only do you want to recognise all other high-street music retailers, you also need to discover the online retailers, the streaming services, the pirate sellers, the already emerging next big thing, and so on. If you were Blockbuster video you would want to be noticing Netflix!

Our final element of the strategic context to map is that of the drivers that may effect change. Drivers are often a combination of factors, actors and players that come together to create a seismic force that ignites a change chain reaction. For example, the combination of ecological concerns, government intervention, emerging technology and car driver behaviour is already leading to a larger market for hybrid vehicles and a diminishing one for those powered by diesel.

Once the thinker group has developed a shared representation of the current strategic context (the existing environment within which the organisation operates), it is pertinent to revisit the questions already asked of the operating model in Step 4 and to then ask these questions of all major competitors. In other words, what do others do better than we do and how is their current operating model superior? Is there anything they can see on the horizon that they are already reacting to that we should take note of?

STEP 6: TIME TRAVEL TO 'WHAT-IF' WORLDS

Wouldn't it be great to be able to see around corners and understand what our futures may hold? Time machines don't yet exist and time travel in any physical sense seems to be beyond our capabilities, for now at least. The very fact we can imagine time travel shows just how advanced the human brain is. Our ability to imagine situations, plan activities and predetermine decisions and actions for any given set of circumstances is fundamental to the survival of our species. Imagination allows us foresight of potential events, even if it is only via means of mental construction. This internal virtual reality provides a safe environment in which we can play with ideas, test hypotheses and practise responses without undue risk to our physical selves. We usually do this in isolation and without placing much conscious thought into how we go about it. When scenario planning we are more structured in our approach to the far-future and we travel with friends. That way we can create a collective understanding of potential future outcomes and a shared vision of the options available to us and the likely course of action in each.

In our modern everyday lives, we're wired for predictability and forecasting. To generate useful scenarios, we need to cast these tendencies aside. We cannot possibly predict the future with any degree of certainty and to attempt to forecast beyond the near-term is pure folly. This is why gambling is so dangerous and addictive – there's no way of confidently knowing a future outcome (unless of course there's some foul play involved).

The most useful scenarios are those that are possible and plausible yet challenging enough to create a shift in the way we think about our endeavours and the environment within which we perform them. Purely extrapolating existing data is not an effective way in which to build plausible future worlds. Contexts can shift unexpectedly and significantly – it is these potential future shifts that we really want to gain some insight into.

While our eyes are set towards the horizon and the far-future (which could mean a period of anything beyond 3–5 years for many organisations but for others 30 years plus) we must also be sure to take a close look at the road immediately ahead. The next sharp corner may be far closer than we think or may be concealed behind a well-placed hedge!

SIGNS

The future is all around us. As we anticipate an event we travel towards the future with a potent mixture of excitement, hope, confusion, fear and all manner of other emotions. Sometimes our minds experience an event as hurling itself towards us as the future collapses into the present – think about that exam you've been studiously revising for. And sometimes, when we least expect it, something in our past catches up with us to wreak havoc or precipitate positive change. In organisations this can take the form of neglected technical debt that accumulates quietly over time. The issue renders the organisation unable to react fast enough to an imminent threat or sudden opportunity. Are some of our past and present-day responses to the evident climate crisis laying the foundations for further crises that we cannot yet foresee or even understand? Our steady-state understanding of a complex system is rarely as good as it needs to be or we think it is.

It's not effective to assume that what is will be. Abstractedly extending existing data and obvious emerging trends is potentially unhelpful and misleading, but there are important lessons to be learned from history. History has a habit of repeating itself. Characters may be different and cycles may alter in length, but there are stories that present themselves in an array of guises like repetitive mantras. Economies, politics, consumer preferences and even global conflict tend to demonstrate cycles over time – repeating narratives that, upon investigation, seem to manifest similar symptoms ahead of each major shift. The tendrils of the future are already interwoven into our present. There are elements of our experience right now that seem virtually insignificant which, over time, will emerge to have been the catalysts for fundamental change. Change that none of us would have necessarily foreseen, but which appears obvious with the benefit of hindsight and an ability to view the macro patterns from the safe distance of the future. Some very early shoots of our future have already shifted into our past; patterns are already in development that will create the next cycle. They may look slightly different this time, but the signals will be there – faint and obscured by our current world view. This is why it is so important to listen to the experiences, opinions and visions of everyone in the room. The smallest insight that initially appears insignificant and irrelevant may be the very one that breaks the future cipher. Our current world view is not the best lens through which to venture boldly into the future.

Preferences also need to be recognised and restrained. Most of us have a view on how we would like to see the future unfold. This individual perspective is influenced by our subconscious beliefs, values and experiences and we place an additional filter of personality upon how we then express it to others. At the simplest level, pessimists tend to expect the world to become more challenging and optimists the opposite. It's easy to write off a viewpoint as overly pessimistic or optimistic, but by investigating the rationale that sits behind the opinion more deeply we sometimes unearth a useful alternative world view or a better understanding of opinions based on experiences that we haven't personally experienced.

Leadership teams are more often overly optimistic about how the future will unfold for them even when they protest otherwise. I like to remind myself of Margaret Atwood's bestselling novel *The Handmaid's Tale* and the research she undertook in its creation.[28] Anyone who has read the book or watched the TV adaptation will be aware that the story is one of an unrecognisable future world where violence and abusive control are everyday life and a theocracy is at the helm of Gilead (formerly much of the USA). The reader or viewer absorbs the story in disbelief that any of the events could actually happen in the real world. The fascinating fact is that Margaret Atwood purposely went about creating the story using only things that human beings had wrought upon other human beings at some point in time in some part of the world. I'm not suggesting that Gilead is about to come into being (let's hope not), but it is important to note that there isn't much that the world is not capable of or willing to manifest. Assuming 'it can't happen here' is not an adequate basis upon which to build a supple strategy.

Signs and patterns are often found in the statements of experts as the current paradigm starts to crumble around them. Gordon Brown, when

Chancellor of the Exchequer in the UK, is famously remembered as having said 'no more boom and bust' not too long before the global financial crisis of 2008 and the inevitable 'bust' that followed.[29] None of us, recognised expert or otherwise, can genuinely predict the future. Time changes everything and what once may have been a fundamentally stable system can be disrupted suddenly and unexpectedly. Somebody somewhere might be desperately trying to raise the alarm, but nobody is listening to them as they are not a recognised expert of the system – a system that's already failing.

PERSPECTIVES AND FILTERS

And so, as we work with the future we need to be mindful of our feelings towards it and our inherent (and perhaps unsubstantiated) expectations of it. We need to observe closely manifestations of the future in the present and hangovers of history in the present that may cause an alternative future to emerge should conditions be supportive. Are there experiences, opinions or situations we have not yet personally experienced that we don't therefore even realise could exist and don't possess within our mental lexicon? Individual thinking performed collectively is a powerful antidote to this situation.

Most importantly we need to watch and listen more than we ever thought we may need to watch and listen, and we need to notice the small currents that start to divert the course of events even if they do so at first in a small way. Once the timeline has shifted we are relegated to playing catch-up, but if we can test the small diversions we are noticing we may just be able to get ahead of the damn burst or have a major impact on the course of history. How might social media alter the way we educate our children or the manner in which we access medical services? How will reality TV affect societal norms and behaviour? How will increasing environmental concerns and our desire for 'just in time' delivery manage to live together? This is what shapeshifters do – they create the future.

There are no all-positive or all-negative future scenarios. Plausible scenarios present threats and opportunities – admittedly these may be distributed unfairly or unevenly but they will both be present. Assuming a given future world is all-bad or all-good is lazy thinking and will lead to a strategy based on a biased view of its potential outcomes or neglecting the consideration of a particular outcome full stop.

Shapeshifters generate alternative futures that are plausible, challenging and present unfamiliar situations where they will be faced with new or fundamentally altered opportunities or threats. Futures that differ to an existing situation enough that they might demand a different response, a new way of thinking, a paradigm shift in the organisation's operating model.

Shapeshifters challenge themselves to believe what they see rather than what they think they would like to see. They look at the fringes of their experience to explore what might be happening just beyond their present field of vision. They switch lenses and shift the angle to see the past, present and potential futures from a range of viewpoints. Shapeshifters notice and interrogate catalysts and challenge inherent judgement biases and expert opinions.

HOW YOU THINK MATTERS

Let's take a moment here to understand just some of the cognitive biases we are subject to. As a species we have developed habits which, while helpful to our survival amongst predators, tend to limit our ability to work with the future in a meaningful way. We typically build our mental models based on a limited number of examples regardless of how representative they may be. Expert opinions, rituals and habits, and frequency of story repetition, amplify existing thought patterns and drive inertia and intransigence. Our beliefs, values and experiences limit our interpretation of these further, particularly if we have not consciously sought to expand these throughout our lives. Where complexity, ambiguity, volatility and uncertainty prevail we find it hard to contemplate the 'whole' of an issue – it's just too big to comprehend and handle. Instead we focus on the achievement of lesser outcomes assuming that our power does not extend far enough to influence larger causes. We wait for others to act, expecting those more powerful, connected and capable than ourselves will take control and lead us all to a better future. As a result, we avoid accountability and relinquish autonomy and agency to an unknown superhuman who is probably sat in a corner with a cup of tea watching Netflix doing the selfsame thing. Our present options typically remain the easiest to understand and so we look to find ways in which we can make these fit a developing situation rather than work to understand and influence the future as it emerges and find new ways of being successful within it. Coupled with our reticence to give up what we already have (no matter how unsuitable it may be) and a pessimistic or optimistic bias, we can see why future thinking is such a challenging pursuit.

BUILDING PLAUSIBLE YET CHALLENGING SCENARIOS

There are two main approaches to building scenarios. Both approaches are equally viable and productive – I often use a combination of both when working with leadership teams.

The first approach is more intuitive and appeals to those who are naturally creative. The idea is to think broadly about the context within which the organisation operates and to generate a number of story segments that start to describe potential future worlds. This is much like the experience of writing a novel; it's a creative process reliant on utilising imagination to build worlds that would be interesting and useful to explore. Any number of scenarios can be developed in this way. Considering the likely future environment and capturing the strategic context it generates leads to the intellectual testing of the ideas. Do they stack up? Could they plausibly happen? How might they come about? What would the storyline be? This approach typically generates lots of energy, and even those who usually consider themselves to be relatively uncreative find their imaginations unleashed.

For example, a pharmaceutical company could explore a scenario where antibiotics were no longer effective against a wide range of diseases, a scenario where all medical provision was privately funded, a scenario where a major epidemic had altered the world, and a scenario where gene technology had developed to such an extent that it had a profound effect upon preventative medicine and lifespan. Each of these eventualities would have a significant impact on the strategy of a pharmaceutical company and each would likely result in the failure of any such organisation that did not radically alter its operating model in preparation. This approach does not place a limit upon the number of scenarios, but it can become unwieldy to work with more than five or six due to the level of detail required of each for them to become useful tools.

The second approach is more structured and appeals to those who are typically focused on process and analytical thinking. Using this method, the team chooses two drivers of contextual change from the drivers they have identified in Step 5 or other drivers that have emerged as discussions have progressed. A four-box model is created around these drivers, setting each on a scale between two varying future outcomes. This approach is useful to generate debate and disagreement (remember, disagreement is good!) regarding which drivers are likely to be the catalysts for fundamental change or paradigm shifts to the operating environment. Four scenarios result, pitching two variables against one another and outlining the future worlds likely to come about from each combination. Each scenario can be given a catchy title that will capture the imagination as we attempt to shift the organisation effectively towards the future.

For example, if we are operating in the automotive industry we may want to consider the future of energy production and consumption patterns against the development of public transport infrastructure in a given geographical area. Four scenarios would result, each representing a different combination of the two major drivers selected for consideration.

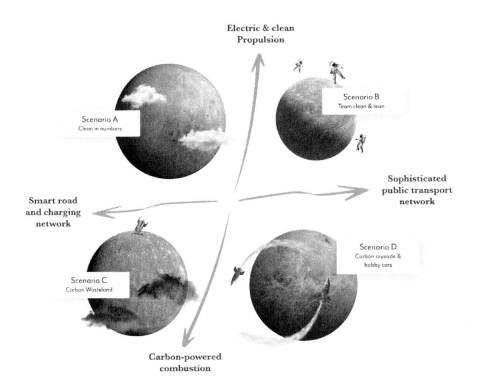

We might decide to have one axis that has the internal combustion engine (petrol and/or diesel) at one end, and electric and other propulsion methods at the other. This can be set against an infrastructure axis where at one end the infrastructure and related technology is specifically developed to support these new vehicles while at the other a far more sophisticated public transport network has been created which has led to a world where car ownership and usage is a thing of the past or at least becoming far less common.

Each of these scenarios will present different opportunities and threats to the organisation. By consciously thinking well in advance of these scenarios coming to pass, not only can the organisation better prepare for each eventuality, it may also be able to exert some influence in terms the direction in which the market moves.

Whichever method is employed, we then need to capture the strategic context that would result, in particular the factors, actors and players that will survive from the 'what is' and those that are likely to emerge as a result of the changes identified. It's useful to explore the peripheral vision of each scenario to alight upon what else might be coming towards the organisation from the future that may have been missed and what may be catching up with the organisation from its past.

SIZE MATTERS

'Go big or go home' doesn't apply to scenario planning. While it's powerful to consider the broadest context and an extensive timespan, it can be equally productive and enlightening to work in a more defined space (perhaps a particular market or technological focus) or to consider the near-future (particularly where this type of activity is an entirely new way of thinking for those involved or major disruptive change is likely imminently). Quality rather than quantity is what really counts here — small can be good if entered into with an open mind and a genuine desire to play in the sandpit of the future. Time horizons can be set far into the future or towards the next strategic planning cycle. A high level of uncertainty in the near-term may necessitate shortening the lens towards a shorter time frame. To gain focus it can be useful to ask questions about the outcomes wanted from the scenarios exercise: What's troubling us about the future? Where do we want to gain clarity? Are we getting excited about the right things? Supple strategy relies upon supple process and open minds — remaining flexible is key.

I've mentioned already that the scenarios developed need to be plausible and challenging, but how do we ensure we aren't playing with predictions and hyperbole? This is where systems and storyboards become important vehicles to capture potential future emerging contexts and how they manifest.

STEP 7: STORIES AND MAPS OF THE FUTURE

The tale of the slowly boiling frogs in a saucepan is now indelibly etched into corporate folklore. Peter Senge, a recognised expert in systems thinking, used the frogs as a metaphor to describe how we tend to react to gradual changes in our environment that have the propensity to harm or kill us. In his book *The Fifth Discipline* he explains that if a frog is placed into a pan of boiling water it will immediately jump out of said pan to safety (having felt the immediate threat to its existence), whereas if a frog is placed into a pan of cool water that is gradually heated to boiling point it will remain there oblivious to the dangerous, and at first subtle, changes to its environment until it is no longer able to take evasive action.[30] I have no idea if this is a true reflection of how a frog may actually behave in these circumstances (and I'm not about to attempt to find out), but it is a very apt metaphor that describes how organisations tend to react (or not) to what is (or is not) going on around them.

At this stage of the process we have generated a small number of scenarios that we think may be useful to our strategic discussions and we have started to capture the strategic context (the factors, actors and players) that will contribute to its formation and existence. By examining these scenarios in greater detail, we can start to identify how they may in fact come about – which events, patterns and behaviours may actually lead to the final destinations we have described. Understanding events, patterns and behaviour is important as they will provide us with indicators that will help us to navigate our course. By taking time to interrogate the process through which a particular scenario may come to pass, we start to identify repeating patterns from history and highlight areas where greater research might be required. This process can also present us with further plausible scenarios that had not yet become apparent from the earlier stages of our discussions.

A shapeshifter knows that the future is a series of unfolding interconnected events – often when it is not immediately obvious where those interconnections may be or what they may drive. To better understand this process, we create system maps to elaborate upon what may be positive and negative cycles that drive or inhibit outcomes. Mapping a system cannot in itself deliver a firm prediction of what the future may hold, but it can provide us with reassurance that the scenarios under examination are plausible. A system map can also identify factors that lead us to an alternative scenario that is more plausible or useful to the organisation's thinking.

System maps allow us to capture the driving forces of a system, their likely impact and where they interact. They capture the feedback loops at play – positive and negative. When adopting a systems-thinking perspective a shapeshifter is looking for how the behaviour of the system emerges from the structure and impact of its feedback loops, and how these feedback loops seed further feedback loops that drive the system towards greater complexity or allow it to decompose towards chaos.

Thinking in systems is the process of understanding how the individual parts of a system combine to form and influence its whole. Organisations, people and the systems they are subject to are unpredictable in a chaotic environment, but we can seek to better understand the mechanisms at play so that we can check the potential validity of our scenarios and, perhaps more importantly, discover indicators that may provide signals along the path towards a particular future eventuality.

A systems-thinking approach accepts that complex systems are just that – complex. It encourages the thinker to consider the whole and to examine the process through which the whole is created. Underlying dynamics are of utmost interest – what are the patterns that determine outcomes and how might these patterns manifest from the chaos around them? Interdependencies and interactions of inherent economic models and devices, ecological concerns and developments, geopolitical structures and evolution, demographical profile, patterns of historic conflict and potential future conflict, psychology of populations and swarm behavioural patterns all combine to generate feedback loops that either support or challenge the development of a given scenario.

A system map allows the visual representation of major contributing factors that have a positive or limiting impact upon a system and therefore a direct effect upon the potential future scenario. Where systems demonstrate balance and the mechanisms to self-correct and reinforce the status quo it is pertinent to identify factors that could throw the system into chaos to identify risks and opportunities that may arise from that disruptive force. In systems that are naturally more dynamic there is an inherent instability and typically a propensity for greater risk alongside greater opportunities from the potential for exponential growth.

System maps can sometimes draw us too far into analysis and a search for evidence that cannot yet exist. A balancing activity is that of storyboarding. Creating a storyline with depth and meaning for each scenario takes us back to a more creative and intuitive approach that can truly win hearts and minds. Generating a visual storyboard, a comic strip or a set of snapshots of points in time on the journey towards a particular scenario is useful as it can later be utilised as a mechanism for others to get involved and engaged.

The best scenarios are typically created using a combination of these approaches. Moving from a range of linear stories to system maps and back again leads to a storyboard that is then ratified through the examination of the systems underpinning its script and then altered as necessary. This can effectively be accomplished as a group working as one team or splitting into two groups each performing a storytelling or system-mapping role for a given scenario. Once this process has been repeated a few times the scenario starts to feel more believable and tangible, and a potential future is more easily visualised. At this stage it is useful to review the strategic contexts captured for each future scenario (the factors, actors and players) and to start to identify some drivers that might already be emerging for a future beyond the scenario itself:

- Who are the winners and who are the losers in a given scenario?
- Who are the trendsetters now and in the future – and why?
- Who might invade the space and what capabilities will allow them to do so?
- What would it be like to actually live in the context generated in this scenario and to experience the journey through which it comes about? And how might this influence opinions and behaviours?
- Which factors have major impacts, and which are less able to be monitored or predicted?
- What do we already know are the inevitable future events or events that have already occurred whose outcomes have not yet fully played out?

Through the shared experience of system mapping and the co-creation of scenario storyboards another level of learning and a shared understanding of the past, the present and the future are ultimately achieved. The whole point of creating scenarios is to make the implicit explicit and to generate insight and clarity amidst volatility, uncertainty, complexity and ambiguity. Process learning – learning inherent within the process – is invaluable; it expands the mind and changes the thinker forever.

STEP 8: CANARIES IN THE COAL MINE

In years gone by miners would lower a canary into the coal mine they were about to descend into themselves. The bird would succumb quickly to toxic gases that may be present and thus alert the miners to withdraw or remain on the surface. These days the term is taken to mean an indicator that can call attention to something that presents a risk (or perhaps an opportunity).

When working with the future it is prudent to take markers from the system maps, storyboards and the scenarios themselves that may signal a change of direction or the likelihood of a plausible scenario materially increasing or decreasing. Shapeshifters make it their business to identify indicators of timeline shifts or the collapsing of the wave of potentiality into a more likely reality. These indicators come together to form an early warning system that alerts the organisation as the future becomes more tangible and gradually takes its physical form.

It can be useful to interrogate patterns of the past to isolate indicators that gave warning to important outcomes ahead of time. With the benefit of hindsight this can seem remarkably straightforward, but it is important to remember that it is always easier to see a pattern once it has fully emerged.

Shapeshifters enable strategy generation and navigation through their deep understanding of the mechanism through which the future arrives and a genuine curiosity throughout the journey. The indicators that the organisation gathers and regularly monitors provide a dashboard of early warning signals that allow it to alter course and influence outcomes to best effect. Shapeshifters collect 'path indicators' that can give early warning signals of particular futures becoming reality.

STEP 9: WIND-TUNNEL STRATEGY

By now we will have a small number of detailed future scenarios against which to plot organisational strategy. Before we start to do so, it is useful and informative to wind-tunnel existing strategic plans against each potential future to examine how they would stand up to the pressures and risks of these various contexts and whether they would best place the organisation to seize and optimise any opportunities they may present. Indeed, could the organisation even survive in its present form, executing its current strategic plan?

In this step of the process the thinkers consider the existing strategy against the current reality and against each of the scenarios to ascertain what still remains relevant, where the strategy presents risk, where opportunities may be missed and where future scenarios cannot be supported by the strategy in its current form.

Often it becomes quite clear that the existing strategy is not well understood by the senior leadership cohort let alone beyond its boundaries. The thinker group benefits from walking through the strategy as it has been set out, ensuring a shared understanding of the strategic options that were considered and the strategic choices made alongside the justifications for each. This process unearths further deeply buried assumptions and historical perspectives that may have the power to blind the organisation to alternative options. Perhaps more importantly it highlights powerful limiting beliefs that may cause the organisation and its leaders to hold back from taking advantage of situations to fulfil the organisation's full potential or to dogmatically pursue existing plans even when they are already clearly inappropriate for the future, whichever direction that may take.

Shapeshifters realise that while strategic dialogue may be ongoing, a strategic plan is conceived and captured at a point in time. Strategic plans that are not scrutinised often and debated deliberately, at best face stagnation and dilution, and at worst take the organisation in entirely the wrong direction by the least appropriate methods for the emerging strategic context. A case of 'wrong strategy' can be a fatal blow that fails to become apparent until the water is too hot (remember our frogs).

This step unearths assumptions, myopias, further path indicators and potential strategic alternatives. The discussion carries the debate towards future implications for the organisation and its people if it remains steadfastly committed to its existing strategy in the event of each of the potential futures depicted by the detailed scenarios. It examines the consequences for the commercial viability of the enterprise, its structure, core processes, critical capabilities and the evolution of the markets in which it operates and the stakeholders it serves. The very integrity of the organisation's existing operating model can be wind-tunnelled against potential plausible futures.

As with any shock there can be a range of reactions to what emerges from this exercise. Some thinkers may feel rather overwhelmed by the problems they seem to have discovered, while others may deny any such problems exist. Optimism and pessimism can erupt at this point, but we all know that each and every future scenario presents a range of risks and opportunities. As a group you just need to work through each of the future contexts to understand how the map of reality will have changed and start to generate options and determine directions that may best place the organisation in each of those futures.

STEP 10: ALTERNATIVE PATHS FOR ALTERNATIVE WORLDS

Our thinkers now get down to the exciting business of generating new strategic options for discussion – ideas that may take the organisation into new markets, alter the fundamental basis of its products or services and meet as yet unfulfilled, or perhaps even unforeseen, needs and wants of its stakeholders. Ideas that may mean the divestment of key parts of the business, the hothousing of pockets of innovation that may drive the future value chain or the total repositioning of the organisation over time.

For each scenario a range of strategic options can be generated and debated regarding their merits, risks, feasibility and likely impact. A strategic path can then be plotted to be turned to in the event of each scenario manifesting, alongside a range of path indicators that will signal the emergence of each of the scenarios. In reality the future doesn't behave in such a linear manner and the truth will likely be somewhere in the middle. A hybrid scenario may develop. The future will emerge via a complex path that combines layers of elements from a number of our detailed scenarios or extend entirely beyond the scenarios already captured or branch out in a direction not yet considered. However, the activity will not have been in vain. The path indicators will be shining beacons lighting the path as the organisation travels along it, and illuminating potholes and alternative routes along the way. With a path for each scenario the organisation now has a pick-and-mix selection of ideas it can test and rehearse ahead of time – a supple strategy that presents options rather than a fixed route that may become blocked at short notice with no plan B.

Organisations that are future-fit understand that this range of options and detailed scenarios gives them choices and insight that places them ahead of the competition when the going gets tough. They have already considered the potential actions and decisions they can take and have rehearsed the future ahead of its arrival – if only mentally. Through their detailed examination of the future, its ramifications and their potential responses, they already have a sense of what to do if circumstances that have some similar elements but are in some way fundamentally different to the scenarios they have already rehearsed emerge. As a result, principle-based decision-making and devolved leadership accountability combine to enable an aligned and fleet of foot organisation to develop, ready to respond to reality as it happens rather than blaming and shaming away from hard truths.

Shapeshifters go a step further. They seek to create the future. They approach strategy creation as a tool with which to bring about the future they want to see. Shapeshifters come to strategic thinking in a manner that is less combative towards their competitors, suppliers and other stakeholders. They want to get the best outcomes for the context within which they find themselves and they work collaboratively with other actors and players to leverage drivers of contextual change and make the most of any manifesting symptoms of an emerging future. To achieve this, shapeshifters influence the future, lobby its constituents, collaborate to co-create and positively disrupt the status quo. With alternative strategies that are firmly focused on future creation, shapeshifters maintain a truly supple strategy and a flexible and workable approach to its implementation.

STEP 11: STRESS TEST SUPPLE STRATEGY

Once strategic options have been considered and choices decided upon for each detailed scenario, go back to the wind-tunnelling exercise and do the same for each of these new paths towards the future. Ask yourself:

- How will each of the strategic paths we have laid down cope with the potential demands of the futures depicted within the detailed scenarios and the routes they may take to emerge?
- Which elements are new to us here and where do we feel discomfort or unfamiliarity as leaders?
- What capabilities as an organisation and as individuals will we need to develop to be successful in each scenario and how can we go about doing that effectively?
- How might the organisational structure need to change?
- Where may there be challenges to commercial operations or funding models?
- Where do we need to be building relationships now to ensure collaboration for the future?

Shapeshifters must face all of these questions and more to be sure that they have the most complete picture of the range of possible futures and plans in place that facilitate how they may decide to respond.

STEP 12: OPERATING MODEL REINVENTION

The previous steps may have determined that the existing business model is not fit for purpose. It may already be showing signs of strain but, more likely, it will limp on into the future until a devastating fatal blow is struck. Organisations unwilling to re-examine and, if required, redesign their operating model will fail more often than not. It may feel safe to stick to the status quo and avoid change at all costs, but organisations that fail to evolve eventually suffer the same fate as the dinosaurs – they die.

Future-fit organisations make sure their operating model is front and centre of strategic discussions. They examine how it provides them with the capabilities destined for future success and they regularly interrogate the assumptions it has been built upon. They reposition the target as soon as it becomes apparent that the predetermined destination is not in their best interests, will take them on a circuitous route or is, in fact, likely to be no longer in existence.

In shapeshifter organisations the target operating model (TOM) is not a fixed destination point that never wavers no matter what.[31] It is a moving target that responds to events and does its best to pre-empt the demands of the future. Its destination, foundations and mechanisms are investigated, redesigned and deployed at speed on a regular basis allowing sharp turns to be navigated and road blocks to be expertly manoeuvred.

Markets and behaviours can change beyond recognition within a single generation, sometimes faster. The retail industry is undergoing disruption due to online sales, the music industry has been disrupted beyond recognition by streaming technology, the car industry is about to be disrupted significantly by new fuels. What next? What may be the change lurking just around the corner that renders the organisation's current operating model inept, then irrelevant, and finally extinct?

Using scenarios to stress test the existing operating model and to wind-tunnel potential new options can lead to game-changing insights or game-making innovations. It can provide protection for the organisation via conscious evolution and allows experimentation to enable the best ideas to take shape in protected environments before they are put to the true test of the future. Operating model reinvention may even be constructed around the need or desire to work collaboratively with other actors and players to make the world a better place. Truly joined up thinking for complex wicked problems!

STEP 13: PUBLISH AND ENGAGE

Step 13 (unlucky for some) might be the first time your thinking truly hits the road and receives feedback from others who are intrinsically linked to the organisation and are painfully aware of its successes and failures, and its inherent strengths and weaknesses. Publishing scenarios as a fait accompli with little prior consultation is a recipe for disaster. The greater the involvement of a wider audience in their review and refinement, and the broader the population of participants invited into strategic dialogue, the more likely a powerful movement can be formed (more about that in Part 4).

In reality, this might be the first time that the scenarios are in a detailed and polished enough format to publish throughout the organisation. And yes, publish them you must, otherwise they will suffer the fate of most strategic thinking and planning – they will be consigned to a shelf as the work of a detached group unconnected to the reality of day-to-day activity, never to be revisited. You know this not to be true as you've built a diverse group of thinkers and worked hard to ensure inclusivity and fair representation but, of course, your well-designed thinking group will no longer be considered fully connected if they have been thinking in an ivory tower while the rest of the organisation has been unceremoniously dumped and left to get on with the business of present day reality.

This is where a virtual Futurological Congress can be critical. The use of a shared platform where ideas can be shared and debated, opinions sought and commitment evaluated can be a great way to involve as many people as possible in the strategic conversation as it evolves. Most people don't feel the need to know every detail of the discussions that may take place but, given a vacuum, they will fill an empty space with what they believe could be true or the latest rumour that the organisational grapevine has given credence to.

There are, of course, some elements of strategic discussion that it would be foolish to share (for example, mergers, acquisitions, leadership changes and funding challenges), but there are a great many elements that can be openly discussed. There is no danger in seeking input into scenario development or contributions to a SWOT analysis; these are purely opinions and you can never have enough data on what people truly think and believe. The more information you can both share and gather, the stronger and more supple the strategy will be.

There is nothing to fear except fear itself. Through transparent engagement, you may just learn something that changes the organisation's future entirely or has the potential to create disruptive change beyond its borders. Shapeshifters take every opportunity to engage with and learn from everyone in their team – absolutely everyone!

STEP 14: METRICS THAT MATTER

For each of our scenarios we now have a detailed picture of what the future may hold, a set of path indicators that notify us should that future seem to be coming into existence, and a strategy and TOM formulated for each eventuality that has been stress tested and rehearsed. The future is not a tame beast; it is fierce, wild and entirely unpredictable. The only thing we do know is that the future will probably not emerge exactly as we depicted within one of our range of scenarios. Instead it is likely to be a combination of worlds or a different world entirely that was, at this time, a paradigm beyond our ability to perceive it.

As we travel into the future we still have a responsibility to the present. An organisation that is fully focused on the future and devoured by its desire to evolve extensively to greet it or create it may suffer in the present and may not ever get to the future it yearns to meet. It may plunder its present in pursuit of the future – not a great way to go.

Shapeshifters know they need to balance the sightline and shift effortlessly between future creation and present mastery. They identify and monitor a small range of metrics that matter alongside the future path indicators identified through the scenarios process: measures of health and vitality that will provide evidence of wellness and performance; data that will inform decision makers that their actions are generating the required results or alert them quickly if risks are identified or results are not as expected.

Shapeshifters look up often enough to adjust their course now in response to the present while manoeuvring steadily and flexibly towards a future that may not yet be apparent to all.

STEP 15: WATCHFUL WAITING

The final step in the supple strategy system is perhaps the most important. Having created potential future worlds, examined the contexts they generate, wind-tunnelled existing strategy against them, developed new strategic pathways towards them and identified path indicators for the emerging future and metrics for present performance, now comes the time to engage in watchful waiting. By that I mean horizon scanning and taking in information from a wide variety of sources to give the organisation the best possible chance of identifying game-changing events and anticipating their future impact.

Events that can cause paradigm shifts to the timeline are not necessarily those of great magnitude or recognised significance in the present. They often come from an unexpected direction or source and can whisper their intentions rather than explicitly signpost the future for all to see. Impacts can reach far beyond the initial context and have effect over significant time frames. For example, consider how the invention of the contraceptive pill has impacted the world of work; just one related outcome being the high number of women of menopausal age now in the workforce performing complex and challenging roles – an entirely new cadre of services and service providers is now emerging linked to this one outcome.

Encouraging people throughout the organisation to take a keen interest in world affairs and engage in creative pursuits or community service can place an organisation at the centre of a powerful web of useful data. Shifting opinions and perspectives are sometimes more noticeable when we engage in activities beyond the typical day-to-day operations of the business we are in. Casual conversations, apparently innocuous press releases and social media exchanges, speculation regarding new technology and interesting research outcomes can spark new ideas or pull the trigger for an indicator of the future that you have already isolated through the scenarios process.

Changes and developments internal to the organisation can be equally influential over time. A new investor will come with a particular set of interests and capabilities. A surprising success in a new product line or the first signs of failure in a long-serving cash cow can be signals that should attract your attention towards a possible change in direction.

Shapeshifters engage in conscious and active watchful waiting. They are not lethargic in their consumption of news and views. Shapeshifters look beyond the confines of their existing environment to scan the horizons presented by their range of future scenarios, and even beyond those. Their interest is in life, the universe and everything.

It's clear by now that the 15 steps of the supple strategy system are a way of being rather than a one-time event or series of events. For best effect, the steps overlap and repeat as necessary with fluidity and grace. Structured interventions and formal events purely set the tone and provide the drum beat, the rhythm through which to develop an organisational personality that has flexibility, agility, collaboration and innovation at its core. Ongoing curiosity, experimentation and dialogue are the keys to avoiding the fate of a dinosaur and becoming a shapeshifter.

Two further elements make the supple strategy system whole. They are not 'steps' in and of themselves, but they are critical to its effective functioning.

STRATEGIC LOOPS

Engaging in scenario planning and diving into the related strategic dialogue takes time and effort. A group of thinkers will have immersed themselves in future worlds and challenged themselves and one another to create the most demanding environments possible to drive the formulation of strategies that will best position the organisation in whatever future eventually emerges. They will have explored innovative approaches and solutions to complex issues and found ways to mitigate risks and exploit opportunities as the timeline unfolds.

Inevitably the world changes as time marches on. What was once a plausible scenario suddenly becomes far less likely or a scenario that was initially discounted as impossible becomes ever more likely to happen (everything is possible regardless of how improbable it may seem at first).

Without a structured approach that ensures the conversation continues, these diversions can be missed, misinterpreted or reacted to inappropriately. The quantity of thinkers regularly involved in the functioning of the organisation's brain and the quality of said thinking is directly related to the actions and decisions the organisation may take and their likely outcomes.

Skip ongoing strategic dialogue at your peril. Building in enduring strategic loops ensures that people come together on a regular basis in a structured manner to continue the strategic dialogue beyond initial interpretations. Each loop will force thinkers to re-examine their assumptions, re-interrogate the present, review the plausibility of the scenarios already generated, drive the generation of further scenarios as the future unfolds and subtly shift supple strategy across the range of alternative timelines as future path indicators start to take shape.

U-TURNS AND LANE CHANGES

Last but by no means least. As the organisation navigates the emerging future the indicators and metrics it identified within the steps of the supple strategy system may present them with evidence that demands immediate action. I have already mentioned that sometimes a U-turn is the strongest and most sensible option available (see page 24). Leaders with confidence and courage know that a well-executed U-turn is a safer manoeuvre than steady acceleration towards obstructions on the path that have the potential to cause great damage or even destruction. At any point in the journey metrics may show that interventions are not having the expected or desired impact, or that the external operating environment has fundamentally altered – perhaps a paradigm shift has come early and unexpectedly.

Game-changing leaders ensure their curiosity is such that connections, information and insight provide advance warning of such potential threats or diversions. Those who are game-makers go a stage further and seek to cause disruption. In either case, shapeshifter organisations make sure they enable U-turns and lane changes when the situation suggests that these are the safest actions for the future sustained health of the organisation. Shapeshifters make every effort to avoid following a stagnant or dangerous strategy for the purposes of ego or avoidance of blame. Shapeshifters keep their options open – they know it's the only sane approach when working with the future.

CHAPTER 6

START WHERE YOU ARE: THE SUPPLE STRATEGY MATURITY MODEL

There's probably some work to do and some changes to make if you genuinely want to work with the future in a meaningful way. It's a rare organisation that automatically approaches strategy formulation in this way and habitually creates supple strategy. Where does your organisation demonstrate shapeshifter DNA and what could it gain from developing shapeshifter capabilities?

To help you answer this question, over the following pages you will find a maturity model that outlines in great detail what it takes to be a shapeshifter. It will provide you with a map of the territory so that you can accurately determine where your organisation currently is on its journey towards becoming a shapeshifter and how it can best evolve towards supple strategy generation. It may be that your organisation already displays some shapeshifter behaviours; alternatively it might be that it is yet to develop any. Whichever is the case, its evolution will be unique and will typically fare better when everyone understands why it may be a good idea, what might be at stake if the voyage isn't embarked upon, where to focus first and how to go about it without destroying all that is good in the process.

The model is, of course, a simplification of a complex human system and so it is unlikely that your organisation will fit neatly and entirely into one stage. Use the maturity model to explore how strategy is currently formed within your organisation and by whom, and to ascertain what type of relationship with the future currently exists. It may be that circumstances have forced you into certain habits of strategic dialogue – have you perhaps slipped back into a more primitive state due to threats or challenges over which you have little obvious control or have these very instances acted as catalysts for significant evolutionary jumps? Once you have a sense of where you are you can then use the model to identify some priority focus areas, practical steps you can take and milestones you can aim to reach. This exercise can underpin a progressive and collective evolution of the elements that make up supple strategy formulation.

The five evolutionary stages are:

1 Reactive
2 Focused
3 Structured
4 Integrated
5 Shapeshifter

Each stage has markers that signal a certain level of strategic dialogue has been habitually achieved. To work out whereabouts your organisation spends most of its time (and therefore within which stage it generally resides) we focus on 10 elements:

1 Impact: the typical level of impact at which strategic dialogue is directed.
2 Horizon: the typical length and breadth of the time horizon.
3 Catalysts: the events that tend to drive the initiation of strategic dialogue.
4 Dialogue: the quality and quantity of strategic dialogue.
5 Choices: the way in which strategic options are generated and evaluated.
6 Governance: the management of strategic dialogue and related indicators.
7 Journey: the way strategic plans are created and allowed to develop over time.
8 Rehearsal: how and when opportunities are presented for practise and immersion.
9 Learning: feedback mechanisms that inform the journey.
10 Agility: flexibility and manoeuvrability as the future takes shape.

STAGE 1: REACTIVE	
Impact	**SURVIVE**
Horizon	• Short- to medium-term time horizon (up to a maximum of five years but typically one to two years) • Based around internal or external known event timelines • Narrow context of existing sector players • Largely predictable outcomes
Catalysts	• Emerging external events with potentially substantial impact • Highly predictable or known future change • Opinions of respected and established experts • Typically threat- or fear-driven
Dialogue	• Strategic conversations limited to senior leadership and proven experts • Little to no appraisal of the existing operating model • Conversation is infrequent and disorderly; heavily influenced by areas of expertise and interests represented in the room • Largely focused on threat avoidance and risk mitigation
Choices	• Strategic options are limited and applied impulsively • Lack of adequate data analysis • Choices are exposed to the bias of leadership preferences • Details and outcomes may be cascaded by leaders of the organisation if they are considered important to the achievement of key strategic goals
Governance	• Strategic planning activity is ad hoc and lacks follow-up • Few, if any, metrics are identified and observed • Data may be skewed, inaccurate or incorrectly interpreted • Version control is limited and amendments are not always discussed and agreed
Journey	• Path is not clearly mapped and few milestones identified • Obvious obstacles are considered but limited identification of potential barriers to success • Strategy is revisited in the event of major problems arising but unlikely to be re-evaluated otherwise

Rehearsal	• Disaster recovery and crisis management rehearsal where required by regulation • Instructions may be cascaded or covertly applied through actions, decisions and behaviours of senior leadership
Learning	• Feedback on strategy is limited • Reactions to events and outcomes as they happen may result in organisational learning
Agility	• Opportunistic yet rigid strategy, known to few and inconsistently applied

– • –

STAGE 2: FOCUSED	
Impact	**STRIVE**
Horizon	• Mid- to long-term time horizon (up to 10 years) applied to a limited number of high-profile projects and ventures. Shorter time horizon for overall organisational strategy • Context extended to include possible future players in areas of particular interest
Catalysts	• Potential opportunity to extend or diversify in terms of markets or products • Predictable future impact of technological development and other contextual changes in chosen focus areas
Dialogue	• Strategic conversations are limited to senior leadership, proven experts and high-potential emerging leaders • Focus is predominantly on extension of the existing operating model to optimise opportunities and/or improve financial results • Strategic conversation can be narrow in focus and may neglect connected elements in related sectors and markets

Choices	• Strategic options explored for focus projects and ventures may be at odds with broader organisational direction • Limited consideration of how broader organisation strategy or activities of competitors may impact choices made • Choices and related decisions and plans are cascaded to those considered critical to successful execution
Governance	• Ad hoc strategic planning activity is supplemented by a more planned approach where projects and ventures are of strategic importance • Key metrics are identified in relation to some important elements • Strategy is owned by key people and they are accountable for version control and appropriate consultation in relation to changes made
Journey	• Obstacles and risks are identified for critical areas, and mitigating activities and decisions form part of the plan • The strategic journey is managed and monitored closely for areas determined to be of strategic importance • Effort is directed at driving activity and pushing through obstacles with resilience and tenacity
Rehearsal	• Instructions are cascaded and there is some mental rehearsal or workshopping of key elements of strategic plans
Learning	• Feedback is focused on priority areas and limited to achievement against predetermined metrics
Agility	• Focused strategy, with tendencies towards dilution over time and competing strategic strands

– • –

STAGE 3: STRUCTURED	
Impact	THRIVE
Horizon	• Short- to medium-term time horizon (up to a maximum of five years) routinely considered within a centrally managed annual planning process • Broader and longer-term time horizon is applied to strategic focus areas • Established process to identify and mitigate risk, and optimise opportunities
Catalysts	• Process-driven • Reliant upon internal leaders and specialists to encourage focus to be applied to areas of potential strategic significance
Dialogue	• Process-driven dialogue and theoretical methodology • Facilitated by internal or external strategic advisors • Focus is predominantly on growth, risk mitigation and exploration of opportunities through incremental development of existing operating model, targeted acquisition and divestment • Formulaic conversation that utilises case studies of previously successful strategies
Choices	• Strategic options are linear and predictable, based on readily available data and historically proven approaches • Extensive internal data analysis and external benchmarking is routinely undertaken • Limited exploration of alternative strategic options should the context fundamentally change • Outcomes are cascaded formally to all involved
Governance	• Strategic planning activity is a centrally managed process supported by well-designed tools and techniques and driven by a focused team • Metrics that matter are identified, isolated and regularly monitored • Responsibility for version control, consultation regarding changes and monitoring of metrics is held centrally

Journey	• Critical path is clearly mapped • Obstacles identified are categorised in terms of likelihood and impact • Effort is focused on driving the strategy through key milestones, mitigating risks and finding solutions to problems as they present
Rehearsal	• Instructions are cascaded and clear metrics are communicated to all • More sophisticated organisations may consider the development of required capabilities and behaviours through experiential learning
Learning	• Metrics and indicators are routinely monitored and level of strategic leadership altered in response to chosen strategic activities • Limited opportunity or willingness to change course without overwhelming data or significant external pressure
Agility	• Strategic process enables structured agility at fixed time points

— • —

STAGE 4: INTEGRATED	
Impact	FUTURE-FIT
Horizon	• Short- to medium-term time horizon (up to a maximum of five years) • Horizon scanning is routinely undertaken • Scenario planning is used to establish likely future operating environment and potential future sector players • Long-term ambitions are established which may require large-scale change
Catalysts	• Curious leaders and critical thinkers across the organisation explore the strategic context and highlight potential future opportunities, threats and paradigm shifts

Dialogue	• Strategic conversation involves a representative cross section of the organisation and is supplemented by relevant specialists and advisors from time to time • Future scenarios are discussed in depth to generate greater understanding of values, opinions and perspectives of future actors and players • Strategies are developed for each potential future
Choices	• A range of strategic options are generated and considered in view of potential future scenarios • Historical patterns are examined and applied to future scenario development to understand how particular options would facilitate or hinder future success • Choices are made through a balance of information and imagination • Information regarding scenarios, emerging indicators and strategic options is available to all upon request
Governance	• Technology is used to create shared collaborative workspaces where strategy can evolve with appropriate version control, consultation and communication • A network of organisation-wide synchronised processes and dialogues is established with leadership devolved into teams focused on business units, function and/or projects • The established planning cycle is supplemented and augmented through pop-up scenarios and strategic conversations • Metrics that matter and path indicators are identified, monitored and reported on
Journey	• A range of potential critical paths is explored and storyboarded • Wicked problems are identified, and efforts are made to progress through them efficiently to maintain direction and speed
Rehearsal	• Storyboarding, workshops, immersive experiences and inventive communication cascades are utilised to ensure potential activities and decisions are rehearsed ahead of time

Learning	• Impact on internal metrics and evidence of external changes are considered and acted upon • Where internal impact is not as expected, or external context fundamentally changes, strategic options are revisited
Agility	• Multiple paths and process learning provide the ability to quickly adapt to a range of possible futures in good time

– • –

STAGE 5: SHAPESHIFTER	
Impact	**CHANGE THE GAME**
Horizon	• Short-, medium- and long-term horizon scanning evident across all areas • Potential and plausible future contexts are explored naturally through an embedded culture of scenario planning and imaginative thinking • Long-term future context is designed and influenced
Catalysts	• Horizon scanning, scenario thinking and future context mapping are organisational habits • Imagining the future from multiple perspectives is core to leadership capability at all levels and is a major driver of strategic dialogue • Positive deviance demonstrates potential new paths
Dialogue	• Immersive and continuous strategic conversation that invites and welcomes contribution from all • Networks are leveraged to raise curiosity and insight • Scope extends to how to create a favourable future scenario and the development of strategy and creation of products and markets to support this • Reflection, refraction and rehearsal are used as foundations for strategy development • World-building and storytelling become central to strategic dialogue

Choices	• Collaborative and continuous exploration of the future drives a range of potentially successful strategic options • Chosen options are selected for their ability to achieve success in a future context alongside their capacity to drive the agenda and shape the future beyond the organisation's current boundaries • Making markets becomes more important than exploiting markets
Governance	• Organisational consciousness is raised through dynamic, connected, learning networks • Technology and face-to-face relationships collide to allow planning cycles to adapt, accelerate and decelerate to suit the environment • Everyone is committed to the conversation, any choices made and the constant need to challenge assumptions • Strategy evolves through the active involvement of the entire community • Governance is light but ensures involvement, understanding, activity and evaluation • Metrics that matter and path indicators are used to inform the reassessment of context and development of strategic choices
Journey	• Storyboards for a range of critical paths are created and linked to potential futures • Path indicators are used to inform the debate and identify which path to take as the future emerges • A range of game plans are co-created and examined for opportunities and threats • Wicked problems are used as opportunities to change the context and shape the future • Meta-tribes work across organisational boundaries to explore potential, examine impact and influence outcomes internally and externally
Rehearsal	• Storyboarding, workshops and inventive communication are amplified through immersive gamification and active experimentation • Informal networks explore potential • Wicked problems present an opportunity to engage with systemic drivers and design novel interventions

Learning	• Strategic loops naturally occur driving a continuously evolving supple strategy • Quality of dialogue, openness to change, awareness of context and process learning through rehearsal and immersion create a learning culture
Agility	• Multiple paths, habitual curiosity, endemic innovation, devolved leadership and a willingness to learn and change provide the ability to adapt to a range of possible outcomes ahead of time and to influence or potentially fundamentally redesign the future

The life stage and circumstances of an organisation can render a Stage 1 (reactive) or Stage 2 (focused) approach appropriate for a certain amount of time, perhaps until a crisis has passed or a known change has made its full impact felt. However, stay locked in these stages too long and the likelihood of becoming a dinosaur before your time is substantially increased.

Let's be realistic, there aren't that many organisations that can honestly say they consistently fulfil every element of a shapeshifter mindset and approach. But, asking some serious questions of the way strategic dialogue happens in your organisation and being open and humble enough to recognise where the organisation habitually finds itself within the supple strategy maturity model is a solid first step towards developing into a shapeshifter.

ASK YOURSELF...

Whereabouts are you on your journey to becoming a shapeshifter? Consider the supple strategy maturity model and ask yourself:
- When thinking about the future, making plans and discussing strategic options, what time span do you typically look to and engage with?
- How much is your conversation based on what you already know and how can you extend the conversation into the unknown or perhaps the unknowable?

- What parameters do you set when considering the context within which you operate? How far and wide do you look?
- What drives you to have a strategic conversation? What has to happen for you to consciously think about the future?
- Who gets involved in debates about the future and how do you make sure the right people are in the room?
- Where's your organisational head at? Is it worrying about threats, optimising results, exploiting opportunities or crafting a better world for you and everyone in it?
- What options do you have and how do you choose between them?
- When was the last time you seriously contemplated the operating model and its fitness for the future, let alone the present?
- Who decides, and how do they make decisions?
- How many versions of the truth are in circulation and who has control of the master plan, if there is one?
- When might you revisit strategic plans and how does this happen?
- How can you be sure that what you have planned to do will work?
- Who knows what to do, and when and how?
- What feedback and learning mechanisms are in place – and who's genuinely listening?
- If you received data that told you your strategy was misguided or wrong, would you turn around or take a new path, or carry on regardless?
- What assumptions underpin your organisation's existing strategy and/or its operating model? What has to be true for your organisation to be successful in its present state and form?

CHAPTER 7

IT'S GREAT TO BE A SHAPESHIFTER

Being a shapeshifter imbues you with a far greater likelihood of working towards the right strategy – a strategy that will take you into a successful future and that is not so rigid that it will strangle and asphyxiate the organisation as it reaches towards new opportunities or identifies new games it can play or, better still, make.

Shapeshifter behaviour is not that of reacting to every external and internal stimulus no matter how insignificant. It is a coherent moulding of the structured and the dynamic. It brings about the evolution of a new heightened level of organisational consciousness that makes the most of dynamic, connected, learning networks. A future-fit organisation (at Stage 4 of the maturity model) is ready and able to change shape so that it can compete effectively in future worlds. Shapeshifters (at Stage 5 of the maturity model) are in the business of shaping change; they work collaboratively with others to build the world they want to see.

SIDE EFFECTS OF TIME TRAVEL (THE BUSINESS CASE)

I know, you're busy right? You and your colleagues are in a perpetual state of being that combines information overload, constant distraction and debilitating fatigue in equal measure. But what if this counter-intuitive step into the unknown provided the keys to a better balance, a steadier focus and a far greater likelihood of personal and organisational success? Supple strategy is a work of art – the art of working with the future. As such it demands space and time to think, and the ability and willingness to indulge in creative activities for at least some of the time. 'It's too much work! We're too busy to think! Pure indulgence! What's the business case?' I hear you cry…

I'm biased, I know, but there are many direct and indirect benefits of engaging with the future in a meaningful way and entering into the art of supple strategy generation.

The very act of engaging with the far-future (however far you can bear to look) is one that will endow you with an almost innate sense of seeing around corners. As events unfold we don't really know what will actually happen next but most of us assume we can take an educated guess. More often than not our educated guesses are wrong, but this important fact does not stop us from acting on our predictions and venturing into the unknown with our gut for company (thinly veiled with some extrapolated data which makes us feel a bit better about our quest).

As the future unfolds multiple timelines are competing to exist and various outcomes have the potential to come into being. Consider the famous metaphor of Schrödinger's cat – a thought experiment, a paradox, devised by Erwin Schrödinger in 1935.[32] He described a scenario in which a hypothetical cat was placed in a box with a vial of radioactive material. Until the box is opened the observer does not know if the cat has succumbed to the radioactive element and died or is in fact alive. His suggestion was that, until the box is opened by the observer, both eventualities exist – the cat is simultaneously both alive and dead. Only when the box is opened, and the cat directly observed, do the two potential timelines collapse to form one reality. His hypothetical cat has been much used over the years by quantum physicists in their attempts to explain quantum mechanics, particle entanglement and the potential for multiple universes. In some interpretations of the experiment, multiple outcomes exist regardless of observation. The outcomes and observers simply multiply and spin off into alternative universes.

We have no way of knowing what is going on in the box until we open the box. The same is true of the future – we have no way of *knowing* the future until it arrives, but we can learn ways to interpret its signals.

Like any skill, the more we practise the better we become. As we engage with the future and examine the patterns as it continuously unfolds, we exercise our minds in the interpretation of facts, events and behaviours. We still cannot know what's coming next and we'll still be wrong a lot of the time, but the very acts of practise and exercise mean that, over time, our intuition becomes influenced by the patterns we have consciously examined – this can only be a positive impact.

Remember those core habits of refraction, reflection and rehearsal (see page 46)? Generating potential future scenarios is a total body workout for these beauties. Practising refraction allows us to perceive the present and future through various lenses and from multiple perspectives, noticing how the landscape alters depending on our vantage point and personal filters. It gives us a greater awareness of the vast array of possibilities and the parallel alternative timelines at play so that we can test assumptions and generate a range of alternative future strategies that would make sense in alternative worlds should they come to be. Reflection causes us to take a peak in the rear-view mirror and become consciously aware of what has got us to where we are. What patterns can we see with the benefit of hindsight that allow us to translate the present and interpret potential futures, and how can we use these to illuminate the path ahead? And finally, rehearsal brings possible strategies to life and allows our prospective memory to inform and power our future memory. We can literally programme ourselves with memories of future questions and actions should particular trigger situations arise.

In a practical sense, the supple strategy system provides access to a wider range of strategic options that will future-proof an organisation. It generates an effective dashboard that supports the organisation as it navigates turbulent times and it delivers able and willing leaders at all levels of the organisation. It unleashes game-changing leaders who are insatiable learners, connected, informed, insightful, focused, valuable, inclusive, believable, authentic and credible. And it builds a platform for game-makers to emerge – the innovative, collaborative, curious and courageous, hungry, playful and self-aware leaders of the future who will change the world.

The supple strategy system provides space for serendipity; the potential to be in the right place at the right time with the best solution and an opportunity to genuinely make your own luck. Process learning results in levels of agility and flexibility that can counter turbulence and navigate ambiguity and complexity with grace.

It drives pre-mortem rather than postmortem, pre-learning rather than 'lessons to be learned', and innovation and collaboration over shame and blame. The supple strategy system provides a scaffold for systemic innovation and the depth of thinking and passionate engagement that powers momentous movements (capable of influencing the greatest naysayers and scariest stakeholders in your midst).

Children learn through play and, through playing with the future, you and your colleagues can learn a lot about one another, the context within which you operate and the possible paths that context may take. The insights generated drive far deeper and more meaningful strategic dialogue and shift individual and team thinking forever.

Shapeshifters use the supple strategy system to shape the future and to take an evolutionary step to become their best selves!

Within the supple strategy maturity model there is mention of positive deviance, meta-tribes, wicked problems and gamification. Moves Two, Three and Four will build upon theses concepts to take your strategy to reality.

THE UK CIVIL AVIATION AUTHORITY

The UK Civil Aviation Authority (CAA) was formed in 1972. It is a public corporation that was established by Parliament as an independent specialist aviation regulator that regulates aviation in the UK and, through its subsidiary, Air Safety Support International (ASSI), is responsible for air safety in British Overseas Territories. The CAA is the UK's airspace design and technical standards regulator, and regulates aerodromes, airlines, UK registered aircraft, pilots, air traffic controllers and engineers. It issues pilots' licences, regulates the airworthiness of aircraft and related training equipment registered in the UK, and oversees the application of security standards at UK airports. It also economically regulates two UK airports and the UK's en route air traffic provider, is a competition authority, enforces consumer legislation applicable to UK aviation, licences UK airlines and runs the tour operator licencing and protection regime ATOL (Air Travel Organiser's Licence). The CAA has a broad and important brief indeed. Although the CAA is a statutory public corporation established by Parliament, it is predominantly funded via charges levied upon those it regulates or that use its services.

Shifts in the domestic and international geopolitical landscape can have a major impact upon the CAA and its operations. Clearly conflict and acts of violence across the globe can necessitate a greater level of scrutiny and surveillance in terms of aviation security and safety. Even apparently more benign political developments can cause a wave of disruption across the aviation industry and therefore those that regulate it. Preparing and responding to specific events is also an important role for the CAA, whether it be responding to weather events such as volcanic ash, air safety events or tour operator failure. As a result, the CAA engages in continuous horizon scanning and scenario planning to best prepare itself for numerous potential eventualities. It also has to ensure it has sufficient organisational capacity and agility to respond to these events.

As an inherently international sector, much of the regulatory framework is established at an international level. The CAA has a close relationship with the European Aviation Safety Agency (EASA). It both contributes to the establishment of European aviation rules and implements them in the UK. It has been intrinsically invested in a strong relationship with Europe (and EASA) and has fostered close collaboration with various European partners for over 40 years (for example, Concorde was the result of a joint venture with France in the sixties). In addition, the CAA's International Group contains CAA International (CAAi), a social enterprise focused upon raising aviation safety standards across the globe. The CAAi is heavily connected to and dependent upon its relationship with both the CAA and EASA. Many organisations could be affected by any form of Brexit and the CAA is no exception. The impacts of Brexit upon the operations, organisation and people, and more broadly the aviation sector, its suppliers and those who use its services, are complex.

At the time of writing Brexit has been delayed twice already and a range of vastly differing outcomes is still ultimately possible. While the most extreme outcome (a no-deal Brexit) has presently been voted against by Parliament, it is still the default legal option should the deadline be reached without further developments.

The CAA's approach to strategic planning has a process at its core but is increasingly intuitive in nature and peppered with opportunistic scenario planning exercises and horizon scanning activities. It has used scenario planning extensively to generate a range of options that depict potential futures arising from a variety of forms of Brexit. This has taken time, focused alignment and the courage to prioritise thinking over doing in a tightly funded and resourced organisation, but has prepared the organisation well for many eventualities.

I asked Tim Johnson (Policy Director) and Ben Alcott (Director International Group) to describe their experience of how strategy is formed across the CAA:

What vehicles have you used to drive the change?

Ben: We've used a lot of scenario planning and horizon scanning. We've then engaged in watchful waiting as the future emerges in clunky steps and stumbles from one set of potential outcomes to another. There are changes to the fundamental strategic context taking place before our very eyes and it's been important to keep focused on our preferred outcomes so that we can influence towards those, while being ready for alternatives.

Tim: We use scenarios for a range of purposes:

1 *Crisis planning: managing and preparing for uncertainty and planning for the worst outcome.*
2 *Broad strategy development.*
3 *Innovation and related risks and potential opportunities: there's no one view of the future and so it's important to engage with a range of opinions as to what might become dominant and where to allocate resource.*
4 *Brexit planning.*

Different people are involved in the analysis and decision-making processes for each, but they are iterative activities and often feed into one another. Everyone from working level teams to the Board is engaged in the process that is now much more of an organic rather than a rigid formulaic process.

For both the Brexit event and planning for the period beyond Brexit, we have generated a range of scenarios which we have then narrowed down to a couple of chosen ones that form the basis of planning and resourcing decisions. These scenarios have been the foundation for lots of collective mental rehearsal and readiness planning. By narrowing down to a small number, we have been able to make them real and decide about what specific preparatory activities we would actually undertake. We've consciously brought groups of people together to explore likely outcomes and mentally rehearse responses ahead of time. This has meant that we've been able to do quite extraordinary things in the event of a particular scenario or crisis actually happening as we've been able to see it ahead of time in our imaginations. Inevitably there's no such thing as perfect foresight, so when we've been in those high-pressure scenarios, we've also been agile enough to learn and adapt our approach as we go along. Our people have been ready, willing and able to perform roles that are far from their typical everyday working lives.

When we look in depth at a scenario we seek to identify its wider consequences, how these may impact upon the sector we regulate and our own organisation, and how to manage our response. We attempt to isolate pros and cons objectively. In terms of Brexit, we investigated different views of the future and how we might manage the discharge of our regulatory roles and our organisation successfully in each of these potential futures.

What's different about the approach?

Tim: We're not scared to think about and prepare for a range of different scenarios, even when those scenarios could involve some different futures and uncomfortable decisions. We are prepared to think and act differently as required, and where necessary seek changes to our legislative and policy foundations – we change shape as and where necessary.

Recognising the more agile and changing world in which we operate, and our need as a regulator to better anticipate those changes, we've created an outward-facing innovation team. It looks at planned and unpredicted changes to the aviation system and attempts to learn from them. Our ability to learn in the context in which we operate rather than 'know' is a real strength. This internally driven dynamo promotes thinking of this type – it thinks all day every day about the future and what trends or specific technologies or operations might occur. To genuinely shift approach you have to create focus, and not allow it to get lost alongside someone's normal responsibilities when up against competing priorities – it needs nurturing. Our innovation team starts the work of engaging with the tough scenarios. They then test their thinking with internal colleagues, stress test emerging strategy for issues, and road test operational plans with external stakeholders such as airlines, airports and the relevant government departments.

As we focus on a couple of scenarios we explore a range of outcomes and identify our preferred outcome. We then work hard to bring that about by building a programme of people and assets around them that can move into action as necessary. It allows us to achieve our strategy for each situation.

What's been difficult?

Ben: Sophisticated scenario planning takes time. Time and resources can be scarce in times of change and so it can be difficult to continue with this important thinking and co-creation when organisational capacity is under pressure. As we engage in scenario planning, other crises emerge that need attention and responsiveness. A large-scale change with potential for massive disruption (like Brexit) can become all-consuming until a clear direction emerges. Imminent change with high levels of remaining uncertainty means we must shorten our time horizon both in terms of scenario planning and strategic planning. The timescale of strategic planning is greatly influenced by the level of immediate uncertainty or perceived threat. At the moment, strategic thinking and scenario planning is running from anything between two weeks to two years. We would like to be more able to plan on a five-year horizon at least, but uncertainty is of a level typically seen over a 20-year horizon and so a short focus is required due to the breadth of possibilities near-term (think of the lens on a camera and what we can bring into focus to capture with any level of clarity). If the short-term holds potential for great jeopardy it makes sense to treat two weeks as if it were a far longer time frame to ensure alternative strategies are mapped and tested repeatedly as the landscape changes just ahead of us.

Tim: In strategy we often think of our job as one of prediction, but we can't predict accurately and with confidence. We have to remain agile to all outcomes and responsive to their challenges and opportunities. For some scenarios, we want to create the best position possible against the likely worst-case scenario to capture a strategy of least regret. In other scenarios, we have more control over the levers and can be more deterministic in our approach. At a point in time you have to decide which priorities to back and devote resource to – to find two or three areas that deserve greater investment or exploration. Sometimes these elements appear in a range of scenarios and are perhaps therefore more likely to come about regardless. Even if you think you can predict an outcome, you can't predict the pace of its emergence. Add to that shifting societal attitudes and our natural reactions and available responses to them – it's a complex mix.

Why have you persevered?
Ben: Failure is not an option. This organisation has to succeed and find a way through. Perhaps find a new path or new paths that will allow our purpose to be fulfilled in a fast-changing and uncertain world.

Tim: We're creating mechanisms to think differently through our strategy process: that's inevitable given the nature of the world, but also engaging for many of our colleagues. As we evolve the process towards a more organic and iterative approach that better suits an uncertain world we learn at every step. We're still learning how to do this stuff; it's a journey – a journey that helps our people individually navigate disruptive change as well as best prepare the organisation for the future.

How do you know it's working?

Ben: Our level of thinking has changed. We're not necessarily personally comfortable with some of the changes on the horizon, but we know the organisation is best placed and has well-rehearsed ideas and plans should the most disruptive outcomes come to pass. This has allowed people to get back to focusing on the day job while they are surrounded by unprecedented levels of uncertainty and potential disruption – it's certainly very VUCA around here, but we're coping well with the challenges that presents.

Tim: Events can prompt people to think differently. With each event comes deeper experience and another layer of thinking capability and we make sure we capitalise on that learning. We're now seeing some truly agile thinking and planning. We have a clear articulation of what we're doing and why in a range of potential outcomes, and our ability to respond well in a crisis has been tested and proven.

What have you learned from the experience?

Ben:

- *Assume the worst-case scenario and everything in between – there will still be opportunities evident within each if you can mitigate and get past the risks.*
- *Decisions cannot be made through fear; they must be formed around purpose. Therefore, a powerful and engaging purpose is key.*
- *When the level of uncertainty and range of outcomes still possible is high it has led to the consideration of strategic options previously dismissed as unfeasible. This renewed interest in alternative ideas is a good thing and can be a catalyst for very positive thinking and change.*
- *It's important to consider where people are on their own personal emotional arc. Can they be detached enough to perform informed analysis and judgement? Where people are personally affected by imminent potential*

change any organisational planning seems high-level and big-picture unless rooted firmly in purpose and a collective spirit of camaraderie. That said, if people are not included a vacuum develops that can become malignant.

- *With the benefit of hindsight, I wish we had started the scenario planning process earlier and been more open to exploring what appeared to be outlandish ideas and options at the time. What we imagined then could not possibly come about has suddenly become eminently possible.*

Tim:

- *We should have done more scenario planning and earlier. We previously undertook some horizon scanning, but we underestimated the amount of flux in the world, particularly related to disruptive politics and technology. As the political context and accepted norms are broken down, unpredictable and unwanted events could come about. It's important to expect the unexpected; not just the micro changes but seismic shifts too.*
- *For scenario planning to be of value we need to have a strategy that seeks to influence and is responsive to those changes.*
- *Focus on the downside to find the upside! What and where are the doors that open as others shut? Where are our boundaries and are they capable of shifting?*
- *There's a point at which you have to stop analysing and try some things. Be willing to create the space to experiment (safely).*
- *Be very willing to change tack if required. It's important for leaders to remain supple to a range of scenarios and not to become over-invested in one particular outcome. Leadership is critical in times of uncertainty.*
- *It's important to have a point of view and to be able to explain the risks and opportunities as you see them. We have a view of where we could go in certain eventualities and we make sure we keep revisiting these as our thinking expands.*
- *Always remember your core purpose. While there are often many new avenues and opportunities to pursue, decide on what you will do on the basis of your core reason for existing (in our case, being an effective aviation regulator).*
- *Don't assume that what you think can't happen won't happen, or what you think is most likely to happen will happen. Brexit is a perfect example of this. Some of our early assumptions about the process and outcome were*

quickly proved incorrect and challenged by emerging events – luckily, we were open to re-examining them. Suspend judgement of what's desirable or undesirable and put personal opinions and emotions to one side when creating alternative strategies.

It can be difficult to think beyond emerging issues of high disruptive capacity, but it is important to do so. Situations with huge impacts and far-reaching consequences can drain energy, stifle thinking and shorten the camera lens to dangerous myopic levels. What might be happening alongside or just beyond the presenting situation while we're all thinking about this over here? What's next or what's emerging right now that may have an even greater impact, heightened risk or myriad associated opportunities? It's easy to miss the next big thing if the focus is too short-term and focused on a single contextual driver.

While the CAA has to focus on what Brexit may demand it is ensuring that it uses other mechanisms to consider the impact of other contextual drivers, such as technology. It is acting like a true apprentice of the future – never assuming superior knowledge and preferring instead to concentrate on connecting to gather information and generate insight. The CAA is a learning organisation. Aware of its shortened attention span it is investing in other ways to bring people together to consider the future. It uses experimentation in the real world to stress test strategies and road test operational plans. Critically, its leaders know the importance of decision-making at all levels and the principle-led autonomy that a meaningful core purpose can engender. The organisation and its people have the courage to change track or direction when evidence suggests they should do so – well-considered lane changes and U-turns are not taboo!

The CAA is looking to bring about the future it wants to see, and it uses its influence and activity focus to further its purpose. Even when the organisation seems to have arrived at a destination, it treats it as a pit stop on its journey to becoming its future self.

PART 2

MOVE TWO:
BUILD A META-TRIBE

In Move One we faced the very real challenge of creating a strategy that is supple enough to cope with volatility, unpredictability, complexity and ambiguity. This is important as the future cannot be predicted and reveals itself in stages that are not uniform or following any obvious pattern. We saw that supple strategy could be created through a process of collectively imagining possible plausible futures and identifying the activities and decisions likely to bring greatest success and least risk within each future context. Most important of all, we focused on ensuring we were not sticking rigidly to the wrong strategy. Critical as this is, culture is arguably even more important. It is often said that 'culture eats strategy for breakfast', and Move Two is all about culture. This move is the process through which we can create a culture that brings together subcultures, a culture that transcends tribes. Our task is to generate a culture that will allow us to shape the organisation effectively and align cohesively behind a set of shared values, beliefs and goals.

Culture runs deep in an organisation. It is its identity, its personality; that complex combination of the traits it tends to demonstrate in particular situations, the capabilities it naturally holds and the habits it has formed over the years. All of which are based on the shared experiences of its people, the natural alliances it has nurtured and the foes it has collectively battled, successfully or otherwise.

Successful cultures propagate their memes just like genes. In other words, without much careful cultivation the inherent behaviours and habits of an indigenous organisational culture will amplify and spread with abandon throughout its being. This can be helpful if, and only if, the culture is one that is likely to support the future ambitions of the organisation. A culture that is congruent with the navigation of supple strategy in the possible future worlds that may be unfolding. A culture that you want to cultivate. Supple strategy is nothing without a strong, coherent, inclusive culture that aligns and galvanises people and amplifies the values, beliefs and habits that will bring energy and determination to the cause.

Culture is a heady mix of beliefs, values and habits that are built upon many things, including behaviour, capability, process, structure, experience, reward and leadership. Cultural roots are planted in the myths that are retold, the legends that are revered and the heroes of battles long forgotten. But are these myths, legends and heroes the right ones for your cause? They may have once been powerful in delivering success, but times change, and people evolve. What may have once been a powerful way of being, may now have many cracks and gaps. The existing culture may prove to be lacking in structural integrity or, worse, counterproductive to the cause. The BP Deepwater Horizon disaster has been largely attributed to a catastrophic breakdown in the organisation's safety culture brought about by a multitude of actors with competing goals and behavioural norms operating independently of one another where collaboration, challenge and co-creation were key to safe operations.[33]

Cultures are tribal in nature. We're all a member of a few tribes – whether we're conscious of it or not. If you consider yourself to belong to a nation, align with a political party, support a sports team or work for an organisation then you are part of a tribe! Tribes typically have a uniform (more obvious for sports teams, but still subtly evident in others), demand an initiation of some description, offer a range of privileges (some of which are intangible and social) and expect certain behaviours and rituals to be respected and others to be vilified. True tribes are connected through shared experience and united in approach. Compelling tribes have a shared consciousness where individual members acutely feel joy and pain at their collective achievements and woes.

Inevitably there is competition between tribes. Competition can be a great driver of team success in many situations. Sales teams thrive on competitive energy and enjoy the game of beating their personal best or outperforming an outstanding colleague. Sometimes competition in a typical organisation can get out of hand, and it can have far less healthy repercussions when it does so. Competition can develop into unhealthy rivalry, hostility and even sabotage. All of these can drain energy, damage culture and ultimately lead to poor outcomes for the organisation. Competition becomes obstructive when it distracts two functions of the same organisation (or two organisations that have recently merged) that, for some reason, have pitted themselves against one another when they would do better to focus on a shared goal. When tribes go to war and seek to further their individual cause at the expense of the bigger picture, an organisation starts to experience wider problems. The cracks can run deep and can critically impact supply chains, employee engagement and customer experience. Disruption, confusion, avoidance of accountability and a lack of collaboration serve to deepen any such cracks and solidify tribal positions. Intransigent tribes can be a major factor in the development and perpetuation of wicked problems (the most complex problems with no clear route to resolution).

We all have an innate urge to belong and to contribute to something bigger than ourselves, and tribes are a powerful conduit for us to do this. We just need to work out how can we convert and focus this tribal urge into a potent force for good.

CHAPTER 8

HOW SHAPESHIFTERS DO CULTURE

As an organisation grows and develops through its early years, its culture tends to evolve naturally through everyday activities and the decisions made by the organisation's early pioneers. In larger, older organisations there is often an established formal culture encircled or supported by a range of subcultures that have built up through the inevitable tribal fracturing and irregular development that occurs across larger groups of people. This fracturing is sometimes accelerated and complicated further by mergers and acquisitions that have taken place.

Regardless of any official organisational values and behaviours that may grace the office walls, the most important culture in any organisation is its informal culture(s). The informal culture is the true culture that pervades an organisation's corridors for better or worse and takes little direction from appointed tribal leaders. In simple terms, the idle chatter at the water cooler, the celebrated events and memories, and the coder in IT who has a substantial and loyal band of followers and who sometimes throws a spanner in the works by sharing alternative ideas or voicing unforeseen risks (and is therefore considered to be an irritating distraction by appointed leaders), all have a far greater impact than any formal cultural programme can ever hope to achieve.

Shapeshifters know this instinctively. As they go about codifying their existing culture or embark upon rebooting their culture to better reflect the demands of the future, they do not lose sight of the fact that culture is a complex phenomenon that has many symbols and artefacts that people may attach great meaning to. Shapeshifters consciously take a big dose of reality to truly understand the cultural undercurrent that really drives the organisation to action or inaction. They appreciate the need to fully understand, evolve and harness the informal culture to deliver the beliefs, engagement and ultimately the capabilities that will shape the future of the organisation.

Shapeshifters work with the real organisation rather than an imagined one that better reflects where they wish they were. They see past the illusion and get down and dirty with the nitty-gritty of multiple tribes, unofficial leaders, unsung heroes and viral stories. Any posters that adorn the corridors espousing values and behaviours are tightly connected to an inclusive and continuing conversation on culture. In fact, you might not even see any such posters adorning the walls in Shapeshifter organisations; superficial cultural collateral is not where they focus their efforts. Their culture runs deep through the everyday actions and decisions of the people who make their organisation work the way it does. Shapeshifter culture is a way of being that everyone is deeply connected to and committed to emboldening. In the absence of posters and other such material collateral, the culture is kept alive through constant discussion and examination; a big cultural conversation that:

- Cuts across internal borders and brings people together to connect on an emotional level and with purpose and causes at the core.
- Captures new legends in the making and makes much of them.
- Deals robustly and fairly with counterproductive behaviours and ideologies.
- Delights in storytelling and the creation of new, inspiring, supportive myths.
- Prevents a vacuum from forming and does the work of connecting people across historical intra-organisational tribal boundaries.

A shapeshifter is proud of the positive deviance in its belly. It delights in the constructive challenge, novel innovation and paradigm shifts in thinking that outliers can bring. Presenting mutations of beliefs, values and behaviours are considered as experiments in the future and are examined for signs of malignancy or the potential to invigorate the next generation or incite the next big idea as the culture evolves.

In a shapeshifter organisation culture is the blood that keeps ideas circulating and provides nourishment and replenishment to its outer reaches. It maintains relationships and forms a dynamic, connected, learning network. Shapeshifters develop a hive mind – a shared consciousness and collective intelligence that combines its many parts into one being. Much like the patterns observed in starling murmurations, the shapeshifter demonstrates levels of cohesion and choreography that others can only dare to imagine. Its collective behaviour is one of a self-organised system working tirelessly towards a shared and meaningful purpose; a sentient being of an organisation made up of many individual people, processes and parts.

HOW TO TRANSCEND TRIBES

Culture is not a one-size-fits-all mantle. It is as individual as the personality and evolving identity of the organisation it calls home. The same can be said of the process of cultural development. There is not one correct way for an organisation to 'do culture' but there are many standard activities that only serve to waste time or cause cynicism amongst its people. There are, however, some fundamental elements that seem to feature more often than not in the more powerful cultures I have observed:

1   A meta-tribe: a tribe that transcends all other tribes is born.
2   A compelling story: tribal myths, legends, symbols and rituals are aligned and believable.
3   A code: behaviour is deciphered – it's easy to work out how to behave and make decisions in a wide range of situations.
4   LOVE: Leadership, Ownership, Values and Energy are all enabled and nurtured.
5   Quantum entanglement: the organisation is a dynamic, connected, learning network.

A META-TRIBE IS BORN

People naturally organise into tribes – usually around areas of common interest or shared experience. Tribes have their own codes of conduct, myths and legends, rituals and emblems, all of which become deeply embedded and meaningful as the tribe develops its identity over time. Catalysts such as hardship, pressure, repetition and deeply shared beliefs accelerate the process and deepen tribal cohesiveness. Tribes can become monsters capable of the most terrible things (there are many examples throughout human history where ideologically-driven political tribes have wrought untold horrors on those they considered to be unworthy or routinely despised), or they can become a magnificent force for good – driving innovation, challenging injustice, lifting human consciousness and improving the world.

Organisations are usually made up of any number of tribes which overlap and perhaps contradict one another. 'Turf wars' and 'empire building' are common language (and practice) in most workplaces. It's quite the conundrum that tribal behaviour is the cause of many headaches, while it's a critical part of a magical movement that brings people together in support of a cause or in pursuit of an outcome. To form a powerful movement, we need the magic of a meta-tribe – a tribe of tribes.

Our first fundamental therefore, is to connect and combine individual tribes into one big all-encompassing meta-tribe. A tribe that transcends the smaller conflict-driven tribes, connecting them and amplifying their energy around a shared vision of the future or a compelling cause. A tribe with its very own story of existence and the morals that story represents. A tribe that has its own recognised heroes and villains, customs and rituals, tribal elders that become role models (nothing to do with age), and tools to make it easy to connect and share. In a meta-tribe, energy is amplified and those who question the accepted order and illuminate the path ahead (like our coder in IT with a substantial and loyal following) are welcomed.

Meta-tribes can cut across geographies, organisations, cultures, languages, race, age, gender and belief systems – you only have to look at organisations with a formidable fan base (think Apple) to see them in operation.

One tribe aligned and galvanised around a shared strategy, meaningful cause or wicked problem is a force to be reckoned with. A meta-tribe that has a common purpose or a common enemy at its core provides power in numbers and strength of conviction. Shapeshifters understand that common enemies are made of wicked problems rather than people or groups of people. They intrinsically understand that to create change you need to connect with people – all people. You need to connect with people who agree with you, those who hold a wholly different view to your own and those at every stage in between. Without connection there is no opportunity to influence outcomes, collaborate and co-create to bring a better world into being. Shapeshifters craft their story carefully to create a script where everyone can intuitively play a positive part.

MYTHS AND LEGENDS AND HEROES

When things are going well, we often do little to interrogate our beliefs to identify any that may be limiting our potential. Under pressure we all too often fall back into our old and well-established stories about who we believe ourselves to be, no matter how limiting that narrative may be. Emotional habits run deep, regardless of whether they are positive or negative, nurturing or painful. Regeneration and reinvention are powerful catalysts for broader change, but they consume energy and time. Established organisations can tend towards the status quo – 'That's how things are done around here' and 'We've tried that before' – rendering suggestions and embryonic innovation dead in their tracks. Or they follow a cookie-cutter culture change programme that demands people and processes fit into the newly designed shapes and defined approaches cascaded to them. Truly shifting a culture is hard work, but the fact that an organisation is typically a combination of smaller tribes and their respective cultures can make it easier to work out where and how to start.

The trick is to find new and exciting myths, legends and heroes that can become a fresh overarching story. A narrative that glues the organisation together into one large meta-tribe while respecting and honouring the various myths, legends and heroes that have gone before and trodden the challenging path to get this far. Denigrating what has gone before without good reason is not a sound foundation upon which to build a reinvention. Celebrating respected elders and showing how their actions and decisions were of their time starts the process of unification and reinvention. Showing gratitude for what has brought the organisation this far (a leader, a product, a behaviour) and then explaining what change is now needed, and why it is needed now, is more likely to successfully bring people along. Castigating the past (a leader who was probably applauded or a behaviour perhaps demanded only yesterday) creates contagious and pervasive cynicism and unease.

Culture is all about myths, legends and heroes that people can connect with and believe in. An inclusive and engaging storytelling exercise allows these to emerge from the substance of the organisation rather than be contrived and dictated by those who are once removed from the daily experience of being part of its engine room. Engaging in conversations in all corners of the organisation enables those with a leadership mandate to ask questions of beliefs, challenge assumptions, understand driving forces and identify levers to leverage that can drive the change they want to bring about. People who bring about change through informal networks and in new ways can emerge as the heroes who deploy positive deviance to lead the organisation into its imminent battles. That IT coder may turn out to be the instigator of the very revolution an organisation requires.

Reinvention is a journey that takes time, debate and co-creation. The least effective form of reinvention takes place behind closed doors and is then delivered as a fait accompli to the masses. The best reinventions make the most of new trends and involve the fans every step of the way!

DECIPHER THE CULTURE CODE

Cultures aren't necessarily secretive by nature, but their very randomness and organic growth patterns render them indecipherable to many people. The behaviours that manifest are rooted in deeply held beliefs and values that have developed over time and as a direct or indirect result of experiences. Without the benefit of having personally gone through each of these experiences it can be challenging to understand just why the individuals within an organisation behave as they do and how this behaviour manifests collectively.

Many organisations attempt to overlay an already complicated and intangible behavioural pattern with a set of simple symbols whose meaning fails to penetrate to any real depth. Bland mission statements and benign visions gradually dilute the vitality of the organisation, rendering it merely a ghostwriter of its own destiny.

Alternatively, organisations seek to develop detailed representations of the cultural behaviours they wish to see without unpacking existing norms and their reasons for being – laying a thin veneer over rough, unchartered and unsound ground. Unwieldy and impregnable behavioural frameworks are thankfully becoming a thing of the past and have always suffered the inevitable fate of becoming the long-term residents of dusty shelves, only sought out in preparation for annual performance reviews at best.

The time for complexity is long gone and the behaviours that suit today may not suit tomorrow. To be useful and sustainable, attempts to capture values and codify behaviours must engage with the complexity of culture to provide a relatively simple representation of major themes that incorporates flexibility. Successful cultures propagate their memes just like successful animals and fauna propagate their genes. Animals and fauna evolve to be better equipped to cope with their environment as it changes. So, too, must an organisation's culture evolve to enable it to develop its identity and extend its cohesive capabilities in response to and in anticipation of contextual changes. The ability to properly decipher, capture and evolve the cultural code is critical to its usefulness and survival over time. A shapeshifter organisation must be able to continually reinvent itself and it must evolve, being informed by the past without becoming constrained by it. A behaviour that was once a powerful attribute may now be, or is about to become, a dangerous liability.

The culture code is a language developed by the organisation and a symbolic representation of culture at a given point in time. Continuous facilitated dialogue is used to extend its reach, translate its meaning and encourage it to habitually evolve. For example, if there are 10 key behaviours it may be that their meanings subtly shift over a period of months, or even weeks in a fast-changing environment. As the organisation matures, the very way in which these behaviours are interpreted and displayed may significantly alter. The 10 behaviours may have a common root that manifests differently in alternative subcultures (how one part of the organisation demonstrates a particular behaviour may be entirely different to another – each manifestation being equally appropriate to the overall culture of the organisation). It may be that only 5 of the 10 behaviours are an initial focus with a different mix becoming appropriate as the journey is navigated – priority behaviours being isolated and consciously evolved at different stages of the organisational journey. Regardless, each of the 10 behaviours must be represented by symbols that have the ability to provoke a response, drive connection and portray meaning.

A powerful culture is a believable culture. If people don't recognise the real organisation in the deciphered code or fail to accept that the desired culture is within reach, they will soon ignore it or, worse, mock it. On many occasions I have found that emerging talent programmes highlight the need for or demand adherence to an applaudable set of values and behaviours that are unrecognisable at board or executive leadership team level. If emerging leaders throughout the organisation look up to see a different culture to the one they are being asked to bring about or subscribe to then, guess what… they will see through it. The best will leave, and the worst will stay and cement the toxic culture already in place. False codes eventually lose all meaning and importance and, in time, lead to impotent cultures. If you profess that a value or behaviour is important, you need to show that you mean it and back this up with actions that leave people in no doubt as to your convictions and intentions. Stating that collaboration is critical and then allowing a highly offensive and arrogant individual to refuse to do so based on their financial contribution to the organisation just won't wash. Either the behaviour is important or it isn't – stand by your beliefs and deal with those who dilute the culture. The very act of rendering an anti-hero (someone who actively works against your culture, whether consciously or not) powerless creates a myth and makes a hero of the cultural custodian (the person who supports the culture you are trying to nurture regardless of the personal costs of doing so) that will stand the test of time and illuminate the path for others to follow.

A simple, memorable and deeply authentic code that is encouraged to evolve and is backed up by those in power will provide huge amounts of positive energy for the organisation's cause.

ALL YOU NEED IS LOVE

Love – a small word with myriad meanings; a series of rather mundane chemical reactions, a powerful maternal instinct, a spiritual connection with a mysterious otherworldly universal energy amongst them. It can achieve the impossible, heal a rift, calm a riot, avoid all-out conflict, save the world!

Spiritual souls have long spoken of love's power to bring joy, shed light on the darkest of times and manifest reality in the physical world. Various gurus urge us to show love in all we think and do, to be 'kind to ourselves' and to practise 'gratitude' towards the universe and the experiences and resources it provides for us. Authors and scriptwriters have bestowed upon love the power to reach through space and time, connecting otherwise insignificant people, places and events to a greater purpose (or script). Love is a major part of our daily lives and it shows up differently for all of us. How can we bring the power of love to our work and harness its energy towards positive outcomes and a better experience for everyone?

I use the word LOVE to remind me of four core cultural pillars:

1   Leadership
2   Ownership
3   Values
4   Energy

These pillars form solid foundations for any meta-tribe. A magical movement cannot survive without a congruent culture, and a congruent culture is fully dependent upon LOVE.

Without courageous, committed, capable and aligned leadership, a movement is fractured and weakened. The collapse of trust is a far faster cascade than the arduous climb taken to build it. Heroes are the stuff of legends and can't be seen to be self-serving or ambivalent – they must be fiercely supportive of the cause. Leadership isn't the preserve of the exalted few, but the responsibility of all. Opportunities to lead present themselves continuously and shapeshifter organisations do their very best to ensure that, when duty calls, their leaders are ready and able to respond or anticipate accordingly.

Overt ownership gives everybody a genuine part to play and provides the framework for successful devolved leadership. Ownership drives slick value chains and a great employee experience, and turns customers into a formidable fan base. It allows the organisation to think and move as one well-choreographed movement.

Shared values drive deep understanding and trust. Without them a movement has foundations of sand. Demonstrating values through behaviour and making examples of those who do (and don't), creates a scaffold for unselfish prioritisation, principle-based decision-making and greater autonomy. Eventually, values drive agility through an innate ability to read situations fast and respond in a way that is naturally congruent with the identity of the organisation.

Energy allows us to get up in the morning and make a difference, to play a part and to positively change the world one move at a time. Without energy a culture is cloying and a movement is laborious. Lively debate, open minds, courageous leaders everywhere and co-creation in pursuit of a shared purpose create a dynamo that powers the movement through friendly territory or troubled waters, regardless of how tough it gets.

A firm foundation for LOVE to blossom within an organisation is the willingness to confront difficulties and differences of opinion openly, compassionately, directly and with a shared investment in a positive outcome. It is unhealthy for subjects to become taboo – a shapeshifter organisation needs to be able and willing to engage with and interrogate its dark side as well as its positive attributes. To this end there are six critical conversations that must be happening at an organisational, team and individual level for a shapeshifter to adapt, learn and grow.

CONVERSATION 1: BUILD

This conversation is all about establishing relationships and starting the job of building a team or a movement around the core values of trust and respect. The conversation is focused on sharing a vision, engaging hearts and minds, and generating buy-in to the future you want to create. This is where the values, beliefs and stories of the meta-tribe are shared and proliferated.

CONVERSATION 2: DEFINE

In this conversation attention turns to the consideration and agreement of desired outcomes and related performance expectations. What is going to be done and how it will be done is the focus of these conversations. Operational alignment of the meta-tribe is founded within this dialogue.

CONVERSATION 3: CELEBRATE

Individuals, teams and movements fast become demoralised and despondent when no acknowledgement of their impact or recognition of their efforts is evident. Taking time to notice good deeds, great efforts and positive outcomes gives people a chance to celebrate success to date and to learn what is working in the present that can be a useful pattern to use again in the face of future challenges. Paying attention to what works is a good habit to catch! This conversation provides a great opportunity for this to happen.

CONVERSATION 4: CHANGE

Even with the most positive intent, sometimes plans don't bring about the outcomes we hope to see or may produce unforeseen negative effects. In these instances, it is critical that individuals, teams and organisations are willing and ready to analyse and discuss how they can change their approach and potentially switch to an alternative track (perhaps even U-turn) to improve impact or avert disaster. People and organisations that regularly hold the mirror up and are open to the reality that they are, of course, not perfect, are the ones that ultimately get the closest to greatness. This conversation is where powerful individual, team and organisational learning can occur.

CONVERSATION 5: COLLABORATE

Independence is great and a strong trait to have, but it's hard to do everything alone and, more importantly, it's often suboptimal to genuine collaboration and co-creation. While independent thinking and personal agency are important, individuals need to be able and willing to work as part of a team. Teams need to be able and willing to come together as part of an organisation, and organisations need to be able and willing to combine their strengths with other organisations to bring about positive change at scale. Where individuals, teams and organisations are truly partnering, collaborating and co-creating with others, their impact is accelerated and amplified. This conversation is where the values of a meta-tribe are seeded and agreed.

CONVERSATION 6: GROW

Learning is core to any system that grows in complexity and capability. Without learning, stagnancy or entropy result. Meta-tribes that discuss their experiences at an individual, team and organisational level create a rich conversation across the organisation where best fit fast replaces best practice (see page 43). Systemic learning drives organisational agility and the nurturing of a dynamic, connected, learning network.

QUANTUM ENTANGLEMENT

The theory of quantum mechanics suggests that at a quantum level some particles demonstrate a fundamental connection to other particles regardless of the physical distance between them. It's as if any change to one of the connected particles is simultaneously applied to (or replicated by) the other. The particles act as if they are of one mind and body – the connection and alignment of state between them remains firmly intact no matter what. The potential of quantum mechanics is yet to be fully explored but it is already clear that these unexpected quantum relationships will drive a paradigm shift in the capacity and capability of future super-computers. In a shapeshifter organisation everything and everyone comes together into a magnificent whole. Each individual part becomes part of a dynamic, connected, learning network that facilitates shared consciousness and the ability to think and move as one.

We can emulate quantum mechanics across organisations by encouraging informal networks, leveraging technology platforms for connectivity and hothousing innovation. We can create a hive mentality, encourage a swarm activity pattern and nourish a dynamic, connected, learning network by consciously moving from small talk to deep talk, and by carrying accountability, devolving leadership and holding all accountable and responsible as custodians of the culture.

Shapeshifters connect the dots in mysterious ways towards an elevated level of organisational consciousness – they become a living movement that thinks and acts as one being, in support of a cause.

CHAPTER 9

START WHERE YOU ARE: THE TRIBAL MATURITY MODEL

As for Move One, on the following pages you will find a maturity model that outlines in detail what it takes to become a shapeshifter. The focus here is on the development of a meta-tribe; a tribe that transcends tribes. The purpose of this maturity model is to provide you with a navigable map of the territory. It will allow you to ascertain whereabouts your organisation currently finds itself and which shapeshifter behaviours it perhaps already displays. It's unlikely that your organisation will fit neatly into any one box and it may be that it shows elements of several. Moving towards becoming a shapeshifter and embedding the habits and behaviours that allow us to transcend tribes is a complex journey with many interdependent and subtle streams. Use the maturity model to determine how culture is currently represented throughout your organisation, and the behaviours and habits that manifest as a direct result.

Once you have a better sense of where you are, you can then use the model to identify priority focus areas and practical steps you can take to shift the culture across your organisation.

As in Move One, the five evolutionary stages are:

1 Reactive
2 Focused
3 Structured
4 Integrated
5 Shapeshifter

Each stage has markers that signal a certain level of cultural sophistication has been habitually achieved. To work out whereabouts your organisation spends most of its time (within which stage it generally resides) we focus on 10 elements:

1   Impact: the typical level of impact achieved by the cultural model.
2   Tribes: the archetypal tribal structure observed.
3   Stories: how the cultural narrative is captured and shared.
4   Code: how culture is captured and represented to give meaning.
5   Leadership: how leaders contribute to a sustainable culture.
6   Ownership: how and when people act as custodians of the culture.
7   Values: how cultural foundations are decided and acted upon.
8   Energy: the sources of energy that drive decisions, activity and movement.
9   Learning: how and when the culture adapts and evolves.
10 Agility: flexibility and manoeuvrability as the future takes shape.

– • –

STAGE 1: REACTIVE	
Impact	SURVIVE
Tribes	• A familial tribe that is built around founders • Everyone outside of the tribe is considered a potential enemy until proven otherwise (can extend to new tribe members until their loyalty is established) • Tribal elders are still in the building; myths and legends that will form tribal origins are still in the making • The tribe is embryonic and fragile to disruption • The tribe is thrown together and has no consciously formed structure or commonly held values beyond those that have developed organically

Stories	• Happenstance delivers the ongoing narrative that informs the tribe's rituals and symbols • Rogues, heroes and villains are characters that have a fundamental impact on the organisation's early trajectory and its 'here and now' • Anti-heroes are often mistaken for heroes due to their force of character and strength of opinion • Culture is informal and not yet understood or deemed to be of importance • Water cooler culture rules without limits • Tribal stories are predominantly focused on the personal battles of tribal elders and their tales of overwhelming success despite potentially insurmountable hurdles
Code	• There is no attempt to decipher the symbols of culture • Limited or no understanding of how culture manifests and how to create shared understanding • Meaning is individual rather than collective, or is collectively established by virtue of the stance of a powerful charismatic founder • Heroes rule and dissent or deviance is not appreciated
Leadership	• Leaders are autocratic and expect to be followed • Leadership responsibility is based on individual charisma and personality • Command and control of the masses with the elevation of a trusted few to advisor status (typically based on loyalty rather than capability) • Do as I say, not necessarily as I do
Ownership	• Decisions are made by founders and their close allies – tight control delivers minimal autonomy for many • Culture is controlled at the top through unconscious actions and decisions • Knowledge and control are closely guarded

Values	• Dependent upon those of founders and major leaders
	• Emergent and appear as events and situations unfold
	• Can be entirely contradictory
	• Precedents being set but not considered
	• Critical conversations are avoided and some subjects are strictly off-limits
Energy	• People- and event-dependent
	• Driven by profit or cause but reliant upon regular interventions by founder and key leaders
	• Predominant energies of excitement and fear
	• Gut impulse over structured analysis
Learning	• Ad hoc and ineffective
	• Cultural errors repeated and replicated
	• Dependent on agility, willingness and openness of key leaders
Agility	• Spontaneous but incoherent and at times chaotic

– • –

STAGE 2: FOCUSED	
Impact	STRIVE
Tribes	• Many tribes
	• Tribes are rooted in factions and fiefdoms – turf wars are part of the everyday scenery
	• The enemy is within – other leaders, functions and business units are considered to be obstacles on the path to greatness
	• Cross-tribal networks are pulled apart before they can form
	• Warring tribes are forced to play nicely but beneath the surface find passive-aggressive ways to dilute the others' strength

Stories	• Competing heroes seek the limelight through competing narratives
	• Power and dominance over peers and their tribes is a common narrative
	• Multiple authoritarian cascades that ensure people in each tribe know how they should think and behave to demonstrate loyalty to their tribe
	• Myths and legends are diluted by varying beliefs of multiple tribes
Code	• Tribes compete to have their culture dominate
	• Many codes that confuse the broader organisational culture
	• Codes lack authenticity and are disrespected and ignored
	• Counterproductive, misaligned and contradictory cultures
Leadership	• Strong combative leaders are respected and successful
	• Power bases dictate how culture is represented
	• Leaders divide the organisation to rule its people
	• Autocratic and demanding
	• Positive deviance is misunderstood and 'problem children' are moved within or removed from the organisation
Ownership	• It doesn't pay to be a custodian of the culture
	• Culture is owned by the few and enforced through punishment and censorship
	• Blame and shame cause most to avoid responsibility for actions and decisions
Values	• Variable and competing
	• Unenforced and only supported when it suits
	• Contribution trumps behaviour – toxic behaviours will be tolerated if commercial contribution is strong
	• Problems are moved within the organisation rather than confronted and dealt with
	• Critical conversations happen to avoid an inevitable meltdown, but some subjects remain taboo

Energy	• Diluted and unfocused • Lack of holistic prioritisation – every leader for himself • Predominant energies of competitiveness, animosity and ambition
Learning	• Sporadic and isolated • Lessons are learned many times but not shared and applied • Contradictory precedents are created across multiple tribes and within subtribes • Mistakes are repeated due to lack of conscious collaboration
Agility	• Tribal warfare and countercultures lead to lack of connection and limited holistic agility

– • –

STAGE 3: STRUCTURED	
Impact	THRIVE
Tribes	• The tribe has advanced to a civilisation or organisational empire • Empire takes the moral high ground towards enemies without (and closet enemies within) • The formal tribe has power while subtribes are unrecognised or negated • Structurally engineered tribes mean that people pretend to play nicely
Stories	• A controlled narrative is achieved through carefully constructed stories • Cultivated heroes play the major roles in formal myths and legends • Process and politics drive shallow meaning • Stability is the order of the day, 'one culture' is an organisational mantra • Culture assumes the future will be as the past or follow its patterns closely

Code	• Culture is captured in a formal code of values and behaviours
	• Informal code is unexamined, refuted or dismantled
	• Code is built upon a textbook understanding of emotional connection and cultural development
	• Culture and code are one-size-fits-all and may not translate for all members
Leadership	• Leaders are anchored in theory and process
	• Leadership responses are planned in detail – robotic, mapped and scripted
	• Emerging leaders are asked to behave one way while senior leaders behave another – culture struggles to pass the 'looking up' test
	• Positive deviance is suppressed or controlled, and alternative thinkers are often labelled as heretics or dissenters
	• Formal hierarchy is where leadership power resides
Ownership	• Key performance indicators and metrics determine how ownership is distributed
	• Matrix management creates many owners for each issue and may dilute accountability
	• Ownership is awarded for performance and an entitlement of those in power
Values	• Clearly audited and sanitised
	• Authorised and cascaded
	• Values create a veneer that glosses over the truthful organisation and its culture
	• Words and figures differ – what we say we want in the literature may be different to what we really want every day
	• Critical conversations are included as part of a structured dialogue process. Some subjects are still considered negatively should they emerge
Energy	• Structured prioritisation is based on linear thinking and logical analysis
	• Commercials, financials and metrics are of utmost importance
	• Predominant energies of thinking, planning and structured action

Learning	• Benchmarking against alternative cultures determines best practice to be applied • Structured feedback loops are supported by engagement surveys • Postmortems encourage the determination of respected precedents • Complexity of culture is underestimated
Agility	• Mechanism allows structured agility at fixed time points

– • –

STAGE 4: INTEGRATED	
Impact	**FUTURE-FIT**
Tribes	• Authentic tribes are built around genuine causes • Enemies are problems not people • Tribes collaborate and combine to exert more power and influence • Disparate tribes are brought together over shared interests
Stories	• Myths and legends are examined and retold • Superheroes cut across tribal boundaries and create new and interesting narratives to inspire people • Stories of successful collaboration are elevated and shared • Suggest or assume that the future will evolve along a predicted path
Code	• The code and its chosen symbols are realistic and allow for current cultural norms • Simple, adaptable and translatable symbols allow all to make meaning from them • Provides principles for guidance in the everyday world • Allows freedom within a flexible framework

Leadership	• Game-changing leaders drive belief through remaining connected, informed, insightful, focused, valuable, inclusive and authentic in everything they do • Leadership is devolved where possible through structured networks • Cultural congruence is expected of leaders and challenged when not apparent • Positive deviance is encouraged
Ownership	• Emotional connection and engagement drive all to take ownership wherever it is possible for them to do so • Individual participation and self-management are organisational habits
Values	• Born of a genuine and inclusive discussion • Vulnerability is shown so that values can be crafted and evolve • People are encouraged to speak truth to power and to challenge behaviours, actions and decisions that are counter to values • Critical conversations are part of the fabric of the organisation and few subjects are avoided
Energy	• Energy is cause-driven through strong emotional impact and connection • Predominant energies are commitment, purpose and a desire to contribute and make a difference
Learning	• Continuous and in the moment • Driven by an individual and collective hunger for progress • Many sources are established to generate best fit for the situation at hand • Collaborative and experiential learning is facilitated and encouraged
Agility	• Multiple paths and process learning provide the ability to quickly adapt for pre-planned shifts to an emerging evolutionary culture

STAGE 5: SHAPESHIFTER	
Impact	CHANGE THE GAME
Tribes	• A meta-tribe is created that transcends all others – organisation moves beyond tribes • The organisation and its people fall in love with problems rather than solutions • The organisation fosters hive mind and thinks as one • Quantum connections are established across the network
Stories	• Myths and legends depict an overarching narrative of beliefs and values that fuel the meta-tribe in pursuit of its ambitions • There's room for everyone to play their part and everyone can be a hero • Co-creation is the process through which the narrative of myths, legends and heroes is collected, collated and then shared • Myths and legends suggest that the future will emerge and give confidence to those navigating a turbulent, uncertain, complex and ambiguous journey
Code	• Evolves and emerges as the organisation develops and adapts • Translations are generated by and for every group and individual • Continuous dialogue and application mean that the culture and its symbols come alive • Testing for relevance is a continuous process
Leadership	• Game-makers emerge across the organisation who are hungry, playful, courageous, self-aware and willing to be novices in the face of new situations • Fully devolved leadership delivers full autonomy • Everyone is a leader – people dare to lead and all have the power to make a huge difference • Principle-based decision-making is the norm • Hive mind has developed into a palpable shared consciousness • Positive deviance is actively encouraged

Ownership	• Comes from playing a meaningful part in an inspirational movement – a shared powerful cause with meaning and energy • Intra-organisational boundaries are in continuous movement to enable people to co-create the future • Self-managing networks are dynamic and lead to synchronised swarm activity • Individuals are custodians of collective culture and its mechanisms
Values	• Evolving and emerging • Effectively translated for meaning and application • Co-created and examined for continued relevance • Trust forms their foundation • Critical conversations are expected and actively encouraged as part of a rich and healthy dialogue that is not limited in direction or subject
Energy	• Energy is self-replicating and creates a dynamo effect • Predominant energies are meaning, sharing, connecting, imagining and changing the world for the better • Activity is cause-driven and purpose comes foremost driving a virtuous cycle (profits will arrive through focusing on the purpose and go on to fund achievement of the cause and related research or innovation)
Learning	• Organisational learning is hardwired into informal networks • Culture pre-mortems and scenarios mean many lessons are learned in advance through experimentation and enquiry • Learning is meaning-driven • Process learning is recognised and respected • Interconnected dynamic learning network means that learning is dissipated across the shared consciousness – quantum mechanics in action
Agility	• Collective intelligence and shared consciousness underlined by a powerful cause combine to create a shapeshifting culture that is agile to the emerging future – pre-emptive shifts evolve over time and emergent shifts spread virally

Each of the five stages may be appropriate at a given point in time, for a particular context or organisational life stage. Imps have a tendency to remain firmly towards Stage 1 (reactive) of the cultural spectrum, while dinosaurs seem to result where giants overstay their welcome in Stage 3 (structured) or where imps suddenly wish to emulate their larger and older peers and their structured and complex bureaucracies in an effort to appear grown-up. Unicorns quickly learn that Stages 4 and 5 are the way to achieve great things. Organisations that are future-fit (Stage 4) are ready and able to face the future and attract the talent they need. Shapeshifters (Stage 5) have the greatest ability to enhance their capabilities and co-create the future with a willing band of fans who genuinely want to be part of the movement and contribute to their cause.

Again, there aren't many organisations that can claim to consistently fulfil every element of the shapeshifter mindset. Those that set out to do so will always develop a more authentic culture that will stand the test of time. Cultures built on a bedrock of authenticity, inclusiveness and trust demonstrate a magnetism that is virtually impossible to emulate through staging and acting, no matter how sophisticated the illusion may be.

You'll notice already that when a shapeshifter focuses on generating a supple strategy and a culture that transcends tribes simultaneously there are synergies to be had. By adopting a holistic approach to the moves they each become integrated with one another and easier to achieve. Already it should be apparent that the four moves are firmly interconnected and best traversed simultaneously rather than as a linear roadmap. Strategy to reality is a complex game of simultaneous moves and networked organisations.

ASK YOURSELF...

Whereabouts are you on your journey to becoming a shapeshifter? Consider the tribal maturity model and ask yourself:

- Who rules your empire and how do they rule?
- How does everyone in your organisation work together to create a great environment?

- Do tribes effortlessly come together to collaborate and co-create or are there turf wars and empires scattered everywhere?
- Can you think of a value that pervades the entire organisation – honestly?
- What stories capture the narrative of how your organisation came about, why it did so and what happened to make it succeed?
- Who are your heroes and how are they representative of the organisation you want to become – or the organisation you are trying to be right now?
- Where does culture get its power – at the water cooler, from its centre or through the network?
- How many cultures exist across your organisation?
- How is culture codified? Are the values and behaviours clear and important to all?
- How do you deal with a toxic culture or an individual who represents the poison within?
- How and when do you check cultural precedents for consistency, relevance and appropriateness?
- Who are your leaders and how do they lead?
- Where in your organisation do the big decisions get made?
- What are the critical conversations that are important to your culture and how are they approached?
- Which conversations remain difficult in your culture?
- Are any conversations still taboo in your organisation?
- How congruent is your culture, and have the values stood the test of time?
- Do the posters on the wall get ridiculed?
- How focused is the tribe and where does it place its energy?
- How curious is the tribe and how does it learn from its mistakes?
- Are people even allowed to make mistakes?
- Who are the custodians of the culture and who can safely voice its problems?

- How accepting is your organisation of different ways of thinking and experiencing the world?
- Is your tribe alive or is it just memorable?
- How can the culture evolve as the world changes around it?

CHAPTER 10

WHY META-TRIBES RULE

Great cultures that power game-changing movements take work, belonging and belief. Aligned and connected organisations where everyone is a leader are far more likely to build the future. Fractured organisations with many tribal factions waste copious amounts of energy just trying to keep the peace. A meta-tribe connects information, shares ownership, devolves leadership and co-creates an identity that is authentic and congruent throughout the organisation. A meta-tribe knows its mind but accepts its many thoughts. It challenges its beliefs where they limit progress but does so in a way that upholds values. It has a cause at its core and a purpose to its power – it knows where it wants to be.

A force-fed meta-tribe is not sustainable. Like a human it must feel its way and learn by experience – its individual parts coming together to tell the stories that inspire them to act in ways that uphold the values that make them proud to belong, find the purpose they want to achieve and make the difference that delivers their legacy.

A meta-tribe makes the most of shared vision and connected behaviours yet dispels the hostility and aggression of unhealthy competition. A meta-tribe formed well thinks as one, acts coherently and amplifies impact. A conscious being of many diverse individuals becomes agile to the emerging future and forges a path into the unknown. The power of convergence is not to be underestimated. A meta-tribe with a better world as its ambition is a tough tribe to stop in its tracks!

SIDE EFFECTS OF META-TRIBES (THE BUSINESS CASE)

Shapeshifters codify their culture in a way that binds people to their cause through a web of deep meaning and belief in a shared future. Engagement and commitment levels in these organisations are far beyond those experienced in organisations with a lesser developed culture or no concept of a meta-tribe.

Shapeshifters shape, align, evolve and mobilise their meta-tribe through structure and process, but not in a way that expends flexibility. Networks overlay structure and experience drives process. Relationships become deeper and more able to stand disagreement and misunderstanding. Transparent and engaging discourse and co-creation activities provide oxygen to agility and evolution.

Powerful new myths and legends are collectively narrated, and heroes emerge from the everyday to drive momentum. Everyone knows they have a part to play and how to play their part.

Memetics drive the evolution of culture and the emergence of new ideas.[34] Creativity and positive deviance nudge the status quo gently into oblivion, fast replacing it with novel innovations that play a leading role in shaping the future. Neurodiversity is celebrated, and positive deviance is encouraged. Assumptions are routinely challenged, and the organisation evolves through the prolific birth of novel ideas.

Shapeshifters think as one and appear to move effortlessly in the mystical synchronised dance of particles linked at a quantum level. They work collectively across boundaries on the wicked problems that will determine their future, and they enhance understanding, forge new bonds and develop greater belief and alignment along the way.

Their culture is congruent – wherever you touch it, it feels and reacts in a way that conveys its purpose and authenticity. This very congruence generates natural alignment around the important issues and a commitment to the shared purpose and common good.

Faced with ambiguity, the culture provides a haven of clarity and the autonomy to act; an ability to make decisions confidently based on a proper understanding of core values and behaviours that fundamentally craft the organisation's identity.

Through ongoing discussion, the culture code contributes to robust and unselfish prioritisation. Making sure the organisation achieves its purpose and the meta-tribe furthers its cause is the number one focus and the rationale for all decisions. People are not left wondering if they should, rather they are given the space and encouragement to consider if they could.

Game-making leaders, individual and collective ownership, and shared and deeply meaningful values combined with the energy of a shared purpose mean that nobody is left behind. In a shapeshifter organisation, there is no room for Mack the Turtle to be left to collapse under the strain of competing priorities, limited capacity and unreasonable demands from those at the top of the pile. Ultimately trust is built on firm foundations that can withstand the inevitable storms.

So, what are you waiting for?

SHAPESHIFTER IN ACTION

THE UNIVERSITY OF SALFORD

The University of Salford began life as a direct result of changes wrought by the Industrial Revolution of the nineteenth century. Declining industries created a need for the re-education of the local workforce and a range of institutions rose up to meet those needs. To cut a long story short, these educational institutes merged, then split, and then merged again in 1996 to become the University of Salford. The university has transformed and reinvented itself many times throughout its journey; it is no stranger to change!

Today the university is a global presence in the higher education sector. With a turnover to rival many large businesses, 4 schools, 20,000 students and 2,500 staff, the university is an important employer, educator and agent for social change in the region. Recent years have seen the creation of a new campus at Media City in Salford Quays, the building of New Adelphi (a purpose-built Arts and Media facility on the main campus) and the development of strong partnerships with some of the biggest and most well-known names in TV and radio media. The university is looking to the future with ambitious plans for the redevelopment of its existing campus and the use of digital and virtual learning environments. Its strategy is all about Industry Collaboration Zones (where partner businesses play a major role in the design of programmes, delivery of learning and provision of opportunities for research). You only have to see the big red 'AMBITION' sculpture in front of the main campus entrance to appreciate that change is a state of being for the University of Salford!

The organisational culture at the university has, of course, also evolved over the years. Change has a habit of shifting a culture regardless of whether such a shift would be a helpful or desirable outcome. Change in organisations can be perceived as positive or negative dependent upon the angle from which it is viewed and the likely impact of the change upon the observer. Experiences of change and the leadership of such change can create unacknowledged and uncontrollable cultural shockwaves into the future.

The university's strategic ambitions demand new capabilities, value-driven behaviours and an alignment of resources and people to be successful. In 2016 the university decided to consciously focus on the way its culture manifested and evolved, in particular through its leadership approach and capability. Its initial goal was to create a leadership framework that would define what good looks like in the context of the university and to clarify and align around core values, behaviours, attitudes and skills. The framework was to provide a scaffold and common language which would enable performance, development and talent conversations so that leaders (and aspiring leaders) could understand what was required of them as a leader of the university.

It would have been easy to replicate the typical leadership framework seen in many higher education institutions, but the University of Salford decided to do things very differently.

From the very start, the university took a keen and genuine interest in the way that its culture presently showed its character. Hangovers from the past were unearthed and understood. Simultaneously, future strategy was examined to find the stretching behavioural challenges for the future that would need to be grappled with. This initial step was the big dose of reality that provided invaluable information regarding the existing cultural norms, transformation hangovers from the past, hopes and beliefs that would impact the future, and the emotional reactions that resulted. It also allayed the fears of many employees that the process was either a window-dressing job (covering up obvious cracks without dealing with fundamental flaws) or the precursor to a painful organisational transformation dressed up in a gown of culture and leadership development.

The university has a small central Organisation Development (OD) team, which itself has undergone much change. From the get-go, this team wanted to do things differently – they wanted to use the process itself as an opportunity to create immersive learning experiences for people across the organisation.

The process of cultural investigation and behavioural framework design was to be a major cultural change lever in and of itself. The team were very conscious that the creation of a behavioural framework was merely the start of a much longer and complex journey and they wanted to make the most of every opportunity to connect and partner with their colleagues everywhere.

The resulting behavioural framework was co-created with a large number of university employees and was also reviewed by a group of students and some local business partners (the true end users of the university's services). The label for each behaviour and the words used within the framework to describe them were very consciously selected for their ability to preserve effective behaviours, encourage new behaviours and stop habitual yet unhelpful behaviours. Language was purposefully stretching, challenging and enlightening, and behaviours were examined continuously to unearth how they could best be applied to a given situation or context.

The summary below gives a taste of The Salford Behaviours:

THE SALFORD BEHAVIOURS	
Connecting	Consciously connects with people to build trusting relationships over time and helps others to form networks that will support them in their work and learning
Inspiring	Communicates with clarity and behaves in a way that engages and influences people to do their best for the university and its students
Evolving	Creates a better future through a constant focus on improvement and innovation
Achieving	Takes accountability to make things happen and see things through for the benefit of the university and its students
Enabling	Trusts and empowers others to deliver results providing support and challenge where appropriate
Learning	Takes personal responsibility for their learning journey and actively contributes to the university's learning culture and the learning experience of its students

Deciding	Objectively and effectively makes decisions in a timely fashion, placing the needs of the university and its students front and centre
Co-creating	Works with and through others to generate the best possible ideas and solutions for the university, its students and its staff
Aligning	Focuses on what is in the best interests of the university and its students, and positively aligns to university strategy
Daring	Courageously navigates new situations and boldly decides, acts and challenges while supporting others to do the same

The behavioural framework was just that – a behavioural framework. What made it different was that the behaviours were 'future-paced and far out' with a genuine recognition and admission that there was much work to do at all levels of and in every corner of the organisation to bring this desired culture into being.

This could have been the end of the process, and for many organisations it is. The university realised that to stop at this point would render the culture change impotent. Instead, the behavioural framework became a fluid starting point rather than the end result. The creation of The Salford Behaviours was the beginning of something far more inclusive, immersive and transformational.

Universities are typically traditional in approach and a top-down communication cascade and embedding process would have been the norm. Culture is all about the beliefs, myths, legends and heroes and the real conversations and habitual behaviours that dominate. For a culture to evolve, its foundations must be able to continually reform and its method of evolution must also evolve.

The university's OD team turned the idea of a traditional rollout programme on its head. They set about changing the university from the inside out and upside down. The team knew that to bring about a change in culture they had to be that culture. They had to demonstrate and be the behaviours they were seeking to infuse, and they had to work as a virus to infect their host without raising levels of antigens (cynicism, avoidance and the like). In a sea of largely traditional thinkers who had experienced many change programmes before (and most likely ably fought them off), the team set about igniting small fires and feeding the flames of a more organic and natural growth and spread. To do this fast they made the most of the super connectors and informal networks in operation across the university.

I asked Robert Ritchie (Head of OD) to describe his experience of the culture evolution so far:

What vehicles have you used to drive the change?

We've done the typical things to ensure the framework remains alive. It's embedded into our employee lifecycle wherever it makes sense to do so, and so we know it is an active part of the living cultural system within the university. The behaviours are everywhere and interwoven into everything. We now call this framework 'The Salford Behaviours'.

Of course, we've ensured that our most senior leaders are supportive of the behaviours and we actively challenge any behaviours from them that seem counter to the culture we've all agreed we would like to see.

This has been supported by several products that are aimed at developing capability and generating powerful conversations:

- *'Leading at Salford' is a programme of quarterly get-togethers where we focus on critical leadership conversations. We use very contemporary interventions, such as storytelling and appreciative inquiry, to ensure that everyone has a voice and all perspectives are explored.*
- *'Salford Conversations' also happen quarterly and involve everyone at the university. Topics are contemporary and sometimes controversial with the aim of eliminating taboos, filling communication vacuums and exploring shared interests.*
- *'Salford Managers' Programme' is a learning offering for anyone who manages others at the university. It focuses on the difficult and critical conversations that shift mindsets and behaviours. It focuses on the human aspects of managing people – less of the how and more of the why.*
- *'Leading without masks' is a learning experience for members of our VCET (Vice Chancellor's Executive Team) – our most senior leaders. It is all about being more human, and daring to show your true self in all that you do. We explore how meaning can replace jargon, and how vulnerability, openness and inclusion generate more powerful followership than fear.*

What's different about the approach?

While the lifecycle integration and learning products have been instrumental, our biggest shifts have come from rather different interventions.

We've used a great deal of disruptive learning. Some of our methods at first feel uncomfortable for everyone involved but can therefore act as a catalyst for a different way of thinking and acting. As facilitators we have made ourselves vulnerable by inviting people to learning events that are far from the norm at the university. One example is our 'Take 10' sessions where a number of relatively unconnected people are invited to a room where they find a box containing 10 items and have a short amount of time to make meaning from those items as a group. On the face of it the exercise seems rather futile, but invariably the group engages with one another through their discomfort and participants start to learn about their own emotional and behavioural responses alongside those of the others around them. We've made every effort to be inventive and expose people to new experiences, challenging ideas and counter-intuitive approaches.

The culture is always front and central when we speak to people across the university. Every conversation is an opportunity to explore its meaning at an individual, team and organisational level, and to connect across behaviours that have great resonance for that person or situation.

We've avoided posters and focused on experiences. The only cultural collateral we have (besides The Salford Behaviours) are some fun items like behaviour paddles and playing cards that we use to support some learning experiences.

What's been difficult?

Initially the team were met with much resistance but over time their persistence and innovation paid off. People started to enjoy the alternative approach and the refreshing way in which they were being invited to not only adopt the behaviours but to actively evolve them in service of the organisation's future and its ability to better serve its stakeholders.

As an OD team we have coalesced around five axioms that have challenged us to do our best work regardless of any turbulence:

1   *We understand and explain clearly where development stops, and others take over.*
2   *We look up and out and ask others to do the same.*
3   *We build the bridge as we walk on it.*

4   *Mindsets and behaviours are our thing.*
5   *We reshape the university about what's strong not wrong.*

Why have you persevered?

It's been great to watch as mindsets and behaviours evolve before your eyes, particularly those of the people formally driving the culture. Our aim has been to untap creativity and to unlock hidden strengths, and we have seen some people and teams achieve outcomes they wouldn't previously have dreamed possible. The purpose of the OD team is to cultivate mindsets and behaviours that will better equip the university in a 'wicked world'.

It's such a different approach and at times it has been incredibly hard work. In the short time since we finished the initial version of The Salford Behaviours, we have already seen significant engagement and impact. The university now describes itself as 'unstoppable' and there is a tangible energy around this which keeps us going.

How do you know it's working?

We don't know who's adopted the framework or not – but that's not the point. The framework is only supposed to serve as a guide to what works here behaviourally. The organisation looks and feels very different to when we started – it is a very different (and hopefully more positive) experience to be a part of the university now.

Incidentally, the reputation of the OD team has massively improved since we have shifted our approach to work in partnership with every one of our colleagues rather than just delivering pre-packaged solutions to them. The team focuses on three things now – connection, community and citizenship. We want to bring people along so that they feel they need, want, must be a part of this. Every day we are noticing changes in people's approaches to learning, growing and change – and these shifts are accelerating.

What have you learned from the experience?

1   *Tenacity is key. Keep going even on your darkest days. This is the sticky bit in the middle, but you need to keep going. It will be worth it…*
2   *Don't bother trying to bring together a 'turbulent network of people' to get things done. Forget the naysayers and the fence-sitters and focus more on*

connecting with like-minded people and friends of the show – the people with open and change-focused mindsets. These are the early adopters and others will follow. If people don't buy in at first, move on to someone else. In short, follow the energy…

3   *The answers are often 'in the room'. Sometimes you don't need to create something from scratch, but instead you can build on and amplify what already is. Ideas become infectious when people are included and genuinely invited to co-create!*

4   *It's a myth that you must always start with getting the most senior leaders on board first. Develop a groundswell (from anywhere) and then include senior leaders when they are ready. Others from across the organisation, including senior leaders, will become curious and want to find out more for fear of missing out. Two years ago, the work we are currently doing with our VCET would not have been accepted. Traditional, limited impact and low-disruption models of learning were the order of the day. We had to earn our place at the table by showing how we had already made a positive impact through doing things very differently (without having been asked or invited to do so). Now our VCET are fully on board and actively want to sponsor, and be involved in, the work we do across the university – we are now trusted when we dare to be different and this is a massive shift in itself.*

Using The Salford Behaviours as a starting point, the University of Salford is yet again reinventing itself. Perhaps without even setting out to do so, the university is fast coming together as a powerful meta-tribe. Shared values are underpinned by enabling beliefs and meaningful values to allow devolved leadership and principle-based decision-making to gain traction. The Salford Behaviours were but a marker in the ground, a line in the sand that represented a new stage of organisational evolution. The real work started after its creation (and The Salford Behaviours are now also evolving as a direct result of these ongoing organisational conversations). The behaviours were embraced due to the levels of inclusion, voice and co-creation embedded into their creation. The process has encouraged storytelling, myth-making and the building of powerful connecting narratives. The purpose of the university has never been clearer, and the best part is that people are unleashing their creativity, inventiveness and courage to dare to be different. A magical movement is fast building at the

University of Salford; a movement that will ensure the university always possesses the energy required for success in good times and bad, and is always ready and able to provide the very best experience for students and colleagues alike.

PART 3

MOVE THREE:
WICKED THINKING

In Move One we played with a range of alternative futures to ensure that our strategy was supple and able to rise to the opportunities and challenges that those futures may present. Indeed, our overall aim was to generate and navigate a strategic pathway that would bring about the very future we would like to see. Move Two saw us transcend tribes through the formation of a meta-tribe that would enable the organisation to act and think as one in pursuit of its goals.

Our next move is equally important to an organisation's future success. In Move Three we seek to innovate in ways that allow us to alter the strategic context irredeemably. The problem with any strategy is that there are typically a range of quite intransigent and established obstacles in the path of its successful fulfilment. Often these obstacles are age-old problems that have until now been avoided. By thinking about these issues in a different way we can make friends with them on our journey so that they present opportunities rather than myriad risks to our future. By thinking beyond complex problems and finding new ways to co-create sustainable progress around and within their boundaries we may, almost accidently, identify the singularity at the core of our powerful cause.[35] This very problem or issue might become our reason for being and turn out to be the vehicle through which the future context remoulds itself.

In a volatile, uncertain, complex and ambiguous environment, just like the post-truth fast show, we need to come up with new, novel ideas. To do this demands that we approach problems in a manner that is less combative and more collaborative, less solution-oriented and more progress-focused. For ideas to gain traction they must attract first followers, and for first followers to become interested it must be in their interests to be so. Wicked problems often get in the way of strategy but can provide the very catalyst required for the formation of a cause with meaning, penetration and momentum. So what is a wicked problem?

A wicked problem is a problem that is too big, complex or difficult to solve. It's the kind of problem that mutates and evolves in unexpected ways and is stoked by a cast of (often well-meaning) stakeholders with, at times, little common ground. The concept of a 'wicked problem' first emerged from social policy, where many actors and complex contexts and histories resulted in problems that exhibited a range of complicating factors. Wicked problems are socially complex and often demonstrate contradictory perspectives which each have a level of validity and authority. Academics, Rittel and Webber cited 10 characteristics which they believed to be true of wicked problems in the social policy arena:[36]

1   *There is no definitive formulation of a wicked problem* – they evade clear definition and so the usual advice to 'define the problem' takes on a whole new meaning.

2   *Wicked problems have no end point where the problem is deemed to be fixed* – they continue to evolve throughout and after any interventions a problem-solver may seek to apply.

3   *Solutions to wicked problems are not true or false, but better or worse* – this dichotomy is in reality a spectrum of shades of grey, dependent upon the perspective from which the problem and potential interventions are viewed.

4   *There is no immediate and no ultimate test of a solution to a wicked problem* – their evolving nature and disparate stakeholders mean that meaningful measurement is challenging.

5   *Every solution to a wicked problem is a 'one-shot operation' that cannot be undone or redone* – interventions have immediate efficacy and limit a safe opportunity to learn through trial and error – therefore every attempt or intervention counts significantly and can have irreparable impact.

6   *Wicked problems do not have a pre-defined set of potential solutions or permissible operations* – due to their unique nature, wicked problems each have their own equally unique, potentially positive and negative interventions which may not be immediately obvious.

7   *Every wicked problem is essentially unique* – therefore there are no predetermined solutions or processes that can be easily applied to resolve them, each wicked problem demands a fresh approach.

8   *Every wicked problem can be considered to be a symptom of another problem* – they are interconnected across large distances in space, culture and time and it is unlikely that they can ever be fully mapped and interpreted.

9   *A wicked problem can be explained in numerous ways* – often dependent upon the party's experience, beliefs and opinions.
10 *The social planner has no right to be wrong* – interventions can create massive ramifications. People therefore need to be conscious of and responsible for the consequences of any actions they generate.

In essence, a wicked problem is one that is typically large (although scale is not always a determinant), transcends borders and is complex in nature. Wicked problems have many causes and no central authority that could force a solution (even if there was a solution available). The parties involved in its resolution are often at the root of is causes, or may be compounding its causes through their efforts at finding a simple solution. Tackling the wicked problem from any angle invariably creates new problems or exacerbates other existing problems. Interested parties tend to come and go throughout the problem's life and stakeholders that remain involved demonstrate changing opinions alongside fluctuating resources and interest levels. Each stakeholder of a wicked problem is likely to describe it entirely differently from its other stakeholders and their particular vision of a suitable outcome may be the worst possible scenario for another group. Just to compound matters, wicked problems seem to lurk in packs. They form a web of such problems that are interconnected, intertwined and interdependent – a wicked web if you will.

If a wicked problem is multidimensional, with multiple causes and symptoms, and socially complex with many stakeholders each with an alternative perspective or interpretation, it seems prudent to accept that such a problem is ever-evolving and may be altered and shifted in many ways. Multiple potential interventions may cause positive progress in the context of a given wicked problem, but the many viewpoints and competing interests cause obvious challenges around goal-setting and prioritisation. Competing and conflicting ambitions coupled with a moving target means that a wicked problem is a tricky (if not impossible) one to fully solve.

And guess what… we're surrounded by wicked problems that are complex, diffuse, vague and resist all logical interpretation. Fast-changing stakeholders, shifting contextual relevance in any given moment and perceived past failures dilute any efforts to make a positive difference. Wicked problems divide opinion, unite factions and exclude outsiders – the very people that may be able to provide previously unheard and valid ideas.

We can all recognise global wicked problems, for example, global warming and our reliance on hydrocarbons; the demise of bees and our continued usage of powerful chemical pesticides and fertilisers; conflict across the globe and our economically powerful defence industry. They are global problems where there is probably no 'right answer', no 'one answer' that satisfies and improves the lot of all stakeholders. They are problems that present a myriad of unforeseen outcomes from any one small and apparently insignificant decision or action, whether or not such decisions or actions were perceived or intended as largely positive or negative.

The biggest wicked problem of all is that we fall in love with finding a solution, a silver bullet that will permanently and completely solve an issue. We know intrinsically that life is messy and just doesn't work that way but still we seek that perfect outcome.

Wicked problems don't have to be big to be wicked! Most of us have a wicked problem or two that directly impacts our daily work and lives, and organisations have their fair share too: the efficient yet safe disposal of toxic waste from a manufacturing process; the raising of sufficient finance from appropriate sources; the development of products to meet the needs of multiple diverse markets; the balancing of profit and financial viability with social conscience and positive community impact – each organisation has its own mix of intrinsic wicked problems. Can you identify the wicked problems within your organisation?

We all have something to gain from approaching these problems differently. We clearly need to think and co-create in a manner that can transcend our tribes and their endemic beliefs and behaviours. So how do we resist our natural animal instincts to be 'right' and redefine success in a way that allows us to make progress day by day, and to learn from our inevitable failures on the journey?

To take a supple strategy to reality, to bring a culture to life and to inject meaning, purpose and drive into our causes and movements, we must dare to engage with the many wicked problems that sit on our path and invite us to get down and dirty in a way that could just change the world. We must identify, demystify and innovate to make progress on the wicked problems that at first glance seem too big or too difficult to solve!

CHAPTER 11

HOW SHAPESHIFTERS USE WICKED THINKING TO INNOVATE

Unsurprisingly, shapeshifters do innovation differently. They think beyond current paradigms and their own habitual interpretations of an issue to develop novel ideas that can meet the future head-on or create the future they wish to see. Where most organisations and people fall in love with a solution and then go about defending and strengthening their position and its justification, shapeshifters know that this approach is pure folly that has limited longevity in a fast-changing reality. Shapeshifters fall in love with problems no matter how wicked they are. They indulge in getting to know the issue intimately from all angles and avoid falling in love with presenting solutions regardless of how tempting they may be. Shapeshifters engage fully with the chaos of strategic context – past, present and future – and the complexity of the problems that sit along their chosen path. They think beyond current trends and existing paradigms and use their ability to see around corners through scenarios to establish 'what-if' worlds for further examination. They focus on the wicked problems that have the potential to make *the* difference. And they engage diverse and diffuse wicked tribes (meta-tribes focused on a given wicked problem) in collective inquiry, dialogue mapping, design thinking and active experimentation to drive systemic, continuous innovation for positive progress. They are the very embodiment of Peter Drucker's assertion that 'the best way to predict the future is to create it'.[37]

Shapeshifters examine the realities of today alongside the wider possibilities of tomorrow, in a controlled and structured environment. They consciously and unashamedly bring together adversaries and strangers through the catalysts of powerful debate, visible progress and tangible impact. Shapeshifters unleash their supple strategy and meta-tribes to create powerful movements rooted in the depths of entrenched wicked problems. Wicked tribes are encouraged to indulge their imagination and engage in collective thinking and co-creation to drive disruptive innovation. A systemic innovation infrastructure and culture is unleashed – in short, disruptive innovation and 'thinking beyond' become organisational habits.

Shapeshifters are constantly on the lookout for anti-patterns; the systemic patterns of activity and behaviour that cause a problem to become entrenched and deepen its negative impact. They recognise anti-patterns for what they are and speak truth to power (that is, they challenge behaviours, habits and processes regardless of perceived status or hierarchy and even when it may be personally challenging to do so) to shine a spotlight on them wherever they find them.

Shapeshifters appreciate the need to extend their thinking beyond basic empathy and logical self-authoring towards a dynamic, connected, shared consciousness that endeavours to fully understand the complexity of the situation it faces from every angle. True empathy, genuine belonging, committed sharing, authentic partnership, curiosity, courage and creative co-creation result in the development of meaningful opportunities to make a difference. Shapeshifters make sure they shift their collective level of thinking beyond that which causes the problem.

Shapeshifters systematise innovation through culture, leadership, structure and networks. Most importantly, they create space for serendipity! Yes, there it is again – the importance of creating time and space to think freely both individually and collectively. Shapeshifters focus on quality input, confident in their belief that game-changing output will come. They dare to experiment and play with a problem, learning to adapt and evolve as the problem changes shape before their very eyes.

Shapeshifters appreciate that wicked problems demand wicked thinking. They use wicked tribes and some wicked love (leadership, ownership, values and energy) to fan the fire of positive progress. Shapeshifters embark on a journey of discovery – challenging the experts and seeking out open minds and positive deviance to find real interventions for real problems. Shapeshifters think beyond…

POSITIVE DEVIANCE AND WHY IT MATTERS

I've mentioned it a few times now and so an explanation is probably overdue. Positive deviance has a role to play in all four moves, but it does its most profound work here in Move Three.

Positive deviance is a concept often referred to but sometimes misunderstood. Positive deviance is the phenomenon by which a relatively simple but uncommon behaviour, process or approach to a problem produces positive results that stand out from the norm. Typically, the alternative strategy is well hidden amongst the complexity of the many approaches to the issue and, without conscious investigation, may never come to light. The behaviour or approach – 'the strategy' – is performed by a subgroup of people or perhaps just one individual – an outlier who does not follow standard procedure or adhere to the accepted rules but successfully navigates their way around or through an entrenched problem in a novel way.

Many organisations seek to identify positive deviants within their organisation but miss the essence of the concept. An individual is only a positive deviant in respect to a particular problem where their approach is markedly different and consistently outperforms their contemporaries. By marking individuals out as positive deviants regardless of context, an organisation misses the point in finding them. While there may be some typical behaviours (for example, curiosity, creativity, persistence) that tend to be demonstrated by positive deviants that enable them to discover and persevere with alternative strategies, these behaviours are by no means reliable indicators that an individual will become a positive deviant across all contexts.

The power of identifying and isolating positive deviance (and the positive deviants who facilitate it) is in relation to finding potentially high-impact and positive interventions for the wicked problem that is being worked on. In this specific context, identifying positive deviance allows the wicked tribe to interrogate existing approaches and isolate any that already show a greater propensity for positive outcomes. It enables them to look beyond the perceived wisdom often sought from the recognised experts and accepted authorities. They can focus instead upon the action learning of those who have lived with the problem and who have shifted their mindset and actions as a result of the direct feedback they have received from this very experience (at times resisting the powerful urge to conform or comply with a higher authority). Because these solutions come from deep within the actual problem, and from the people most affected by it, they have greater credibility and attractiveness to all stakeholders once eyes have been opened.

In their book, *The Power Of Positive Deviance: How Unlikely Innovators Solve The World's Toughest Problems*, Richard Pascale, Jerry Sternin and Monique Sternin suggest a four-step process that allows positive deviance to rise to the surface:[38]

1   Define the problem.
2   Determine common practices.
3   Discover uncommon but successful behaviours and strategies through enquiry and observation.
4   Design an action learning initiative based on findings.

This process, while apparently simple, unearths strategies that may demonstrate positive deviance in a given situation and isolates those who have invented and regularly perform such strategies. These strategies are the very actions and decisions that allow these people to achieve greater success when compared to their peer group despite the fact that they face similar barriers and obstacles.

The process allows the wicked tribe to view a problem from multiple perspectives and reframe the issue. Through collective inquiry they can spot and map emerging exceptional strategies; strategies that do not respect the existing rules or perceived boundaries of relevant knowledge and therefore have the power to become powerful interventions and solutions if applied more broadly or consistently. The very act of experimentation by positive deviants has already shifted the problem and provided clues as to which ideas may work against the odds, despite appearances to the contrary.

The final stage encourages formal and informal networks to be leveraged in the collective pursuit of progress. By identifying further similar examples of positive deviance and the people who demonstrate its particular contextual behaviours or who apply the strategies identified as game-changers, the invisible threads of organically developed workarounds can crystallise into a web of meaning and light the path to broader solutions.

In organisations, this can often be found where successful workarounds have been implemented in response to outdated processes or intransigent ways of thinking. Where wicked tribes uncover and work with the energy of positive deviance, the resulting co-creation and collective innovation can lead to magical interventions that change the world and create the future.

HOW TO THINK BEYOND CURRENT PARADIGMS

You won't be surprised to learn that there is a pattern to wicked thinking, a process that can be replicated across most contexts. These nine steps will allow your organisation to think beyond with confidence.

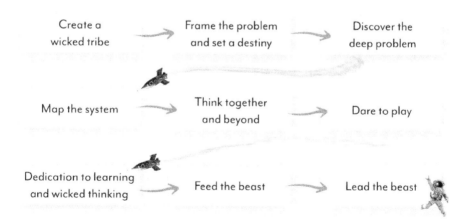

STEP 1: CREATE A WICKED TRIBE (THE SOLUTION ARCHITECTS)

Our first challenge is to gather our architects; a group of people who will become our 'coalition of the willing' and who will work collaboratively to deeply understand the opportunities, obstacles and intransigent problems that may have a material impact on the journey from strategy to reality or might in fact provide the very launch pad required for that journey to be successful. Our architects need to be drawn from far and wide and deep within the belly of the organisation to form a diverse and inclusive wicked tribe that's not bound by the doormen of hierarchy, length of service or background.

To open minds enough to dilute, mute or switch off our own personal echo chambers we need to talk widely and deeply, and not just to those who agree with us. If we demonstrate genuine curiosity and courtesy to those who have opinions that challenge our very beliefs and values we have a far greater propensity to learn and innovate.

A problem shared is a problem halved – or at the very least better understood. The wicked tribe should be constructed to consciously bring together groups of people from different positions in the system not forgetting end users who should also play a major part. All members of the tribe focus collectively on the problem and work exclusively to innovate and create ideas that may nudge it (or parts of it) in a favourable direction. As the tribe progresses in its work it may shed members and gain new ones. For example, the identification of signs of potential positive deviance may provide an opportunity for the tribe to be enhanced by the inclusion of the disruptive innovators; those who were responsible for inventing and adopting the alternative strategies identified.

The wicked tribe must fall in love with the problem rather than any potential solutions. It is only by understanding the problem and all its dark and secretive nooks and crannies that the most impactful and disruptive, yet often simple, innovations come about. Our architects must become explorers of the problem and seek to experience it from all angles, connecting people, ideas and information trans-discipline and across all boundaries, real or imagined.

A well-formed wicked tribe naturally drives wicked thinking.

STEP 2: FRAME THE PROBLEM AND SET A DESTINY

All innovation is directed at solving a problem; whether that problem is already appreciated or not by the majority of those affected is a secondary factor. Some of the greatest innovations that have shifted the contextual environment beyond its existing parameters have been born of problems that had not yet been recognised at the time. Using scenarios to see around corners enables a wicked tribe to recognise problems that are yet to be fully appreciated.

If the wicked tribe isn't looking to find yet undiscovered problems but is grappling with a very real issue in the here and now that has proven difficult to resolve, chances are they are dealing with a wicked problem. Unfortunately, wicked problems are not loners by nature – they tend to hunt in packs. Wicked problems resist interpretation and certainly can't be defined in the typical manner. They are a set of smaller problems organised into a complex interconnected, inter-related and interdependent network – a wicked web. To scope the boundaries within which the wicked tribe should start to work, the tribe needs to fully understand how this particular web works; the contributing sub-problems and additional wicked problems that cluster at its edges.

Before detailed mapping starts in earnest, the wicked tribe needs to think about the past history of the problem and the patterns that history displays, the present experience of the problem and the impacts it has upon stakeholders – remaining alert for weak signals and emerging indicators of the future that are evident in the here and now, and finally how the problem may manifest in the future and what risks and opportunities this may present.

A consensus needs to be reached by all members of the wicked tribe regarding the desired outcomes of a suite of interventions. The wicked tribe thus creates alignment around a powerful reason for making this positive difference. The wicked tribe must mindfully develop a fundamental cause which can drive a ravenous thirst for ideas and a hunger for improvement, around which a powerful movement for positive change can ultimately grow. Sophisticated wicked tribes also pay great attention to galvanising around a set of shared values that will later inform activities and decisions, improving the likelihood of gaining traction for ideas and broad engagement with the changes required.

STEP 3: DISCOVER THE DEEP PROBLEM

Those of you familiar with the great Douglas Adams's *The Hitchhiker's Guide to the Galaxy* will recall that, within the story, a group of pan-dimensional beings (who manifested as mice on earth) construct a supercomputer named 'Deep Thought' to provide them with the answer to 'the ultimate

question'; the question of 'life, the universe, and everything'.[39] After
thinking for millennia Deep Thought breaks its silence. It does so timidly
and reticently as it has a hunch that the pan-dimensional beings will be
somewhat disappointed with its answer – which is, of course, 42! When
asked to explain how 42 relates to the question asked, Deep Thought is
unable to provide an answer and it becomes apparent that the question has
not been particularly well thought through. In an effort to calm its masters,
Deep Thought offers to design its successor – a computer that will dwarf
its intellect and computing capabilities. A computer that will contain living
beings as part of its programming. A computer, yet to be built, that will
provide clarity regarding the ultimate question and explain the significance
of the number 42 – a supercomputer called Earth!

It is clearly important to ask the right question(s) in a way that can be
interpreted effectively. Without a voyage of discovery, it is relatively easy to
identify ideas that may have little to no impact on the overall problem or,
worse, may cause great harm. This happens where the questions asked of
the problem and the deep connections of information and people within the
problem have not been sufficiently probed and understood. The discovery
phase is an opportunity for the wicked tribe to get underneath the bonnet of
the problem and to understand the mechanisms and patterns that drive it at its
core. A big dose of reality that goes deep and wide allows for outcomes to be
better connected with fundamental issues rather than presenting symptoms.

The wicked problem must be examined from all angles and multiple
perspectives – as many perspectives as is humanly possible. To do this,
contribution should be sought from all stakeholders and end users or
participants to the problem's system. By connecting with all involved with
the problem by way of experience, contribution or previous attempts at
intervention, the wicked tribe can gather data that demonstrates the widest
range of experiences. This input is critical both to the subsequent mapping
of the problem system (the wicked web) and the generation of a range of
potential interventions. Research can provide ancillary data by way of peer
benchmarking and the examination of applicable regulatory requirements,
existing performance metrics and cultural indicators that are relevant to the
issue.

Critical input will be that of directly impacted stakeholders and those
in authority already seeking to make a positive difference. Wicked tribes

that genuinely and curiously engage with the problem itself and its array of participants have a greater chance of unearthing assumptions, highlighting potentially limiting beliefs and identifying any areas where positive deviance has already had an unexpected impact.

Wicked tribes ensure they understand the questions they are trying to answer.

STEP 4: MAP THE SYSTEM (THE WICKED WEB)

We're often faced with situations that we failed to predict when taking actions and making decisions with genuine positive intent – we know that, right? Chaos theory suggests that a small change can bring about a greater (and often unexpected or unintended) change (of variable and probably unrelated proportion) elsewhere in a system (think of a butterfly causing a major weather system on the other side of the globe). There's a pattern to everything, and if we understand that pattern in some small way we are far more likely to be able to determine our focus and amplify our impact. We need to truly appreciate and seek to understand the wicked problem as a system – a complex system of actors, histories, activities, decisions, experiences, knowledge, physics, economics and so on, that are all inextricably connected. Remember, most wicked problems are a network of sub-problems that may also be wicked and may only interrelate at their very edges or deeply at their core. It's a veritable web of wicked problems!

We're never going to map the system perfectly, but an attempt to do so greatly improves our ability to identify change levers and isolate outcomes. Mapping the system of a wicked problem is a demanding task and it can be difficult to know when and if you've gone far enough while ensuring you don't remain at the system mapping stage for evermore. The wicked web is complicated, and it is only by mapping it visually that a sense of its complexity can truly emerge. A visual map provides a tangible representation of the many interconnected elements that contribute to and impact the issue, and manifest as symptoms of it.

Alongside the patterns that are responsible for successful navigation of the problem it is also useful to make a concerted effort to notice and capture the anti-patterns. That is, the endemic patterns that are counterproductive and create a vicious cycle of failure or difficulty. In hindsight, the very process of identifying and isolating anti-patterns can often provide the moment where the penny drops in terms of deep understanding and discovery of the levers available within the system to effect positive change.

For it to be truly effective, the system map should incorporate key actors and their opinions and habits, the metrics that seem to genuinely matter in term of measuring its progress positive or otherwise, evidence of any potential positive deviance for further exploration and the context that surrounds the problem (political, economic, social, technological, legal and regulatory, and environment factors alongside competitor behaviours and the other problems or wicked problems that rub up against it or reside within it).

A thorough mapping exercise can help the wicked tribe to collectively challenge assumptions and widen their previously held perspectives. It is often virtually impossible to fully understand another's experience until we walk in their shoes and so the opportunity to spend time alongside end users in their natural environment and, from that, to capture a storyboard of the user experience or a journey map is also a very useful exercise. Interventions that work in theory or show a tangible improvement in one environment may detrimentally affect another or fail to have any impact. There is truth in every perspective and only shades of grey when dealing with socially complex problems. Opinions and beliefs are an individual's truths, but the reality of a situation is perhaps oscillating between a number of positions. The truth is often somewhere in the middle of a range of embedded and emotive perspectives or oscillating between them.

Following the co-creation and collaborative display of a substantial system map it is often possible for the wicked tribe to start to identify and isolate 'nodes of opportunity' where a single intervention may impact several symptoms, to improve the experiences of many or act as a catalyst for wider change. These nodes can go on to become levers that can be leveraged to great effect as the creative process unfolds and active experimentation evolves.

Mapping the present problem system alongside potential future problem systems (that incorporate any known and imminent changes to the contextual environment) can help to highlight factors and actors within said system that have the propensity to create disproportionate movement over time. This process can identify levers to leverage in future transformation efforts.

Change is largely behaviour-driven. Isolating habits, understanding their root causes and drivers, and observing how new habits are formed within the system are all powerful pieces of knowledge that can be used to support change or drive a paradigm shift in behaviour.

Collective inquiry alongside relevant research and tangible system maps help the wicked tribe to identify interesting patterns that may be hiding in plain sight. The problem puzzle starts to take shape in a way that can be interrogated and that provides a basis for testing. Metrics that matter (valued by all involved or recognised for their importance to subsets of the population) will start to emerge as objective parameters that can be applied to measure the success of any interventions. If the tribe is a diverse representation of the organisation and its stakeholders, a greater cross-organisational understanding will develop that can be just as effectively applied to other problems and situations.

STEP 5: THINK TOGETHER AND BEYOND

Once the problem has been analysed and understood by the collective of the wicked tribe and each individual within it, the excitement of creative innovation can commence. At this stage it is worth asking each of the tribe to explain and outline which they feel are the most interesting systemic patterns, where they consider there to be the greatest opportunities to be exploited and risks to be mitigated, and perhaps most importantly why they think this way.

We want our wicked tribe to think and act as if it were one organism, optimising the synergies created through shared knowledge and understanding based on a firm foundation of shared values and vision. But we want to avoid 'groupthink' at all costs. Groupthink is an unhelpful phenomenon typically seen in teams that work together over long periods in a relatively closed environment. The desire to maintain harmony in a group or to conform to its established norms can mean that its members avoid challenging assumptions, questioning rationale and voicing dissenting or contentious opinions. This behaviour keeps the group friendly of course (at least at a surface level), but renders it entirely ineffective. The inevitable result is incomplete analysis of a situation and dysfunctional decision-making. By cutting itself off from external influences the group starts to believe its own hype and heads tenaciously in a direction that may be incredibly counterproductive. Groupthink becomes self-perpetuating due to the lack of outside influence, challenge or opportunities for feedback. With this in mind it is critical for the wicked tribe to include the following four elements in their thinking process:

1   *Individual reflection*: individuals in the group have the time and tools available to enable them to consider a problem (and their emerging beliefs and opinions in relation to it) in a structured way that pushes them to question assumptions and quarantine underlying filters, beliefs and prejudices that may be influencing their analysis and judgement in this context. They are actively encouraged to reflect upon the issue and generate some early ideas for progress. Regular meditation can powerfully enhance the mind's ability to perceive situations in new ways and appreciate inventive insights when they strike. Journaling is also a useful habit as it provides a medium through which patterns and levers can be noticed by an individual over time. Habitually capturing thoughts, opinions, emotional reactions and lessons learned surrounding an issue can facilitate the emergence of powerful insight.

2   *Counterargument*: individuals are encouraged to speak to others within the wicked tribe and to venture beyond its boundaries to test their hypotheses with people who may have an entirely different belief system so that they can challenge and evolve their internal representation of the problem. The idea is not to corral and influence others towards their way of thinking, but instead to consciously seek challenge and therefore the expansion of understanding through the mental maps of others. To really understand why other people think very differently about the same thing.

3   *Collaborative inquiry*: the wicked tribe is formally engaged in facilitated structured thinking exercises that examine and validate all perspectives. Through this process the tribe creates meaning, purpose and a solid basis for invention. It can then start to connect the dots to posset ideas through collaborative innovation techniques.

4   *External input and challenge*: the tribe resists the urge to mark its own homework and invites others to observe discussions and review outputs with a view to seeking constructive challenge and feedback that will elevate thinking and dialogue to a more sophisticated level and blow apart echo chambers.

Tribes that think and play together stay together, but we want our wicked tribe to be an open-minded and progressive tribe that can find novel solutions to old and intransigent problems and the new problems that suddenly emerge as the future unfolds. It cannot do this if it is bound to established norms and avoids conflict. In the post-truth fast show where volatility, uncertainty, complexity and ambiguity are the norm, it's the novel ideas that challenge the status quo, perpetuate a chain reaction and seismically shift the contextual dial. When working with wicked problems of the present and the future, there is no definitive solution that will save the day, no predetermined pattern for success. Progress demands compromise and is achieved in the messy and gradual navigation of shades of grey. Real creativity is required, and this is troublesomely bridled where tribes are reluctant to rock the boat.

For the tribe to be successful in its endeavours, when it thinks together it needs to do so in a structured way. By this point in proceedings it has developed a sound individual and collective understanding of the issue and has started the process of sense making. But it can strengthen these even further through its creative activities spawning a virtuous circle of ever-expanding shared consciousness. Its task now is to connect the dots into new ideas and inventive subsystems that may have a sustainable positive and extensive impact. As Steve Jobs once commented, 'creativity is connecting things'.[40]

Most people don't consider themselves to be particularly creative. This is largely due to the perception that creativity involves artistic tendencies. While a level of creative flair is undoubtedly helpful to the tribe, creativity in the context of wicked problems and disruptive innovation is often more about a deep systemic understanding of the problem and an ability to recognise patterns within, paired with a curiosity regarding the future and how a system can be manipulated to behave in a different way. Disruptive innovation comes about from a process of thinking that may be subconscious for a naturally creative individual. This is great news for most of us! It means that we can follow a process that is likely to generate insights that previously eluded our minds. We just have to give it space and time to happen – that space for serendipity again! Pure magic can seem to occur if we go a step further and perform this process within an environment that encourages alternative thinking, amongst critical friends where a safe space for mental deconstruction is always available.

There are many practices and techniques that can be deployed to enhance thinking at both an individual and collective level. Here are just a few:

Design thinking: a method where divergence and convergence are used in a structured way to generate ideas, create prototypes and draft tests that can ascertain the likely impact of ideas. There are many subprocesses within design thinking and the exact approach may differ from one situation to the next. It is used extensively in the development of new products and is particularly useful when considering how to make progress on wicked problems (most exceptionally successful products are built around a wicked problem that is evident in the present or anticipated in the future).

Collective inquiry: the process by which a group aims to understand an issue as a collective, in an integrated manner. The process can be used to steer the wicked tribe to prioritise the elements of the system it wants to focus upon and then to delve deeply into each of these to discover knowledge, generate ideas and ascertain how to test proposed actions for feasibility. The process of collective inquiry extends beyond the boundaries of the tribe to investigate the experiences and reactions of those directly affected by proposed ideas. The conversations that result lead to even deeper and broader awareness and the emergence of further insight and ideas – hybrid innovations. A period of reflection then follows where the problem is reframed given the information gathered, and further cycles of ideation and experimentation are then designed.

Dialogue mapping: this method involves the creation of a visual diagram of the dialogue that takes place around a given problem and the ideas that emerge. It is useful in terms of capturing the actual reflections and opinions of the group and can provide useful context when considering beliefs and established operating models. The core idea is to listen, summarise and validate the conversations that take place. There is no room left for misunderstanding and groups can robustly test both positive and negative reactions to ideas voiced. It is a useful partner to design thinking.

Any form of collaborative display facilitates the development of a shared understanding and ideation process, and can be combined very effectively with the storyboards generated as part of a scenario planning exercise to co-create effective interventions for future worlds and alternative timelines.

Cross-fertilisation: this technique involves the application of ideas from disparate and unconnected sectors or disciplines, or substantially differing cultures. The purpose is to shift mindsets to an alternative frame and to explore how innovations that at first look may seem entirely irrelevant may provide lessons regarding the problem at hand. By considering another group of people with a vastly different set of experiences, values and beliefs to the wicked tribe and how they may approach an issue, alternative and sometimes powerful insights can be gained leading to genuinely mould-breaking innovations.

What-if worlds: this technique draws heavily on the ideas within scenario planning (see Chapter 5). The aim is for the wicked tribe to consider the problem through the lenses of alternative future worlds or to anticipate how perspectives might shift should a particular path be chosen or intervention applied. The approach not only reframes the problem but also reframes the context within which the problem presents itself. Typically, this can have a significant impact on how the problem manifests, the level of importance of the problem, or may provide sudden awareness of how the presenting problem will soon be replaced by a new one that will be far more significant. Tribes that use this opportunity-driven approach to problem-solving often find that it shifts their priority focus areas substantially and allows unusual and novel ideas to bubble up. What-if worlds can be used very effectively to generate ideas and solutions that have the potential to change the game or even make a new game!

Curiosity: at the end of the day innovation boils down to simple curiosity. Wicked tribes that are driven to pursue progress and seek to turn the status quo upside down show a tenacious hunger for more information and leverage their formal and informal networks to provide a diverse range of ideas. Unafraid to ask pertinent and, at times, contentious questions, the curious wicked tribe naturally challenges the 'as is', questions authority, unearths embedded assumptions and genuinely explores the potential outcomes of multiple ideas. Wicked tribes learn like toddlers exploring the world with wonder and fascination – and questions… lots of questions. The questions, 'What if?', 'Why not?' and simply 'Why?' are repeated until they get to the truth of matters and possible reasons not to try something fall away. Courageous conversations and daring dialogue that is at times uncomfortable is often the midwife to disruptive innovations that were not allowed to go away quietly by their proponents.

STEP 6: DARE TO PLAY

I've already mentioned that tribes that think and play together stay together. But did I mention that they also learn faster? When we watch children play they are obviously having great fun, but there is also a very serious side to play. Play has an evolutionary purpose that we seem to disregard as we enter adulthood, preferring instead more studious learning methods. When it comes to disruptive innovations, playing is the only game in town. Trying things out in a real or simulated environment is the only way our wicked tribe can get a sense of how an idea may play out in the real world. Some things that sound great on paper fail at their first contact with reality. Interaction with the human race and its habitual behaviours has been the death knell for many lauded inventions.

This stage is all about designing experiments that can safely test the feasibility, impact, sustainability and extendibility of an idea. In truth, experimentation is not a one-hit wonder but a cycle of tests that will present data to highlight the next steps on the path or the available alternatives to be chosen from at each stage of the cycle. Sound experiment design is critical. It must, wherever possible, take place within the real system of the problem but with warning bells and safety valves identified and primed.

Wicked tribes that dare to experiment, play with a problem in the only way possible that can take ideas beyond two-dimensional plans. Well-designed experiments can extend understanding of the system and its likely reactions to potential interventions on a broader scale. It may be that the wicked tribe decides to test the comparable validity of a range of options by experimenting with each of them separately in a discreet area of the problem population or system. However, it is important to remember that once the system is altered it will not rebound entirely to its previous shape and state. Any intervention will change the system forever and wicked tribe members therefore must be careful to be sure to have examined potential outcomes sufficiently prior to deployment.

Wicked problems are complex, and their systems are interconnected and interdependent. Attempts to solve a given wicked problem often lead to unforeseen consequences within its system or elsewhere in the wicked web. Change demands psychological and social evolution – cultural and behavioural change in an organisation. It's not possible to understand a problem or the potential impact of a solution until these have been applied in experiments and allowed to evolve. The interventions themselves may alter the problem or its context in ways the tribe does not expect.

Feedback loops are critical. Wicked tribes have a duty to identify the metrics that matter (those metrics that will provide them with a live feed of the impact of their experiment) alongside a comprehensive understanding of the levers available to them should a negative impact be detected. An experiment in the name of innovation is one time when a U-turn or a change of lane must take place if the data suggests damage is being done. Experiments provide a useful mechanism for the fast identification of failures and to move forward quickly to alternative ideas, but this demands close monitoring and decisive action on the part of the tribe.

A suite of multiple experiments is a useful way to not only test ideas but also to generate awareness, understanding and engagement. Testing many interventions can not only quickly demonstrate which are likely to have a quick, large and sustainable impact, it can also lead to hybrid models that were not apparent prior to the experiment or the emergence of positive deviance before your very eyes. Cycles of experimentation across context, groups and time provide valuable insights that can be applied to the next move. An agile approach that takes stock on a regular basis and makes adjustments as user experience is better understood, delivers more positive progress than a traditional long-term fixed project plan with predicted milestones and determined outcomes. This approach allows the wicked tribe to test the impact their ideas are having on the wicked web. Small, short-term changes can lead to long-term and wide-scale impacts. The wicked tribe has a duty to generate sustainable and resilient progress that is supple in the face of an unpredictable future.

STEP 7: DEDICATION TO LEARNING AND WICKED THINKING

This step is a holistic presence that needs to pervade all other steps of the innovation process. Wicked problems demand commitment to the cause, entanglement with the movement and adroit navigation of the gradual procession of advancement and retreat. Most importantly, wicked problems demand dedication – a collective dedication to learning. Wicked tribes that live to learn and open their minds to the exploration of alternatives, that may at times appear random or disconnected, generate innovations that can change the world.

Wicked tribes need to appreciate the importance of working on a wicked problem and the genuine and valuable benefits that they can bring about through innovation. When working on a wicked problem with a wicked tribe I always ask them to consciously adopt these principles throughout our thinking and debate:

- Adopt an owner mentality: ask 'How can we best add value to "xyz organisation" over the longer-term while ensuring we deliver and protect against risks in the short- to medium-term?'
- Think about the future while remembering the past, and fully experiencing the present.
- Consciously and purposefully disassociate from your personal organisational position and professional identity to avoid being inappropriately led by your current role, the protection of the status quo or an allegiance to a particular discipline.
- Think 'factors' and 'ideas' rather than 'personalities' and 'positions'.
- Be curious about the perspectives, perceptions, experiences, beliefs and knowledge held by others, and appreciate that there is never one right answer to any problem. Walk in their shoes and play in their playground!
- Speak up and bring your experiences and knowledge to the table. Be honest about your beliefs and values and raise opportunities, constraints, benefits and risks constructively and openly in the room.
- Be open to the exploration of new ideas and possibilities, and don't be restricted by 'what has been' or 'what hasn't worked before' without proper examination and good reason.
- Align as a team but courageously question authority and challenge groupthink wherever it may appear.

- Fall in love with the problem in all its complexity and individuality, and focus on the debate in hand.
- Dare to experiment and be willing to fail. When you do fail, learn fast – and then dare to change your mind and your approach; dare to be different!

Wicked problems don't tend to disappear in a puff of smoke at the introduction of a perfect solution. Instead, by their very nature, wicked problems evolve and adapt. If you make friends with a wicked problem it will remain a friend for life and, like a true friend, it will change in response to your friendship. The same is true in reverse; entanglement with a wicked problem will change you and your tribe forever. Extended understanding and expanded consciousness mean that things will never be the same again for the problem or its actors. Fall in love with a wicked problem – you never know quite where it will take you and where you will take it!

STEP 8: FEED THE BEAST

Innovation is a beast that requires constant feeding and attention. Shapeshifter organisations place great value upon creating environments that support its needs and developing capabilities that can feed its ravenous appetite. Innovation, while a creative art, is scientific in that it is systemic. For innovation to become an organisational habit, the culture, structure and processes of that organisation must point towards the value of disruption and support people as they bring it about. In shapeshifter organisations these interrelating social, structural and procedural systems are devised to create the right mood and mindset.

There are some core foundations to embedding a system of innovation. Culture is, of course, critical and the formation of an aligned and primed meta-tribe as outlined in Move Two is often a prerequisite. The tribal analogy can be taken further with the generation of multiple wicked tribes each formed around a particular wicked problem of importance to the organisation and its stakeholders. This act itself can signal a clear intention to innovate collectively.

Ideas spread virally across the system of the organisation. Informal networks are often more powerful and have greater tensile strength than their formal counterparts. For sustainable systemic innovation to take hold, networks need to be encouraged to form and given the space to evolve. Networks that cut across the divisional and functional structure of the organisation are the ones that will typically seed disruptive ideas and enable them to permeate the organisation's infrastructure in a way that takes hold and generates fans of the movement and crusaders for the cause. Finding ways for networks to work together on areas of shared interest, or opportunities to create diverse networks whose membership requirements have no connection to everyday operations, provides a skeleton to work with and through. Add technical and virtual support for an ever-ready, ever-connected innovation network. There are some great cloud-based apps and systems available that can be used to support creative efforts across geographically spread organisations.

When feeding the innovation beast, there's much to be learned from the gaming community and the 'world designers' who bring gaming masterpieces to life. There's a pattern to games that can be helpful when considering how wicked problems might behave within alternative worlds or when certain strategies are deployed. The constructs within games that drive gamer behaviour can also be replicated within organisations and wicked tribes to encourage and reward progress.

Game-storming and gamification can both be used to great effect to create a fun innovation habit that just keeps on giving!

GAME-STORMING

The idea of game-storming is to provide an opportunity for a particular scenario, innovation or strategy to be tested in a fabricated world. That world is made up of boundaries, parameters and controlling factors to emulate a context of interest.

The first task is to imagine the world within which the idea is to be tested – the sandpit within which the wicked tribe will play purposefully with the ideas it wants to better understand. This world is constructed of boundaries, rules, norms and artefacts that provide a contextual system that will allow the game to be played. If you think of any well-known computer game you will notice that the world has a different set of rules to the everyday world we live in. There are specialist artefacts that only reside within that world or are perhaps significantly different within that world, and it has a reward system that draws the gamer into the fictitious story. The reward system is more obvious than that which is in operation in the real world (extra lives, special powers, elevation to higher levels, admittance to secret areas) but it uncannily resembles the reward system that more subtly does just the same and provides motivation for action in real life. Once the world is created and everyone understands its rules and boundaries, play can start in earnest. The aim is to try to achieve the goals of the tribe using the innovations or strategies suggested within the social constraints of the fabricated world. This play activity, while great fun, can provide powerful insight and seed further ideas for testing. Improvisation within the game allows substrategies, workarounds and anti-patterns to also be tested and their patterns recorded. Role-playing provides an opportunity for tribe members to take a walk in the shoes of others and experience the frustrations of the system for those less powerful within it. Game-storming can be an incredibly illuminating experience for those wanting to change the game or even make new games for the future.

GAMIFICATION

Gamification has become a bit of a buzzword in recent years and seems to have been applied to describe learning that has anything remotely resembling a test of knowledge somewhere within. This situation has done gamification a great disservice. It is capable of far more and has many interesting applications.

Similar to game-storming, gamification is based on the construction of a world, but this time it's a world that meets the needs of the movement you are attempting to create. Our aim is to promote and sustain a culture that will actively support innovation and the behaviours and mindset that requires. So how can gamification help us to do that?

Worlds and cultures evolve over time through the narrative they tell and the beliefs they hold about themselves. Gamification provides a mechanism through which to steer that narrative and challenge embedded behaviours that are not helpful while building new habits through repetition and reward. Gamification involves a mixture of elements that can be many or few dependent on the complexity of the issue and the nature and level of change sought. 'What-if' worlds and simulation exercises are constructed around the desired future narrative or strategy – in this case systemic innovation.

Storylines and plots, quests and challenges are used alongside meaningful incentives (prizes, extras, opportunities) to engage and excite the tribe to play, learn and evolve. Gamification provides a platform for social storytelling through stories that are co-created and authentic.

DEDICATION'S WHAT YOU NEED!

To systematise innovation the organisation must become the system it wants to see – it must shapeshift in real time, guided by the feedback it receives from the innovations it trials and strategies it employs. This takes time and tenacity to bring about. Connectivity is key to the development of a supportive culture, an organisational mood that supports and encourages innovation. Structure and processes also need to align but be supple enough to shift as the context evolves. It can be useful to treat the shapeshifter organisation and its complex social constructs as a wicked problem in and of itself. Dedication is a core value for shapeshifter organisations:

- A dedication to purposeful disruption, provocative questioning, storytelling and myth-making to gradually embed legends, heroes, rituals and symbols that have innovation at their core.
- A dedication to learning, risk-taking and daring to challenge assumptions or question authority.
- A dedication to investigate and navigate ambiguity and to set up the organisation's processes, structure and reward mechanisms in a way that is congruent with an innovative culture.
- A dedication to the nurturing of formal and informal networks.
- A dedication to a different way of leading.
- A dedication to create momentum for the cause.
- A dedication to thinking beyond current paradigms and shatter perceived limitations and constraints.
- Most importantly, a dedication to the problem and making positive progress rather than unquestioning dedication to a specific solution – dedication in a supple way.

Feeding the beast is a tough challenge, but with perseverance and tenacity the beast can be tamed. Dedication's what you need!

STEP 9: LEAD THE BEAST

Dedication to a different kind of leadership is a potent lever of change for shapeshifter organisations. The aim of a shapeshifter organisation is to evolve through game-changing leadership towards game-making leadership. From game-changer to game-maker is the path to tread. Game-makers are the emerging edge of leadership – leadership that subconsciously forms, breaks and reforms connections across its shared consciousness so that new levels of collaborative thinking and co-creation can be achieved.

Game-makers move away from the quest for immediate solutions to focus on the systems that surround and pervade the problems solutions are sought for. They are the leadership equivalent of the computer that follows Deep Thought in *The Hitchhiker's Guide to the Galaxy*. A biological computer with a shared neural network at its core – experiencing, experimenting and enhancing everything they come into contact with. Game-makers design the future and the products and services that will be fundamental to its reality. Game-makers are:

- **Hungry**. Game-makers are constantly curious and persistently ask the questions that shift perspective, unearth assumptions and alter the collective consciousness forever. Learning is fundamental to their being and they are internally driven to make big leaps.
- **Playful**. Game-makers enjoy grappling with an issue and learning how to make positive impacts through fun and games. They take play seriously and play with a purpose. Games, experiments and simulations are their go-to activities.
- **Courageous**. Game-makers dare to challenge the established way of operating and the establishment that enshrines and protects it. They question authority and shake the foundations of the status quo. They bravely step beyond to fail fast and fall forward.
- **Integrated**. Game-makers are super-connectors and create fluid networks that adjust and evolve in response to opportunities and threats. When plugged in they contribute fully to the shared hive mind allowing the tribe to swarm as a flock; to think and act as one inclusive and diverse being.
- **Vulnerable.** Game-makers know their strengths and limitations. They are self-aware enough to know when they are out of their depth and

to tread carefully but purposefully to test new waters. They open their minds to new information and are willing to change when a different approach is required.

- **Humble**. Game-makers know that magnificent ideas and compelling causes are born of humble beginnings. They see danger in knowing it all and are willing to become novices over and over again. They are apprentices of the future.

- **Dedicated**. Game-makers are dedicated to the cause. Their purpose is pure and simple – to positively change the world one move at a time.

- **Deep**. Game-makers fall in love with the problem and not the answer. They seek to understand the ultimate question of 'life, the universe and everything' and are not distracted by the foretold answer of '42'! Game-makers are most at home deep in the problem they have fallen in love with.

CHAPTER 12

START WHERE YOU ARE: THE WICKED THINKING MATURITY MODEL

Over the next few pages you will find a maturity model designed to help your organisation make wicked thinking a habit. The model is written in such a way that you can use it to work out how your organisation currently tends to think, innovate and create, and where it might best make great gains by altering its approach. Wicked thinking is in part a game of confidence and removing the organisational shackles that hold creativity in check. As in previous moves, the maturity model is by its very nature a greatly simplified representation of a complex human system. Use it to develop a common language and drive open and honest conversation about the capacity for creativity and quality of collective thinking across your organisation, but don't fall into the trap of becoming wedded to each and every indicator – that will just stifle the very creativity you wish to create. It may be that your organisation finds new ways to think and innovate that have not been captured here!

As in Moves One and Two, the five evolutionary stages are:

1   Reactive
2   Focused
3   Structured
4   Integrated
5   Shapeshifter

Each stage has markers that signal a certain level of systemic innovation has been habitually achieved. To work out whereabouts your organisation spends most of its time (within which stage it generally resides) we focus on 10 elements:

1   Impact: the typical level of impact achieved by the approach to innovation.
2   Discovery: the ways a problem is defined and investigated to be understood.
3   Architects: how the organisation comes together to solve problems.
4   Destination: the level of outcomes sought and how these are reached.
5   Mapping: how the problem is captured and displayed.
6   Thinking: the level and approach to thinking through a problem.
7   Creation: the process of generating ideas and strategies, and how these are applied.
8   Environment: the culture, structure and processes that support innovation.
9   Learning: how and when problem-solving and innovation adapts and evolves.
10 Agility: flexibility and manoeuvrability as the future takes shape.

STAGE 1: REACTIVE	
Impact	SURVIVE
Discovery	• Problems are investigated when their presence or impact become threatening to the survival of the organisation • Investigation is ad hoc, driven by the interests of and impacted by the values and opinions of the investigator • Limited understanding of the problem beyond its obvious effects
Architects	• An individual or small group of individuals who are relatively senior in the organisation or expert in their field • External experts may be called upon to contribute • Lack of voice across the organisation and power is unevenly distributed

Destination	• Solution to the presenting problem is the focus of activity • Justification or promotion of a preferred option, idea or solution • Innovation for the sake of innovation – to look like an innovative organisation • Lack of integration and alignment with strategy
Mapping	• Likely to be relatively disorganised and spontaneous • Limited understanding of the full stakeholder map and the range of perspectives and experiences within • Mapping focuses on process and structure at the expense of culture and context
Thinking	• Thinking is unstructured and driven by the interests of the architects or additional emerging problems and ideas • Groupthink or lack of alignment lead to unfruitful outcomes • Debate is thwarted by the power exercised by founder authority • Focus is on the present and predictable near-future • Predominantly restricted to the experiences and needs of the organisation
Creation	• Ideas tend to be measured in relation to the credibility or charisma of the person presenting them • Fads and trends that have been encountered by the architects can unduly influence ideation • Innovation is largely left to the creatives • Ideas are deployed untested or fail to see the light of day • Innovation is seen as a one-time operation and fix • Tendency towards shiny new things
Environment	• Attitude and approach to innovation is dependent upon the opinions and beliefs of founder leaders • Anti-patterns within the organisational system are not recognised as such • Structure and culture are left to their own devices • Innovation is not considered to be an everyday activity or is expected of everyone with no supporting tools

Learning	• Ad hoc and ineffective – no structured feedback loops to evaluate actions and decisions • Interventions are deployed with limited testing and few adjustments made in real time as negative impacts emerge
Agility	• Reactive and incoherent – muted impact beyond immediate issues

– • –

STAGE 2: FOCUSED	
Impact	STRIVE
Discovery	• Innovation is directed at targeted areas of strategic interest • Problems are identified that will support the areas where innovation is considered to be required • Problems will be separated and investigated deeply in isolation • Some bias evident due to targeted strategic focus and the opinions and beliefs of people involved
Architects	• Drawn from senior leadership and those with experience and knowledge of the problem area • Forward-looking organisations may include emerging leaders and high-potential technical talent • External consultancies are brought in where internal experience and knowledge is limited • Diversity is limited by perceived scope of problem
Destination	• The identification and isolation of a truly innovative idea that can carry the organisation's future success • Finding solutions to presenting problems or those that are expected due to imminent contextual changes

Mapping	• Targeted area of interest is mapped in detail • Maps of knowledge, experience, stakeholders, processes, structures and context generated – some capturing of cultural indicators likely • Stakeholder opinions and beliefs are investigated and captured • Simple levers for change are identified
Thinking	• Benchmarking of competitor organisations and early trailblazers • Facilitated dialogue to ensure debate is properly focused and structured • Some evidence of groupthink or over-attachment to a particular solution or way of working • Predominantly restricted to the needs and wants of the organisation in a given context • Present and future contextual requirements are examined
Creation	• Ideas confined to the target area and limited exploration of cross-fertilisation or impact of interventions • Fads and trends may cause a rush towards or away from a solution or idea • Innovation is a structured process that is supported by creative experts • Some testing of ideas within targeted strategic areas • Innovation is confined to those areas that strategically demand it • Tendency to only value high-impact innovation and big leaps
Environment	• Innovation is performed by a select and special few • Innovative culture is strong in some areas where innovation is considered key to organisation's strategic ambitions – less so in other areas • Great ideas in unsupported areas receive limited attention or resources • Creative efforts across the organisation are not joined up and can result in counterproductive ideas and interventions • Testing and experimentation is limited but where evident may be large-scale hothouse environments

Learning	• Extensive learning in some areas is hindered by limited connection to and feedback from others • Lessons are learned many times but not shared and applied • Ideas are replicated, and mistakes are repeated due to lack of conscious collaboration
Agility	• Fractured and focused creative efforts lead to an unbalanced organisation that relies too heavily on some areas or ideas – golden children that may or may not deliver

– • –

STAGE 3: STRUCTURED	
Impact	THRIVE
Discovery	• Strategic planning identifies recurrent problems and areas for targeted innovation activity • Investigation and analysis are structured and supported by best-practice tools and techniques • Investigation is thorough and involves all known stakeholders • Extensive understanding of identified problems and obstacles • Potential areas for creative focus are identified and likely acceptance of attention assessed
Architects	• Centralised organisation development, performance optimisation and performance excellence teams lead the process, coordinate activity and control the dialogue • Functional and divisional leads suggest or select those to contribute from their teams • Voice across the organisation is awarded to those who are a cultural fit, perform in their roles, show promise and behave well • Centrally managed high-potential and future leader programmes become involved as architects on a permanent or temporary basis

Destination	• To generate ideas that can optimise and exploit opportunities and solve problems that present threats now or in the future
Mapping	• Problems are fully scoped and comprehensively mapped to include structure, stakeholders, context, culture and behaviour, process and policy • System maps identify potential areas for intervention, change levers and possible evaluation metrics • Detailed maps are held centrally and can be accessed on request
Thinking	• Structured thinking is facilitated using skilled external or internal consultants and facilitators • Dialogue mapping may be used to isolate and validate contributing issues and ideas to take further • Collective thinking is formally arranged; individual reflection is encouraged but not well supported • Best-practice tools and techniques are applied • Focus is on the past to identify patterns, the present to ascertain reality and the future to identify opportunities and risks • Opinions require objective justification, empathy is a stage of the process rather than a pervasive enabler • Process can be rigid and inflexible to tangential conversations and insights
Creation	• Innovation takes place at a pre-planned time in a creative space and is supported by creative internal or external consultants; there's a figurative 'diary note to be creative' • Best-practice tools and techniques are deployed in a structured pattern to work through a predetermined creative process • Elements of design thinking are incorporated • Ideas are objectively measured using metrics that matter • Steady progress on all creative fronts is measured through programme plans and milestones • Innovation is a process that can be repeated • Preferred solutions become the driving forces of future change programmes • Tendency towards tried and tested − following in others' footsteps and standing on the shoulders of giants

Environment	• Structure, process and policy is supportive of controlled innovation and problem-solving • Change programmes are built around key innovations, ideas and strategic interventions • Culture is manufactured to support controlled innovation and related initiatives • Innovation is considered to be an everyday process that can deliver great ideas if the process is followed and suggested tools applied
Learning	• Benchmarking successful organisations provides a pattern to follow both for innovation itself and the ideas it may generate • Structured feedback loops are supported by stress testing • Postmortems identify lessons learned and how to apply them to other situations • Complexity of wicked problems is underestimated
Agility	• Governance, process and culture allows coordination of innovation and structured agility at fixed time points

– • –

STAGE 4: INTEGRATED	
Impact	**FUTURE-FIT**
Discovery	• Complex and fluid problems are appreciated for what they are; wicked problems • Intransigent issues that cause distress, distraction or deviation are analysed as they come to the surface • Strategic plans are explored for evidence of wicked problems • Investigation and analysis are supported by tools and techniques that best suit the problem at hand and the context within which it manifests • Investigation is systemic and fluid and allows for discoveries to influence direction

	• Deep understanding of a wicked problem from all perspectives • Potential areas ripe for innovation are explored as they become apparent through strategic dialogue and scenario planning • Investigation reads between the lines and seeks to identify positive deviance and/or potential for game-changing innovations and interventions
Architects	• Diverse wicked tribes are created from across the organisation and beyond its boundaries; membership is not limited by hierarchy or expertise, but driven by experience of the problem and hunger for change • Organisational leaders encourage tribes to form where there is a possibility of disruptive change or innovation • Tribes are largely self-organising under the guidance of formal organisational leaders or informal leaders with strong influence • Voice across the organisation is awarded to those with direct experience and understanding of the issue or proven innovation skills in complex contexts • External stakeholders are brought into the wicked tribe to support thinking and design
Destination	• To take a fluid and agile approach to problem-solving and innovation • Create innovations and design interventions that will change the game regarding an intransigent and socially complex wicked problem • Predicting problems that may become socially significant to find the next big idea
Mapping	• Detailed mapping of all layers of the issue including context, stakeholders, structure, culture and behaviour, process and policy, historical patterns, known future changes, prior interventions and their impact, contributing values and beliefs, and differentiation between core issues and symptoms

	• Nodes of opportunity are identified and highlighted with greater research undertaken in these areas • Levers for change and potential evaluation metrics are highlighted • Obviously interconnected problems are identified and interdependencies captured • Maps are living documents held on a shared repository and fully accessible to the tribe
Thinking	• Structured and creative thinking is supported by internal and external facilitators or, in more confident wicked tribes, managed fully by tribe members • Diversity of thinking is encouraged and celebrated – disagreement is considered to be a thinking asset through which new ideas can be born • Collective thinking is rooted in the habits and network of the tribe and continues outside of formal events and workshops • Individual reflection is supported by best-fit tools and techniques – journaling and co-coaching form part of the tribe's thinking practices • Focus is on the past to identify and map patterns, the present to fully interpret reality from multiple perspectives and capture weak signals and emerging indicators of the future, and the future to explore multiple alternative futures and the paths that lead to them • Values, beliefs and habits are explored in the same level of detail as opinions and judgements • Empathy is pervasive and informative to the thinking process • Process is fluid and agile to respond to events and developments as they emerge
Creation	• Innovation is pervasive throughout the wicked tribe and seeps into the everyday lives of all members of the organisation • Best-fit tools and techniques are deployed, and emerging tools and techniques are explored through experimentation • Positive deviance is actively sought and investigated • Experiments are designed to test ideas and interventions in pilot areas

	• Simulations are used to explore the likely impacts of experiments, ideas and interventions on the mapped systems • Experimental outcomes are used to inform a further exploration of the problem and a re-mapping of its system • Potentially disruptive innovations are hothoused in secluded incubators • No solution is all-bad or all-good – each idea has merits and a hybrid idea may eventually emerge • The wicked tribe falls in love with the problem and finding ways to make life better for all involved becomes a major element of their work • Tendency towards changing the game and finding new and novel approaches to problems old and new (and yet to be experienced)
Environment	• Culture is the major driver of innovation supported by congruent structure, process and policy • People are given space and time to innovate and ideas are given time to gain traction or fade • Formal and informal networks that span organisational boundaries are actively encouraged to generate a diverse thinking pool • Leadership is devolved and decision-making is principle-based • Daring to challenge assumptions, challenge authority, question the status quo or suggest a new way are all highly valued behaviours • People innovate in the moment and have the autonomy and accountability to make a positive difference large or small
Learning	• Experimental cycles and incubator outcomes provide rich data for individual and collective learning • Pre-mortems and simulations provide safe learning environments • The problem-solving and innovation process is viewed as a learning exercise • Learning is shared unselfishly across the tribe • Driven by an individual and collective drive for positive impact • Multiple sources via data feeds and social networks are established to generate best fit for the situation at hand

	• Risk is rewarded, and people are encouraged to fail fast and fall forward • Complexity of wicked problems is considered a rich learning field
Agility	• Multiple paths and process learning provide the ability to quickly generate big ideas and strategically important innovations that can meet the future

– • –

STAGE 5: SHAPESHIFTER	
Impact	CHANGE THE GAME
Discovery	• Wicked problems are understood to be part of a greater complex system of interrelating, interconnected and interdependent problems: a wicked web • Horizon scanning is a habit and alternative futures are constantly investigated and interpreted for their disruptive potential • Strategic plans seek to find future wicked problems that are not yet evident and are ripe for disruptive innovation • Intransigent wicked problems are re-examined as a wider web of interrelated issues to find potential positive deviance within their midst that can be amplified or translated to other areas • Discovery is supported but not limited by best-practice and best-fit tools and techniques • Playing with emerging tools and techniques and inventing new ones is integral to the discovery experience • Research and investigation are driven by the collective curiosity of the wicked tribe and its supporters – new voices are allowed to influence direction • A deep and broad understanding of socially complex wicked webs across time zones and timelines is collectively developed • New games are identified way before they start to emerge, and the future is scanned for areas in which new games can be built

Architects	• Many diverse wicked tribes work seamlessly and collaboratively across a dynamic, connected, learning network • Neurodiversity is considered critical to the understanding of socially complex wicked problems • Tribes form informally in response to a potential opportunity or an interesting wicked problem • Tribes are self-directing, and membership is fluid • Voice is extended to all with an interest
Destination	• Ensuring the organisation can remain successful regardless of what future emerges • Sustainable disruptive innovation • Exploiting the opportunity to be the first to make a real difference to an intractable wicked problem through disruptive thinking, product or technology • Becoming a game-maker that creates the future through the generation of new markets and end-user needs
Mapping	• Generates a map of the wicked web as a living system that is impacted by human behaviour and contextual change • Nodes of opportunity across the web are highlighted and mapped in detail • All time zones (past, present and future) and multiple timelines form part of the territorial map • Change levers are tested and impacts mapped • Collective display is represented explicitly and innovatively and shared widely to engage beyond the wicked tribe.
Thinking	• Connected thinkers use individual reflection, collective inquiry and co-creation to deepen their individual and shared understanding • Wicked problems, positive deviance, systemic thinking and networked learning all bring about wicked thinking (thinking that can not only change the game but can generate ideas that invent new games) • Disruptive thinking is a habit • 'What-if' exercises, game-storming and meditation help the wicked tribe to think differently from the get-go

	• 'Nothing is taboo' – outlandish ideas have airtime and potentially take shape as disruptors • Positive deviants within the context of the problem form part of the wicked tribe • The tribe invents its own tools to supercharge thinking • Shared consciousness emerges as the tribe thinks and acts as one being with many coherent yet different parts – hive mind and swarm intelligence are evident
Creation	• Innovation and invention pervade beyond the wicked tribe and are core foundations of organisational culture • Tools and techniques are selected as required and set aside once their usefulness has expired – attachment is to co-creation rather than the method of creation • Positive deviance and outlier performances are reimagined for potential new ideas • Ideation is a collective way of being with space and permission to connect with the problem physically, cognitively, emotionally and spiritually • Alternative worlds are constantly created and explored • Experiments are progressive acts of problem-solving and invention, evolving the problem and changing its fabric • Big ideas are let loose freely in the real world with confidence that thinking and understanding have been to such a level that impact and reaction have been well-rehearsed • The problem and its progression become central to the cause • Tendency to want to positively change the world one move at a time – making new games in the process
Environment	• Wicked thinking and innovations are the foundations of an agile culture • Structure, process and policy are minimal – networks, behaviours and values hold more importance • Humbleness, daring and courage combine to make everyday heroes • Leaders are born of behaviour rather than hierarchy • Change is expected, embraced and encouraged

	• Wicked thinking and innovation are the root of sustainable high performance • Gamification is used to drive invention and related behaviours
Learning	• Wicked tribes connect to form a dynamic, connected, learning network where information and ideas are freely shared and explored • Lessons are learned through the very act of thinking about wicked problems and playing with ideas • Learning is cause-driven • Refraction, reflection and rehearsal generate powerful lessons through deep thought and experience • Process learning is endemic and automatic • Interconnected dynamic learning network means that learning is dissipated across the shared consciousness – quantum mechanics in action
Agility	• Wicked thinking drives big ideas that have the power to disrupt reality beyond recognition. A creator of new worlds, the organisation becomes a game-maker

Each of these stages may be appropriate at a given point in time, for a particular context or organisational life stage but, yet again, it's clear that a shapeshifter approach provides the best chance of survival and success. Generating a supple strategy, cultivating a culture that transcends tribes and developing a pattern of systemic innovation and wicked thinking simultaneously delivers multiple benefits. Each move can be used alone to great effect, but a more sophisticated and integrated approach greatly amplifies the impact they can have. Put simply, the four moves work better together.

Most organisations are perfectly capable of becoming a shapeshifter but many fail to do so. Sometimes the journey appears too daunting or it becomes impossible to work out where to prioritise. Organisations that embark on the journey will inevitably improve their innovative capabilities. Systemic innovation is but a pattern, and patterns can be emulated. The key is in the dedication towards doing so and the level of tenacity and perseverance shown when the going gets tough. Those that start the journey find it creates a momentum all of its own – very soon they are thinking beyond!

ASK YOURSELF...

Whereabouts are you on your journey to becoming a shapeshifter? Consider the wicked thinking maturity model and ask yourself:

- When do you consciously think about solving the problems that could make a real difference to your organisation and the world it operates in?
- What level of complexity are your people confident to engage with?
- How effectively does your organisation horizon scan?
- How does your organisation ensure it understands the underlying mechanics of a problem and is not distracted by manifesting symptoms?
- Which tools and techniques do you use to aid exploration, analysis and understanding?
- How comprehensive is your analysis of the context within which you operate?
- Does your organisation actively engage with wicked problems?
- Who gets to think about wicked problems in your organisation?
- Do your people fall in love with the problem or become attached to solutions?
- How do people come together to think and create in your organisation?
- How do creative teams organise themselves and what processes do they use?
- Who has a voice in the past, present and future of your organisation?

- How much clarity has been achieved in terms of where innovation can add value to your world?
- Is innovation commonplace or reserved for the creative few?
- Do you map problem systems and, if so, to what level of detail?
- Who has access to your analysis and thinking?
- Is ideation a lonesome activity or a collective enterprise?
- How does your organisation's culture support and encourage disruptive innovation?
- How comfortable is it for people across your organisation to challenge authority, question the status quo and rock the boat?
- How do you evaluate and select potential ideas and strategic interventions for further development?
- How do you predict the impact your interventions and inventions are likely to have, and how do you then test reality?
- Where do your organisation's best ideas tend to come from and how do they emerge?
- Which ideas get support and how are they supported?
- In hindsight, how many great ideas has your organisation failed to promote?
- How is learning shared across your tribe?
- How connected is your tribe and how are they supported to think and co-create?
- How disruptive have your organisation's ideas been? Have you ever changed the game or made an entirely new game?

CHAPTER 13

WHY WICKED THINKING'S SO WICKED

Whatever your ultimate ambition, innovation is the only game in town. People and organisations that stand still eventually lose their connection to the present. Reality doesn't stand still and, if you choose to do so, it is only a matter of time before you are severely out of touch and left behind. Many dinosaurs have come crashing down to earth having ignored the warning signals sometimes screaming at them from within their own ranks. Remember the Kodak story and that moment of truth in the seventies that could have radically changed its future outlook and success? Weak signals of the future are always around us in the here and now, and patterns of the past are forever repeating themselves in subtly altered guises. The near-future bears down upon us at pace eagerly followed by the far-future that might seem entirely unrecognisable until the power of hindsight is applied.

As a child I would often watch *Tomorrow's World*, a programme that attempted to give viewers a sneak peek into the future.[41] Many of the inventions profiled never made the light of day, but some did. Similarly, science fiction of the day suggested how we might live, travel and communicate. The smartphone, for example, bears an uncanny resemblance to *Star Trek*'s handheld device that allowed crew to ask Scotty to 'beam me up'.[42]

Imagine watching with wonder at future magical marvels, such as a cooker that could cook dinner in seconds (a microwave) or a machine that could record TV programmes so that you could actually choose when to watch them (a video recorder). Both were hugely important technological advances that drove fundamental shifts in attitude and behaviour, and, one could argue, social structure. New markets and constellations of products clustered around them. The video recorder at once told us that we could control when we wanted to watch something and that, yes, we could indeed 'have it all' and see two programmes that schedulers had seen fit to air simultaneously – modern-day streaming has a lot to thank the video recorder for.

What weak signals are already scattered across our experience that presently seem no more than fantasy but might, one day, closely resemble an invention that has changed the world? What can our imaginations dream up now that would not only change the game in our favour but might also have the potential to bring new games into being; games that we can't yet properly imagine given our distance from them but that we could be instrumental in bringing about?

- How can we build on the shoulders of giants or rock the core of current experience such that a new world emerges?
- What disruption can we wreak that will shape the future and positively change the experience of many people?
- Where are the anti-patterns that drive negative behaviours and abhorrent experiences that we could reverse with the right ideas and levers for change?
- How can we better understand the complex systems at play in the wicked web and where can we ethically experiment?
- Where does the next chain reaction begin?
- What small idea gives birth to the next paradigm shift?
- What invention will next change the world beyond recognition?
- Where are these ideas?
- Who's playing with these prototypes?
- When might the next one show up?
- Who might be its creator?

SIDE EFFECTS OF WICKED THINKING (THE BUSINESS CASE)

The positive impacts of thinking beyond and developing a culture and mindset of systemic innovation are easy to see. Those organisations that have achieved this level of consciousness are scattered like diamonds in the rough around us, and it can be clear to all when they enter and leave that space.

Beyond the obvious benefits of strategic success and differentiation, there are many side effects that also bring glory and joy to an organisation and its people.

Systemic innovators tend to have a loyal and admiring fan base that eagerly awaits the next iteration of a well-loved idea or the emergence of something truly game-changing. The experiences of end users and clients improve as products and services are designed in response to real and challenging problems they may experience in their everyday lives. Where stakeholders are actively involved in the design process, customer and end user engagement breaks all records. Future issues are brought to the fore long before they are truly problematic, so that people can better prepare in advance.

Employees enjoy the time they spend in the organisation and feel a genuine warmth and pride for its achievements and their contribution to them. They enjoy the space to think, the autonomy that's afforded to them and the ownership they can muster. Everyone is able to be a leader and hierarchy holds no bounds. People feel inspired, engaged and empowered to change the organisation, and perhaps the world.

Collective learning becomes an organisational habit. Networks form around common interests and there is a general sense of inclusion and tolerance, belonging and community. Principles guide decisions and the organisation is alert and responsive to the unexpected. Improvisation, rehearsal and simulation drive collective problem-solving and the co-creation of compelling narratives.

Ideation is not an activity reserved for the 'creatives'. Innovation is the way of responding to everyday issues. Supple strategy emerges from sustainable solutions that flex and evolve as contexts change over time.

People learn how to embrace conflict and have courageous conversations, confident that their relationships will remain strong and intact. And remember, teams that think and play together stay together!

With curiosity, and dedication to a cause, wicked thinking allows individuals and organisations to think beyond and to bring the future into being. And, once we have the idea, how do we create a movement that can move mountains – a force that can change the world? That's the job of our next and final move…

WORLDFIRST

When Jonathan Quin and Nick Robinson left their respective corporate roles at global banking organisations to set up WorldFirst back in 2004, little did they know the impact they would make upon the financial services sector and the many individuals and businesses that would be served by it over the course of just 15 years. WorldFirst was born out of a desire to provide customers with a real alternative to the big banks. Jonathan and Nick knew it was difficult and too expensive to move money around the world and so they set out to change that. The rate of growth at WorldFirst has averaged over 40 per cent per year and the organisation has won numerous business awards and appeared in the *Sunday Times* Virgin Fast Track list multiple times. In February 2019 WorldFirst was acquired by Ant Financial, the financial arm of Alibaba (the Chinese owned e-commerce giant) for an undisclosed sum. Another change journey is now beginning.

WorldFirst has had some periods of very high growth where it managed to innovate with abandon, living up to its self-identification as a market-leading, multi-award-winning, bank-beating, rapidly-growing, fun-loving international payments company. Its success has been largely due to a powerful sense of identity and purpose, a hunger to innovate and the courage to dare to go to new markets, where others have failed or recoiled.

When you enter the WorldFirst world, it fast becomes apparent that a core strength is the identification of wicked problems with great potential for progress. WorldFirsters (the noun for a collective gaggle of WorldFirst people) display insatiable curiosity and a hunger to make a difference to the world regardless of how challenging the path might turn out to be. Their values are simple: open, collaborative, courageous, selfless, curious and accountable. These six words drive their behavioural moral compass very effectively.

The senior leadership team at WorldFirst is different to most too. Some of its members have grown up with the organisation and there is a vein of entrepreneurship, vision and foresight that connects every member. Despite scaling significantly over a short period of time the entrepreneurial, ambitious and enabling culture has remained firmly intact. Jonathan Quin, at the helm, has become adept at gathering talented people around him who are equally as passionate about the success of WorldFirst and its ability to deliver amazing products and experiences for customers. WorldFirsters talk about products and situations in terms of the stories they bring about – their work is one of creating great outcomes and happy endings for the stories of their customers' lives and businesses.

There are many examples where WorldFirst has developed innovative solutions to intransigent wicked problems, but one stands out. The creation of The World Account was in direct response to a complex wicked problem that refused to go away. While it's now super-easy to purchase goods online and international shipping is improving significantly, the payment functionality for most people has remained hugely problematic. To remain successful, small businesses need their customers to be able to buy, pay and receive their goods seamlessly and fast. The payment process was (and still is) the weak link in this chain and WorldFirst decided it would like to fix it (or at least make it an infinitely better experience for all involved).

The World Account is basically a multi-currency account. Businesses around the world can register for free and are given a platform with their own bank accounts around the world. This allows them to receive payments in a range of currencies locally from their customers or to pay their suppliers locally. It turns international payments into local payments, which are faster, cheaper and less complicated. It makes a complex payment system simple. I asked Katie Brownridge (Chief of Staff) to describe WorldFirst's approach to innovation:

How does WorldFirst approach innovation?

We routinely engage in a great deal of horizon scanning. This is augmented by a very genuine connection to real customers in real time. By staying connected we can be better informed regarding emerging themes, problems and opportunities. This information inspires us to evolve existing products and services and invent new ones to make life easier.

Jonathan keeps very close to real customers of all shapes and sizes. He doesn't do this via a structured engagement programme, but instead nurtures genuine relationships and demonstrates a keen interest in customers' experiences in an authentic way. He thoroughly understands the customer problem and how WorldFirst can help or hinder it because he is one. He actually uses our products as a customer and is therefore very alert to the end user experience.

The big difference here at WorldFirst is that we really do give a damn about our customers and we make sure that everyone in the organisation does so too. We get as many people as possible close to the reality of our customer experience. Our people know our products inside out.

Our first focus is always to ascertain the purpose we are attempting to serve or the customer pain point we're trying to address. From here we can outline a vision of a destination experience for our customers – not necessarily the solution that will provide it. Typically, we then engage a small group to kick ideas around. We widen the group as ideas move into reality and as we start to operationalise and plan execution.

Ideation is often a spark from an individual and we do everything we can to create space and nurture an environment where these ideas can flow and be noticed or picked up for further evaluation. Careful socialisation then helps us to test the feasibility and potential impact of an idea while starting to build a coalition of supporters. When Jonathan (CEO) first explained the idea of the World Account to friends and acquaintances in a social setting it was very well received. This bolstered his belief that the idea was inventive and impactful, and was the right thing to do. It also provided an early testing ground for idea development and galvanised a group of early adopters.

What's different about the approach?

We involve customers in beta testing, but we do so using Agile software development by launching software in a real environment rather than a 'sandpit'. Customers are very honest about teething problems – where we may have considered the issues minimal and not worth investing in, our customers tell us honestly otherwise.

We go 'live' with a product relatively early in its development – immediately as an MVP (minimum viable product) has been achieved. This takes some courage, but with appropriate communication a friendly advance customer group can rapidly advance product development. We often create a beta for testing in the real environment which enables genuine experimentation in the real world with real customers and their genuine caveats, obstacles, preferences, etc. As Jonathan says, 'If you just give clients a beta product with no explanation, and it's not great, they'll hate you for it, but if you ask them to help be a part of creating the future product, they'll ignore the issues.'

By daring to share early we gain a greater level of acceptance and engagement with end users. This allows us to gain insight and accelerate product development, which ultimately drives user uptake and market growth.

What's been difficult?

We're a fast-growing organisation. Our technical capability from an infrastructure perspective is high, yet our fast scaling had resulted in a level of technical debt that we were also dealing with alongside the development of the World Account. The resulting complexity of technical development made prioritisation more challenging and slowed us down.

Also, our launch rollout plan and regulatory requirements meant that some areas of the organisation had the product available for their customers earlier than others. This caused some frustration and teams were champing at the bit to get hold of the World Account for their markets. There's a fine balance to be struck here in terms of keeping WorldFirsters engaged and ensuring they (and their customers) don't become disenfranchised while they wait. Internal and external communication and excitement levels have required careful management at times.

Why have you persevered?

We believe in WorldFirst, we believe in the World Account, and we are committed to our purpose. We are therefore prepared to motor through obstacles to make the difference we want to see.

By working on this problem, we have identified other customer pain points where innovation will provide great leaps in progress – we're working on those ideas now!

How do you know it's working?

The World Account has been successfully launched and adopted by customers across the world. We have now launched the World Account in multiple countries and take-up is accelerating.

It's a living product in that we are always looking to improve it and our customers' experience of it. The feedback we receive drives us to continually refine the product and create add-on products and services. We're happy to still be learning about what the product could do next – that's where the next big idea comes from.

What have you learned from the experience?

We are now firmly working as an 'agile' organisation (though we use a combination of waterfall and agile techniques to bring strategy to reality). We couple activity sprints with the clarity of an end goal and a target date for achievement. These processes are now firmly embedded but in the early days, development teams could waste time managing process rather than production and engagement. Thinking about process and team structure is a worthwhile activity and can make a huge difference to decision-making and prioritisation capabilities further down the line. Understanding our velocity and great prioritisation are critical!

We thought we were launching an MVP; in hindsight we probably didn't. We launched the product at an earlier stage of development than we might have planned to, but this generally worked. It has taught us that to engage early and dare to show the rough edges builds a band of loyal followers who want to contribute to the product's evolution. We have learned so much this way – bringing ideas in from a wider group is most definitely the way to go.

It's vital that you hold your nerve if you know something is right. Keep on at it until you get it right.

WorldFirst thinks differently to many organisations and is clearly proud to do so. It shows courage to share early and effuses a determination to engage with diverse groups of people to bring about positive change to complex wicked problems. WorldFirst's daring approach allows it to learn fast from failure and to adjust products and services quickly in response to the reactions it receives from its customers. WorldFirsters (CEO included) take a walk in their customers' shoes; in fact, many of them are customers themselves. A wide variety of perspectives and experiences are explored, interpreted and, perhaps most importantly, valued. These inform subtle variations in product design or launch approach for different markets and cultures. As a result, WorldFirst can engage in genuine co-creation beyond the borders of its own organisational walls.

WorldFirsters have a hunger for improvement and consistently engage in wicked thinking. A product is never felt to be quite 'good enough' and there is a constant drive to make it even better. WorldFirsters are exceptional in their quest for learning and capacity for disruptive change. Game-changer behaviours are often evident. WorldFirst is the archetypal apprentice of the future – its journey of discovery is ceaseless, it never assumes it has 'the answer' and has continually evolved its vision as it gets closer to achieving it.

PART 4

MOVE FOUR:
MAGICAL MOVEMENTS

The fourth and final move in our strategy to reality supersystem is the creation of a movement capable of moving figurative mountains. A movement that harnesses a tidal wave of positive change that can sweep obstacles from its path, obliterate the most complex of problems and scale the heights of the highest peaks. Make no mistake – this is the final and brutal hurdle where many strategies fall. Supple strategy, meta-tribes and wicked thinking can bring the organisation a long way, but until they break the barriers of its own walls (structures, culture, limiting beliefs and many more), ideas and innovations remain impotent in their ability to impact the far-future.

In this final move our task is to align the meta-tribe and amplify the power of collective intelligence in support of the cause and in pursuit of the future you wish to bring to pass. This move is not for the faint-hearted; travellers of its path can become wearisome and full of doubt along the way. That's why it is so important to remain focused on the first three moves as the journey proceeds. Like a relay, it's a team effort of moves in which every move has a critical part to play. Shapeshifters look up and out beyond their borders to find fans and cheerleaders who can share the weight of the cause and accelerate baton changes.

Wouldn't it be great to create a movement with energy, agility and momentum, connected at its core by courageous, capable and empowered people; empowered leaders everywhere, who are ready, willing and able to make informed decisions and take bold actions through the mechanisms of devolved accountability and authority alongside full autonomy? Strategic alignment, hive mind and individual agency bring swarm intelligence to life so that the movement can mobilise quickly and effectively in response to and anticipation of any situation.

CHAPTER 14

HOW SHAPESHIFTERS BUILD MAGICAL MOVEMENTS

Shapeshifters approach change as a fluid human activity rather than as a set of planned programmes and processes. They intuitively know that a shared vision of the future, collectively held principles and values, and a compelling reason why they aim to do what they do, will create greater movement than a set of deliverables, milestones and accountabilities. Shapeshifters have the confidence to relinquish overall control (probably because they are under no illusion that they had control in the first instance). This acceptance of 'what is', embracing of 'what will be' and not knowing how that may emerge, and the courageous navigation of a shared adventure of discovery, create truly magical movements that often go far beyond the wildest dreams of what at first seemed possible.

Shapeshifters unleash their wicked tribes and unearth positive deviance so that disruptive innovations can truly lead the way forward from within the trickiest wicked problems. Zones of accountability, widespread autonomy and proactive action based on foundation principles replace process and policy as the means through which people can take up the leadership mantle with the trust and belief that they can truly make a difference to the cause they hold dear. Energy is amplified and focused on the most important things, at the best time, in an effective way. Courageous enough to clear the decks of outdated notions, abandon worn-out customs and challenge those who fear to do so, shapeshifters clear the path for strategy to become reality and do the groundwork for big ideas to take hold without limitation. Where there is fear and doubt they build confidence. Where there is inequality they seek to include rather than build walls. Where there is cynicism, pessimism and doubt they contribute optimism, innovation and practical support.

Shapeshifters allow magical movements to work their magic!

THE MAGICAL MOVEMENT A B C

Magical movements are all unique; each has an identity that evolves as it grows. They are brought into being from a variety of events and experiences, and are not of process and policy born. Their stories depend upon many variables, and their time to lift off can be long or short (at times appearing immediate). It is often unclear why one movement fails to connect and inspire while another takes hold and grows into a global phenomenon. Some of this is down to luck: a well-timed idea, a well-connected founder, a well-funded cause. There's some truth in luck, but to believe in it unquestioningly is to accept failure without hope! Luck may seem magical, and perhaps in some ways it is, but I'm a firm believer that you can make your own luck or at least make it far more likely that luck will be ready and waiting once you are fully prepared to accept it.

The diversity of magical movements makes it impractical or indeed impossible to set out a cast-iron process for their successful formation, but there are some fundamental ingredients that seem to form part of the spell for each and every one!

AMBITION

A magical movement has an insatiable hunger for change. It has an inherent drive to create positive progress. It aspires to succeed where others have failed and demonstrates a potent desire to positively change the world. Ambition that is collective and aligned is a powerful force for good.

BELIEF

For magic to take root there needs to be trust and confidence in the movement's ability to deliver. A fundamental and widely shared belief in the validity of the movement's chosen cause and the potential of the movement's focus and activity to make a difference to that cause are critical foundations for the arrival of magic.

CAUSE

Magical movements are built around a powerful cause – a reason for being or a motive for action; a principle, belief or purpose that is fundamental to the movement's ability to attract people, resources and attention; a thing of importance that can give meaning to those who experience it or seek to change its course; a central tenet that holds the movement together whatever storms it may encounter.

Magical movements have a quest at the heart of their activity – a problem they want to solve, a change they wish to see, a group they want to help. They are constantly seeking the truth of the problem, searching tirelessly for the ideas that might create paradigm shifts, and painstakingly working to bring about a better future in the heart of their domain.

DEDICATION

We encountered dedication when considering the creation of cultures that transcend tribes and the application of wicked thinking in the context of wicked problems. For a movement to become magical, dedication to its root cause is a critical component of longevity and impact. Some movements appear to disappear in a puff of smoke just as they enter the magical stage. The ones that stand the test of time are those that are truly collectively dedicated to whatever it is they were born to do.

Dedication is a major driver of success. It's often just when all feels lost, and the pull to give up and surrender to the invisible forces that seem to be conspiring against every move is great, that a small decision or action, insignificant in the journey to date, suddenly dispels the storm clouds and gets the magic flowing.

ENERGY

Without energy the movement is dead or soon will be. The force, vigour and capacity to act are held both individually and collectively. Movements that pay attention to the well-being of their members and seek to provide them with the resources required to do their work and make tangible progress are those best placed to change the world. These movements amplify the individual energies available to them in a way that combines into an energy field capable of sustaining the movement through good times and bad. Energy comes from many sources and magical movements are clever and agile to connect and exploit these in pursuit of their cause. Sudden surges in energy are not uncommon where movements make an unexpected discovery, connect with new audiences or happen to be front and central to an event that unexpectedly changes the world.

FIRE

Magical movements have fire in their bellies. They are emotionally connected to their cause and this shows. Their passion speaks to a wider audience and inspires people to listen, to act and to join the movement. When the fire is absent the movement is dull; when the fire is lit its warmth can be felt from afar and people travel great distances to sit around its hearth.

GUTS

Magical movements and their people are courageous in their actions. They challenge the status quo, dig out assumptions, question authority and rock the boat. Magical movements have the audacity to hold up a mirror to inequality, inadequacy, injustice or inaction and the guts to lead the way regardless of the fearsome monsters they may face on the path. They dare to dream and show strength of character to bring the wildest pipe dreams into reality despite the forces working against them. It takes guts to start a movement and to bare your soul, to seek support and to ask others to get involved in something before it really has legs.

HEROES

Magical movements have many heroes. In the most magical movements there are heroes everywhere. The movement is not merely a vanity project for an individual or a chance for a small group to exert power over the many. A genuine magical movement gives everyone the opportunity to become a hero of the cause. Heroes who have made humbling sacrifices, trodden perilous paths, facilitated significant progress, sparked disruptive ideas and worked tirelessly across differing factions to co-create a better future are the stars of the story and the true guides of the cause.

IDEA

The post-truth fast show presents more than its share of wicked problems. In a volatile, uncertain, complex and ambiguous world it's the novel ideas that hold sway. Magical movements have a big idea or a novel invention that threatens to change everything. The idea may be an old one that has been repackaged to suit the current situation or a fast-emerging future, or to appeal more directly to an audience. The movement's big idea may in fact be quite a small idea in the greater scheme of things, but it must be an idea that has the capacity to bring about major change, to shift perspectives, to open minds, to design new games and make brave new worlds. Magical movements have an idea with big ambitions and lots of pulling power.

JOURNEY

The path taken by a magical movement has many forks in the road. The movement's heroes are forever presented with unenviable choices regarding which direction to take and what actions to prioritise. In the future path lies the plot that will take the movement forward in ways it cannot yet predict or interpret. The path already travelled gives rich soil from which to grow the identity of the movement and tell its story far and wide. Living in the moment of the journey and capturing its twists and turns gives meaning to the movement that cannot be derived from anywhere else.

Magical movements watch their step and record their progress in ways that are more akin to the telling of myths and legends rather than plans and milestones. They narrate their story mindfully and share it with travellers they meet along the way, knowing that the very act of doing so may change the ending in ways they cannot know. Storytelling makes the journey an intrinsic part of the goal.

KALEIDOSCOPE

The future is an ever-changing prospect. Future worlds cannot be predicted with any certainty, but they can be imagined and used as playgrounds for adventurous explorers. For a movement to retain its magic it must be ever agile to the future and understand the alternative timelines that may cross paths, weave webs and swap ideas as it comes into being. Magical movements keep a fluid sense of the future by viewing it through multiple perspectives and various lenses. They consciously play with the future as if rotating a kaleidoscope and viewing the patterns created by the ever-changing placement of the crystals within. Magical movements make every attempt to see around corners from many angles.

LEADERS

The most magical movements have precious little hierarchy. They operate around a central purpose, much passion and a series of guiding principles. Leadership is devolved, and accountability, authority and autonomy are the responsibility of all. Everyone contributes directly to the cause. There's nowhere to hide. In magical movements there are leaders everywhere and everyone is a leader.

META-TRIBE

Magical movements are a meta-tribe. There are no factions or warring subtribes, no fiefdoms with overlords or turf wars between heroes. The magical movement meta-tribe exists to further the movement's cause and seeks to build an environment where this can best come about. Thinking as one and acting as a coherent collective, the magical movement develops a shared consciousness which allows it to respond congruently yet fast. The meta-tribe consciously extends beyond the immediate movement and encourages fickle fans to become superfans – not groupies but fans with purpose, first followers who will become its next generation of able and willing leaders.

NADIR

Magical movements never forget where they came from and don't pretend the journey has been easy. They remember and use the lowest points in their fortunes to spur themselves on to even greater things. They think back to where they started and reminisce over their valleys of despair as a reminder of how far they have travelled as a collective. For many movements the journey is long; reflecting on the difficulties that have thus been overcome is a good habit to have. Magical movements don't get seduced when fame and fortune come to call – they know they often prove to be unreliable friends. Fads are many but magical movements outlast them every time.

OPEN

Magical movements are open. They are open to people and ideas and remain so even when under attack from those with closed minds and fixed world views. They use information, collaboration and co-creation as their most effective defence mechanisms and never fall into the trap of hiding from a difficult truth. Being open to new ideas, novel inventions and diverse ways of thinking makes the magical movement more likely to change the world. Peaceful revolution is their approach to waging war on intransigent wicked problems.

PRINCIPLES

Shared values and principles create a scaffold for devolved decision-making. Principles are tested in tough environments and precedents are always set mindfully. Foundation principles give form to beliefs while guiding principles provide a framework for operations and a route map for robust prioritisation. Hive mind and swarm intelligence can be unleashed when movements pay full attention to the principles they seek to live by.

QUANTUM

Magical movements show quantum entanglement. The factors that contribute to problems and solutions show spooky action at a distance   where one part moves another responds, like a carefully choreographed dance across vast distances in time and space. Principles are so embedded and communication moves so fast that it is as if people exist in two places at once and ideas span horizons of time. An action on one side of the world creates movement so fast that it seems simultaneous. Impact appears as if by magic.

REACH

Magical movements have reach. Their ideas and commitment to the cause radiate outwards towards new audiences, and the movement grows organically like a biological being. Super-connectors accelerate progress and take the idea of the movement to new realms. A magical movement has natural reach and extends this exponentially over time.

SHIFT

Paradigms are torn apart and collective consciousness is shifted forever when magical movements come to town. Coming into contact with these movements at their edges creates a chain reaction that causes both the movement and the external party to evolve. Spiritual, emotional, physical and cognitive shifts are all the work of movements large and small. Magical movements are shapeshifters in and of themselves as they metamorphosise towards a more complex and connected being. The complexity of the world can only respond and alter as the magical movement becomes part of its intricate web of wicked problems and novel solutions.

TRANSLATION

Magical movements know they must translate their message for the masses in order to gather any momentum. Complex problems and ideas are woven into stories and retold in multiple languages using plotlines that have meaning for diverse populations. People can interpret the movement's aims, approaches and activities to understand what's in it for them, how they may benefit from its work and how they might become involved. They are immediately able to identify how they could make a difference, play a part and become the change.

UNKNOWING

Always learning, the only thing a magical movement knows is that it can never know it all. Curious to the end, magical movements approach every situation as a learning experience. They enter new contexts and cultures with open hearts and minds seeking to genuinely understand. They encourage engagement and feedback from their outer reaches to their very core to ensure their cause is not misunderstood, their belief diluted or their actions rendered impotent. The magical movement approaches the future and its problems with excitement, intrigue and a determination to get down and dirty with the many versions of the truth, knowing that they will never reach a point when they have all the answers.

VELOCITY

Need, greed and speed can be harbingers of doom for an enterprise, but a movement does need impetus and pace for it to remain relevant and survive. Standing still is not an option. Movements that stand still are fast overtaken by the future and the events that herald its arrival. A magical movement keeps ahead of the present but maintains a pace that is sustainable and a velocity that can deliver value.

WICKED PROBLEM

Magical movements have a wicked problem at their core. A wicked problem that they have fallen in love with and committed to for the long haul. A wicked problem that they realise they cannot solve alone, but will work on forever with partners who share their ambitions and add value to the cause. Movements that form partnerships with other movements where causes are connected or problems are interdependent are more likely to see significant shifts in the areas they seek to improve. Magical movements fall in love with problems and don't become attached to a particular idea or person in the pursuit of positive change.

X FACTOR

Magical movements have the X factor. As a collective they are charismatic and have a natural magnetism that draws people in. They attract attention and use it fairly and freely to further their cause. It's exciting to be part of a magical movement and people in numbers want to be associated with its ideas. Magical movements use fame and fortune to further the cause rather than line their pockets!

YES

Magical movements start with 'yes'. They reflexively think 'How can we?' and 'Why not?' over 'Why should we?' and 'It won't work because'. Members of the movement embody the concepts of 'If not now, when?' and 'If not me, who?'

'Yes and' is heard in place of 'Yes, but'!

ZENITH

The magical movement imagines into the future to visualise a time of great prosperity and success, when the peak it is attempting to collectively climb has been conquered. This future is imagined regularly in all its glory, and collectively captured into a variety of formats that allow for a shared sense of vision to pervade the movement. Magical movements know exactly what magic they're trying to achieve and how the magical future might look.

CHAPTER 15

START WHERE YOU ARE: THE MAGICAL MOVEMENT MATURITY MODEL

This move is no different to the previous three. Magical movements have a number of key ingredients to their spell and it pays to know which ones you already have, which ones you need and whether there may be some easy wins that can be applied. Moving towards becoming a shapeshifter and creating a magical movement is not an easy journey and there are no guarantees that your first attempt will find success. If you take a look at how change and transformation currently tend to happen throughout your organisation and the behaviours and habits that manifest as a direct result, it can give a good indication of where to start.

The final part of the maturity model, outlined over the next few pages, attempts to map the progress of an organisation as it evolves towards becoming a shapeshifter and finds itself entangled with or central to a magical movement. You can use it to determine which stage your organisation is at and which ideas you can start to put into action. Remember, the maturity model is purely a tool through which you can take a shared view of the organisation and open a conversation about the way change currently happens (or not).

As in Moves One, Two and Three, the five evolutionary stages are:

1   Reactive
2   Focused
3   Structured
4   Integrated
5   Shapeshifter

Each stage has markers that signal a certain level of change leadership and movement making has been habitually achieved. To work out whereabouts your organisation spends most of its time (within which stage it generally resides) we focus on 10 elements:

1   Impact: the typical level of impact achieved by existing movements.
2   Cause: the degree to which a cause is identified as central to a movement.
3   Membership: how people are encouraged, invited or instructed to get involved and the reach achieved.
4   Governance: how movements are managed across the organisation.
5   Partnership: how people work with others and the degree to which this happens.
6   Symbols: emblems and badges and how these are used.
7   Leaders: who leads the charge and makes the big decisions.
8   Influence: how communication and public relations contribute to the cause.
9   Learning: how and when learning and education form part of the movement.
10 Agility: flexibility and manoeuvrability as the future takes shape.

– • –

STAGE 1: REACTIVE	
Impact	SURVIVE
Cause	• Cause is profit- or survival-led • Energy, passion and focus on the cause can fluctuate depending on level of resources available • Cause is based on founder or key leader perspectives and typically remains so • Profit and commercial viability win when they come into conflict with the cause • Cause identified may be short-term, limited scope and minimally disruptive or 'too big too quick' (highly disruptive without consideration of potential consequences beyond a limited understanding) • Where a broader cause is identified it may be poorly bolted on to existing commercials – 'made to fit' • 'Firestarter' fire may fizzle or erupt into an uncontrollable inferno
Membership	• Uncontrolled and unregulated • Tendency to depend upon who you know rather than experience or dedication to the cause • Membership can be restricted to a small clique of selected individuals
Governance	• Ad hoc movement with little or no governance or control mechanisms • Direction and activity of the movement is under direct control of founder or key leaders
Partnership	• The movement is naturally competitive both within its walls and with external individuals and groups • Limited inclusivity and 'winner takes all' mentality • Partnerships are short-lived and commercially driven
Symbols	• The cause is held up as a 'one-man band'; a vanity project that disciples may follow if they choose • Key people are profiled as symbols of the movement

Leaders	• Leaders can be ambitious for the cause without reason • Change is pursued for fame and fortune • Movement leadership is charisma-dependent
Influence	• Influence is sought via unerring and unquestioning belief • Belief can be vested in the wrong things • Strong beliefs are sometimes held without question or reason • Beliefs can be foisted upon others • Ideas and interventions are ad hoc and lack impact and influence • Negative influence can be wrought through lack of understanding of the cause
Learning	• The movement may learn from failures and large-scale disruptions after they have occurred • Learning is focused and directed on a narrow range of interests and factors • Education is used as a blunt tool for influence rather than to deepen understanding • Problems lead to witch-hunt behaviours • The movement seeks to be lucky, but luck is largely left to its own devices
Agility	• The ability to be agile is directly related to the ability of movement leaders to be so. The movement can decide and move fast but may prove rigid and unyielding. The agility of these movements can be seen as a yes/no dichotomy

– • –

STAGE 2: FOCUSED	
Impact	STRIVE
Cause	• Genuine causes within defined areas of the organisation may be based on strategically important wicked problems or areas likely to play well with audience • Causes across the organisation may collide, contradict and conflict • Leader perspectives, topical issues or big personal stories within the organisation underlie causes selected • Energy, passion and focus are dissected and applied across causes • 'Smoke signal' many fires with little control and limited connection
Membership	• Many tribes compete for members • Members are selected and conscripted due to their place within the organisation or expertise in relation to the cause • Membership is restricted to function or operational unit
Governance	• Multiple movements demonstrate differing approaches • Movements are individually governed and controlled within functional and operational unit boundaries • Cross-organisational governance is diluted • More sophisticated organisations may have some element of central co-ordination of activity
Partnership	• Movement members and supporters want to understand 'What's in it for me?' • 'Hero wars' make competing internal movements unlikely to collaborate and co-create • Movements are internally focused and unaware of the partnership possibilities beyond organisational boundaries
Symbols	• The movement is represented by collateral and energetic internal communications • Badges and emblems are tangible and proudly displayed • Case studies are used to create stories people can connect with • Resources are used on collateral • Hero wars are captured across the organisation to fuel competition for scarce resources

Leaders	• Movement leadership is capability- and capacity-dependent
	• Leaders use the movement to further their cause rather than lead progress of the movement's cause
Influence	• Influence is diluted through lack of alignment and multiple causes
	• Pockets of belief create conflicting ideologies
	• Early adopters are likely to select a movement early and stick with it regardless
	• Influence beyond function or operational unit is limited
Learning	• Movements vary in sophistication; some may have feedback loops and a conscious approach to learning
	• Learning is focused and directed on a particular movement and doesn't connect the dots between movements
	• Learning may be shared between movements in an ad hoc fashion, dependent upon informal relationships
	• Problems lead to a blame game
	• Movement seeks to win
Agility	• Agility is fractured by competing and potentially counterproductive movements and is largely dependent upon the capability and mindset of appointed leaders
	• Focused movement may be agile

– • –

STAGE 3: STRUCTURED	
Impact	THRIVE
Cause	• Constructed shared vision of the future
	• Strategically important wicked problems provide foundation to cause
	• Organisation aims to be a force for good for strong public relations, consultation and engagement

	• Cause can lack meaning to many • Energy, passion and focus heavily controlled • Sophisticated central heating system rather than many fires
Membership	• Tribe of tribes with attempts to create alignment and minimise conflict within and between • Hierarchy and predicted future potential have a major bearing on tribe membership
Governance	• Movement is controlled centrally via rules, policies and procedures • Central change, transformation or organisation development team play a major role in the governance and control of coordinated movement • Plans and milestones ensure strategically relevant activities and interventions are prioritised within the movement • Movement becomes one of many transformation streams often rolled up into communication and engagement planning
Partnership	• Structured partnerships are generated when they present commercial benefits or strong PR opportunities • Collaboration is structured, managed and controlled • Co-creation is facilitated to enable the movement to progress along a planned trajectory
Symbols	• Posters, frameworks and guides capture the accepted operating model of the movement • The code of the movement is transcribed to explain how it applies to each individual and why they should find it important • Heroes and villains are constructed to give momentum to the movement and meaning to the cause • Storytelling is centralised to ensure consistency, alignment and appropriateness to the cause
Leaders	• Leadership is hierarchical, and leaders are selected via a robust process • Organised, educated and prepared leaders engage with the cause in a pre-planned manner

Influence	• Belief in the cause is managed and manufactured • Minds are captured at the expense of hearts • The movement tells members what to believe in and how to best demonstrate that belief – one-size-fits-all allows little room for alternative messages • Influence is planned, and stakeholders are actively managed
Learning	• Feedback loops are designed into the formal mechanism of the movement • Learning is organised, structured and facilitated across the movement • Best practice and theoretically based approaches are encouraged • Problems lead to structured postmortems • The movement seeks the truth
Agility	• Agility is possible but dependent upon structure and process allowing for it within planned programmes of change. Bureaucracy and avoidance of contentious issues can slow change within the movement and create the risk of standing still or sliding backwards • Structured movements may be agile in pockets or slow to get turning

– • –

STAGE 4: INTEGRATED	
Impact	FUTURE-FIT
Cause	• Socially important wicked problem provides foundation for cause • Cause provides destination where problem is minimised or overcome • Organisation is looking to become a genuine force for good • Many fires consciously set and tended

	• Cause is deeply meaningful for people throughout the organisation – people can identify with it and want to make a difference • Energy, passion and focus are connected and invigorated through cause-related informal networks
Membership	• Organisation-wide meta-tribe is created and cultivated • Meta-tribe is cause-led • Meta-tribe is assumed to include all organisation members and adopts an inclusive approach that respects and actively encourages diversity of thinking • High-energy meta-tribe that seeks to share its energy beyond its walls
Governance	• Transformation and organisation development are features of all roles • Control of the movement is diffused across the organisation • Decisions are principle-led and based on shared values • Stories and front-line accounts form the basis for rule setting • Real-time feedback loops give credence to prioritisation
Partnership	• Collaboration and co-creation across the organisation are actively encouraged • Partnerships with outside organisations and individuals are utilised where there is mutual benefit • Future 'frenemies' are made of competitor organisations and movements in order to make progress and influence change on a broader scale
Symbols	• Myths, legends and heroes emerge with little intervention • Fun artefacts and memorable slogans are created to encourage belonging, conversation and playfulness • The code is translated into multiple meanings – no one-size-fits-all • The story and the journey are important symbols of the struggle to make the world a better place • Time spent and effort expended are highly valued and respected

Leaders	• Leaders are everywhere, and there is limited hierarchy or chain of command
	• Accountability, autonomy and agency are devolved throughout the movement
	• People demonstrating game-changer behaviours naturally emerge as leaders
	• Leaders are committed to and focused upon the movement and its underlying cause
Influence	• Hearts and minds are captured through compelling stories and meaningful causes
	• Belief grows as understanding of the cause and confidence in approach develops through experience
	• Stories, experiences and diversity of thinking impact ideas and provide regular healthy challenge to central ideology
	• Movement demonstrates influence beyond its borders
Learning	• Feedback and evaluation are natural elements of the movement's dialogue
	• Learning is fluid and core to the decisions and activity of the movement
	• Best fit is explored, tested and then applied
	• Pre-mortems seek to spot problems and plan possible interventions before they arise
	• The movement seeks to learn
Agility	• The movement ventures forward on its path but is capable and willing to alter course with evidence to support such a change
	• 'Yes but' is the manner in which integrated movements shift position

– • –

STAGE 5: SHAPESHIFTER	
Impact	**CHANGE THE GAME**
Cause	• Cause is made up of a number of interconnected wicked problems – a wicked web • Being a force for good is the organisation's reason for being • The cause is central to everything – everything the organisation does, decides and says • Dedication to the cause is naturally high within the organisation and beyond • The cause is of such a scale in terms of complexity and impact that the organisation exists to further its progress • Energy, passion and focus naturally adjust as the organisation navigates the cause retaining enough fire in the belly for major energy surges – the cause is on fire
Membership	• The meta-tribe extends beyond organisational walls • Connected and dynamic – agile to new information and intuitively feels shifts in the wicked web • The meta-tribe is open to all and fluid in membership • End users and experienced individuals are actively invited to contribute and belong • Tribal energy acts as a magnet to pull people in from far and wide – the meta-tribe has pulling power
Governance	• Governance runs in multiple directions – movement has clear linkage to supple strategy and vice versa • The movement engages in real-time principle-led decision-making and prioritisation • Organisation and transformation are naturally occurring side effects of the everyday activities of the movement • Myths and legends form compelling stories that create precedents for the basis of choices and actions • The movement is self-controlling and governing • Experiences from the front line, feedback from stakeholders and observed impact of interventions combine to create a live web of movement control

Partnership	• The movement is fluid in its boundaries and naturally absorbs people and organisations with whom it can collaborate and co-create • Partnerships based on trust and shared interest extend beyond the borders of the original organisation • The movement's journey is a valued part of the change process – the movement recognises that its very journey and experiences may alter the destination it reaches in a way it cannot predict • Connection and shared consciousness expand beyond the original movement to create supportive satellite movements
Symbols	• Disruptive behaviours and ideas are powerful emblems for the movement • Positive deviance is held up as an example of where the movement 'works with' rather than 'does to' • Symbols are used to question cultural norms and suggest or ask what might be next at the leading edge • The quest is inherently present in all symbols and emblems • Movement members have tangible pride in the movement and all it involves – they become the movement's most powerful symbols of meaning and purpose • There are no villains – only potential partners • Heroes are everywhere, and every opportunity is taken to share their stories (no matter how short or insignificant they may at first appear)
Leaders	• Leadership is a lever of change for all members of the movement • Wicked thinking provides plenty of opportunity for natural leaders to emerge • People with game-maker characteristics lead informal networks that form, dissolve and reform as required • Capacity to decide and act is held at an individual level – people are trusted and empowered to do the right thing for the cause • Respected leaders are highly courageous and authentic in their connection to the cause and their commitment to the movement

Influence	• Deep and broad understanding of the cause and tangible commitment of all to the cause develops belief far and wide within and beyond the cause • Influence extends far beyond the movement's obvious boundaries and attracts people and resources towards it in support of the cause • The positive energy of the movement radiates out and absorbs those it meets • The movement's reach is greater than its size, age or resources might suggest • The movement has ideas with pulling power and outcomes that many want to be connected to • The movement creates a shift where paradigms are (quietly or loudly) torn apart and collective consciousness shifted forever • Quantum entanglement creates spooky action at a distance
Learning	• Learning is continuous and shared • The movement and all its members are open to learning and shifting positions following greater exposure to and experience of the cause • A kaleidoscope approach creates a playground for the cause and its explorers – the crystals are consciously shifted to explore effect on the wicked web • Movement is willing to go back in order to move forward. There is free movement in all directions • Learning happens simultaneously across the shared consciousness and results in an ability to hold and examine multiple perspective levels • The movement seeks to evolve in all areas – spiritual, emotional, cognitive and physical • The movement embraces 'unknowing' and the unknown
Agility	• The movement knows where it has come from and the cause it wants to impact, but is flexible and agile in how it gets there and exactly where it may end up • 'Yes and' gives the shapeshifter multiple strands of possibility

Each of these stages may be appropriate at a given point in time for a particular context or organisational life stage but, yet again, it's clear that a shapeshifter approach provides the best chance of survival and success. Simultaneously generating a supple strategy, cultivating a culture that transcends tribes, developing a pattern of systemic innovation and wicked thinking, while creating a magical movement, delivers multiple benefits. Each move can be used alone to great effect, but in reality, they rarely ever exist fully independently. A more sophisticated and integrated approach greatly amplifies the impact each move can have. It's a no-brainer – the four moves work better together.

Most organisations are perfectly capable of becoming a shapeshifter, but many don't. Perhaps the journey is too much to take in or it becomes impossible to work out where to start. Organisations that set out to become a shapeshifter will have some level of movement at their core. Magical movements are each unique, but they all share some common ingredients. The trick is to sprinkle these ingredients lavishly but carefully across the organisation. Organisations that decide to believe in magic start to find their world becomes more magical.

ASK YOURSELF...

Whereabouts are you on your journey to becoming a shapeshifter? Consider the magical movement maturity model and ask yourself:

- Is there a tangible cause at the heart of your organisation?
- How compelling is the cause?
- How powerful is your organisation's purpose? Does it win hearts and minds or leave them cold?
- Who in your organisation decided its purpose?
- Are there competing causes across your organisation? Can these work better together to create something bigger?
- How do your people describe what they do when talking to their friends and family?

- How proud are you and your people of what your organisation achieves and strives to achieve?
- How interested are your clients, end users and external stakeholders?
- Who manages how the movement goes about achieving its ambitions?
- How many people are committed to the cause and how did they get involved?
- Does the movement work well with other parts of the organisation or external groups and stakeholders?
- What reach does the movement have within and beyond the organisation?
- How inclusive is the movement?
- How is change managed throughout the organisation?
- How has the movement changed its approach as a result of lessons it has learned on the journey?
- What change has the movement brought about?
- What symbols and emblems does the movement use and how are these shared?
- What happens when things inevitably go wrong?
- How and when is success and progress celebrated?
- How can people best spread the word?

CHAPTER 16

THE MAGIC OF MAGICAL MOVEMENTS

Magical movements are strategy, culture and innovation all combined with people to bring about change in the real world. Without people a movement cannot move!

Magical movements are elusive beasts. They sulk in corners waiting to be tempted into the open or sit just around the corner waiting to ambush us as we stroll absent-mindedly through our lives. When a movement is needed it can be slow to manifest but, once given space and permission to grow, it can surpass all imagination. Our imagination has a limit and as a species it is difficult to bring about something that has not yet been imagined. That's why movements move in steps. The steps can be giant or they can be small, but each one lays out the red carpet of a slightly shifted shared consciousness that can then imagine just a little bit further than before.

Movements can get out of control and that scares us. Movements with best intentions and a positive and powerful cause at their core can run ahead of themselves and use unhealthy methods to bring about change. Ends don't justify means. The means is just as important as the outcome – the journey and its impact have a lasting effect on the sustainability of progress.

Magical movements move fast. They are entangled and connected, driving simultaneous actions and decisions across a networked hive mind. Magical movements display the curious features of quantum mechanics and move magically in front of our eyes in ways that contradict what should be possible.

Magical movements make memories, and these memories help to seed new movements. Recalling how belief in a cause brought about massive social change over time, whether directly involved or indirectly affected as an observer, gives inspiration to the potential for further future change.

SIDE EFFECTS OF MAGICAL MOVEMENTS (THE BUSINESS CASE)

Movements are tricky beasts that don't always appear when you would like them to do so. Change programmes, activity streams and milestone maps have an important place in organisations, but when it comes to fundamental change they can leave people dry. A movement built around the elements listed in Chapter 14 can bring magic to any transformation, often when least expected.

Concentrating on the creation of a movement rather than a change programme results in a more emotional connection to the journey and the cause underpinning it. When a team of people come together to make the world a better place, even in some small way, they start to experience connection, synchronicity and collective insight in ways and to levels that a project plan just cannot initiate.

Creating a magical movement enables the organisation to achieve some very tangible outcomes. The organisation will align around a common cause, helping to create the meta-tribe required. Decisions will be made based on principles and values rather than rules and flowcharts. Priorities will be established, and the organisation will act with focus and purpose. Devolved leadership will develop across the organisation to empower all and move decisions to the lowest possible organisational level – generating a far greater sense of autonomy, authority and accountability for everyone.

Less tangible but equally important, the formation of a magical movement encourages a culture of wicked thinking; a culture where it is normal to collaborate across functions and borders, and where people are capable and willing to co-create the future. Magical movements give rise to formal and informal networks and fundamentally alter the structure of the organisation towards a fluid matrix or connected network of individuals and teams. The magical movement provides a firm core for the structure of the organisation and the design of operational processes – each should only serve to further the cause.

Activity sprints push the organisation to move at pace, fail fast and fall forward. The magical movement knows what it's trying to achieve and why this is so important and so it accepts necessary change, adapts to disruption and accelerates transformation with relative ease.

Leaders are developed and unleashed at all levels and leadership is no longer dependent upon or constrained by a hierarchy. Transition agility is quickly evolved at individual, team and organisational levels. Positive deviance is encouraged and celebrated and the organisation is able to make the most of the X-men and women who have found new ways of working or possess unfamiliar capabilities.

A magical movement tells stories that are co-created, well structured, thoroughly engaging and fun, while grounded in reality, authentic and clearly demonstrating what's in it for people to follow, contribute to or join the movement. Human factors and individual actions have big consequences in magical movements – it's the small things that change the world.

Magical movements make difficult decisions that may just save the day and then follow through on their promise to the cause. They are courageous, connected and confident enough to dare to change track or make a U-turn should metrics suggest outcomes are not as expected or the external environment has fundamentally changed. The movement knows there's no shame in turning back and retracing its steps to find a better path should conditions deteriorate or circumstances change.

Just a century ago the world was a vastly different place. We have made progress, great progress, but there is still much to do on so many fronts. Collective crises in confidence give rise to protectionism, exclusion, ambivalence and antipathy. The anti-patterns of progress that repeat patterns from the past are better left there.

Magical movements that matter don't have to be large; your frustrating problem, your small idea, your cause with meaning, might just be the one that ignites a magical movement and changes the world!

How can we confidently, collectively and collaboratively step forward into the future, a better future that we co-create with everyone around us – valuing all and leaving nobody behind? Magical movements make the step changes that weave the wicked web into something entirely different. New problems arise in the vacuums left by progress and this is where our opportunity hides. Let's not repeat the same mistakes – let's make some new ones and learn on the journey; let's make a pledge to positively change the world one move at a time.

Magical movements can become the stuff of legends and give rise to a swathe of ordinary everyday heroes!

THE UK CAA INTERNATIONAL GROUP

The UK Civil Aviation Authority (CAA) was formed in 1972. It is a public corporation that was established by Parliament as an independent specialist aviation regulator that directly or indirectly regulates all aspects of aviation in the UK, and its subsidiary, Air Safety Support International (ASSI), is responsible for air safety in British Overseas Territories. The CAA's primary role is protection, of those who fly and the overflown. In safety, the CAA regulates air navigation service providers, aerodromes, airlines, UK registered aircraft and airworthiness organisations. It regulates pilots, air traffic controllers and engineers, and the associated training organisations. It also issues licences for pilots, engineers and air traffic controllers. In security, it oversees security standards at UK airports, and in consumer protection it runs the ATOL (Air Travel Organiser's Licensing) scheme and economically regulates those with significant market power, such as Heathrow Airport Limited. The CAA has a broad and important brief indeed. Although the CAA is a public corporation of the Department for Transport (DfT), it is predominantly funded via charges levied upon those it regulates or that use its services – it receives no direct government funding other than for specific projects specified by the DfT.

Like any organisation, the CAA is organised into functions. One such functional area is its International Group (IG). The International Group is committed to supporting the sustainable success of air transportation by raising the standards of aviation across the globe, to protect those who choose to fly, as well as those who don't. This purpose is completely aligned with that of the CAA.

There are three functions within the International Group:

1   The International Strategy and Engagement team works with global and regional organisations and agencies such as the International Civil Aviation Organization (ICAO) and the European Aviation Safety Agency (EASA) regarding policy issues.
2   The State Safety Partnerships programme engages with individual States, their industry and UK industry to drive safety performance management and risk mitigation where there is a clear benefit to the UK public.
3   CAA International (CAAi) provides technical advisory, capacity building, training, examination and licensing services internationally. It is committed to supporting ICAO and EASA with its services as well as working with many National Aviation Authorities around the world, and it generates 'profit with a purpose', redeploying funds to where they are most needed.

CAAi is self-funding in that it generates profit from the work it performs with the aviation industry, national aviation regulators and other organisations across the globe. While it contributes financially to the UK CAA funding model it clearly has a very different operating model to its parent. CAAi must remain profitable in order to successfully deliver upon its ambitious global aviation safety goals. Historically, CAAi was run as a consultancy arm of the CAA and this had set it apart from the rest of the CAA in terms of culture and process.

When CAAi recently became part of the newly formed International Group (IG), this transition provided the necessary catalyst for rethinking the way CAAi positioned itself both in the external market and as part of the UK CAA. The time had come to rethink relationships and to find a better way to represent all the great work that CAAi had delivered, is delivering, and is yet to deliver. The positioning of CAAi and its identity were fundamentally changing – CAAi was about to reinvent itself!

CAAi took time to deeply think about what it stood for as part of the IG and the wider CAA. Everyone became engaged in the debate and it quickly redefined its purpose, its mission and the vision of the future it would like to deliver.

VISION

A world where every state has a sustainable aviation system protecting those who fly and those who do not

MISSION

Developing fundamental partnerships and growing our influence worldwide to tackle major aviation challenges and achieve consistent standards of regulation across the globe

PURPOSE

We exist to improve aviation standards sustainable across the globe, connecting states with expertise from the UK CAA and developing our partners' people to help them lead the aviation world of tomorrow. Where our activities make a profit, we reinvest a sustainable proportion to extend our reach and fulfil our purpose

These three statements were co-created by the whole team in collaboration with key internal and external stakeholders. Their capture enables everyone to know the general direction of travel and to make principle-led decisions with confidence. The explicit mention of reinvested profits in support of purpose engages a far wider audience with the CAAi's activities. For many who had previously taken little interest in the team's activities, this was the catalyst that attracted them towards the cause.

Fundamental to this shift was CAAi's decision to become a 'social enterprise'. Social enterprises are businesses that are set up to change the world. Like traditional businesses they aim to make a profit, but it's what they do with their profits that sets them apart – reinvesting or donating them to create positive social change. They:

- have a clear social and/or environmental mission set out in their governing documents
- generate most of their income through trade
- reinvest most of their profits
- are autonomous of the state
- are majority controlled in the interests of the social mission
- are accountable and transparent

The ambitious transformation was conceived and delivered in super-quick time. Already the evolution of culture, acceleration of innovation, engagement with the cause and palpable commitment to the cause shows all the early hallmarks of a magical movement.

I asked Ben Alcott (Director International Group) to describe his experience of how this magical movement has evolved:

What vehicles have you used to drive the change?

The shift to a social enterprise has vastly shifted perspectives and perceptions. The fact that CAAi is now operating as a social enterprise and is obliged to meet the criteria set out makes our purpose very real and our commitment to it very transparent. The authenticity of what we stand for is clear for all to see.

The industry (and the world) is going through a period of unprecedented change. Change of this magnitude can be unsettling and the uncertainty and volatility surrounding it can cause people to lose focus on what needs to be done. By consciously aligning around a co-created purpose we have lit a path that can provide direction regardless of the complexity and ambiguity we are working through. There is genuine power in a collectively created and agreed purpose in times of great uncertainty and change.

Finally, we've placed quality dialogue front and centre. Regardless of the noise and distraction of everyday operations we have made space and time to talk and listen, to interrogate and investigate, and to collaborate and co-create. We have fully engaged with wicked problems and potentially disruptive innovations.

What's different about the approach?

The fact that we have aligned around a common purpose has created a culture where people feel empowered to make the decisions they need to make in support of it. This has led us to be less guided and distracted by fear or protectionism (organisational or personal). Fear and protectionism cannot be allowed to take over decision-making – this is never a sustainable business strategy.

What's been difficult?

The greatest difficulty has been finding and protecting the time required to get everyone within the CAA to recognise and understand the purpose and why it's different to the previous model. The effort has been very worthwhile, but it has, at times, been difficult to ensure we are fully aligned with all that is going on. We have been very careful to interrogate big decisions to check they are aligned to our purpose and likely to further the cause so that we set the best precedents early on. People inside CAAi are now believing in it and are clearly fully committed to it.

Why have you persevered?

It's been great to see how these changes have positively changed the way the UK CAA feels about CAAi and, indeed, how CAAi feels about itself. CAAi has a lot to offer and makes a massive contribution to the global aviation sector, sovereign states, country and regional regulators and, of course, users of aviation services. We are certainly not there yet; changing culture across the CAA in how they think about and engage with CAAi is taking time – shifting a thousand people isn't easy – but we have made some significant progress and this is what spurs us on.

The transformation has allowed the organisation to navigate a time of unrivalled uncertainty while remaining operationally functional and optimistic. Internal competition is reducing as our efforts are now firmly directed at furthering the cause and achieving our purpose and mission. This is now the guiding star that supports people through challenges, disappointments and unexpected change.

How do you know it's working?

- *Our purpose has already created great clarity and alignment.*
- *The social enterprise has tangibly brought CAAi closer to the UK CAA without losing viability, commercial approach and entrepreneurial essence.*
- *There is an increased commitment to stakeholders and clients in times of threat and change. CAAi has not retreated into introspection or avoidance of issues and is now consciously starting to explore how we can further extend the reach of our capabilities where it fits with our purpose to do so.*
- *It's gathering a momentum of its own. Once belief is evident the shifting of the organisation is becoming more automatic (like an autopilot in an aircraft). We still intervene when it goes off course, which it does from time to time, but more and more it is steering its own path.*

What have you learned from the experience?

- *Belief is key to successful outcomes. Belief in purpose, belief in the cause and belief in our ability to have a positive impact!*
- *Be aware of personal opinions, historic experiences and underpinning beliefs that may affect judgement, actions and decisions. As you venture on a joint journey like this, it's important to understand where everyone is emotionally and cognitively with regards to the change and any other situations and changes going on around them.*
- *Be sure to include, engage and communicate with everyone. Do your very best not to allow vacuums to form as they can quickly be filled with misinformation that fast grows legs and can derail the team, however well-meaning. Openness and transparency are not always easy, but they typically lead to better outcomes and greater commitment.*
- *Use formal mechanisms, such as strategy documents, website updates and the usual communication channels, but dialogue is most important. Talk about issues as they arise and jointly interrogate decisions as they are made to ensure they set the precedents you want to see. Decisions, precedents, role modelling and example setting are immensely powerful.*
- *The power of purpose is not to be underestimated!*

CAAi might just be in the early stages of a magical movement. It is engaging fully with wicked problems and as a result it has broken down significant barriers and forged strong relationships where there were previously difficult links. Its shared vision of the future, collectively held principles and compelling reason why are providing it with energy, agility and momentum. By harnessing everyone in its reinvention, CAAi has made the most of the diversity of thought and experience within its teams. It has become a better-connected organisation that is now more able to be agile and decisive through a combination of individual agency and a fast-developing hive mind. Everyone has the opportunity and encouragement to be a hero for the cause and everyone is genuinely committed to that cause. It is actively seeking to learn from its experiences, its people and its stakeholders and focuses on building a future that its vision broadly represents. CAAi is brewing a tidal wave of positive change based upon a deeply meaningful cause that many believe in. An ambitious force for good with true dedication to its shared cause, CAAi is building a magnetic and magical identity.

PART 5

BUILD A
BETTER WORLD

We are lucky enough to live at a fascinating point in human history. The long-established models of civilisation are in the process of being disrupted in front of our eyes. Societal values, economic systems and ecological impact are all transforming on our watch. Are we content to watch or could we have a positive impact on the world through our individual actions and those of our organisations? Has there ever been a greater opportunity to pull together and co-create a better future for our planet, our descendants and the animals and fauna we are privileged to share this planet with?

While the four moves can take strategy to reality for an organisation seeking to be successful in a complex, volatile and fast-changing context, they can also be applied to some of the broader issues that face humanity. Equally, by using the four moves to establish longevity for your organisation, you can ensure you and it have a voice in how the future unfolds.

Leadership, influence and critical examination of what really constitutes success all play a part in lifting the four moves off the page and into reality.

CHAPTER 17

IT'S LEADERSHIP BUT NOT AS WE KNOW IT

The four moves work in tandem to create a strategy to reality supersystem that can accelerate your organisation through trouble and strife towards a future filled with opportunity. It's a complex undertaking and one that requires great leaders who have the capacity and capability to guide themselves and the organisation along the many paths it will venture.

Leadership is critical, but the sort of leadership most organisations fixate upon just won't cut it! Leaders born into hierarchy who have collected a replicated set of capabilities defined by and developed within the organisation cannot hope to have the breadth and foresight to lead the charge. A few may intuitively know what's needed and have the natural mindset of openness and curiosity that just about carries them through. Still fewer may become great leaders through luck or happenstance – being in the right place at the right time with the most appropriate capabilities for the situation and the capacity and authority to use them. The odds aren't great though…

Awareness is increasing and curiosity is building regarding our educational infrastructure, constructs and approach, and the range of unintended negative impacts it appears to generate. There seems to be a largely accepted yet unfortunate ability within existing educational systems to spectacularly dissolve creativity and expertly hide the talents of our children beneath cumbersome syllabi and multiple evaluations. Children with talents that don't neatly conform to the range of subjects available, or who perhaps become interested in learning earlier or later than their peers, are not well catered for. The conversation around this wicked problem is gaining volume and the embryonic movement already developing to create a shift and change the way we educate is gradually picking up momentum.

The same issue is also present in organisations across the world. Many of the leadership capabilities that used to bring about successful outcomes will not work in the post-truth fast show. The environment demands something different from leaders. People want to see their leaders' struggles and connect with them on a human level. Leadership is no longer the domain of a privileged few and where this bastion remains it is fast crumbling.

An outdated view of leadership pervades many organisations. Even organisations open to change where leadership is not the exclusive endpoint for a chosen few, still define and develop capabilities along a well-worn path. There are lots of interesting opinions regarding the leadership competencies that will drive success in the next century and great ideas for how to develop these effectively, but most organisations remain attached to modular leadership programmes with contrived experiential components. Existing leadership programmes provide a two-dimensional map, but they are not and never will be adequate territory for learning. Leadership development as we know it is not fit for purpose!

Talent pipelines have had their day too. Let's be honest, we've all seen examples where the talent pipeline has been busy in the art of distraction as true leaders naturally emerge, against all odds, from an unexpected vicinity stage left.

Rather than learning to lead, leaders need real opportunities to learn through leading. This process can't wait until they are officially considered to be leaders in the traditional sense. Being part of a movement that is built around a meaningful cause, where they can develop a sense of agency and hone the principles upon which their decisions are based, is invaluable in a world that never remains the same. Playing with reality and being committed apprentices of the future provides plenty of options for learning. Considering alternative timelines, reflecting on repeating patterns, co-creating with like-minded and vastly differently minded individuals and groups, all expand an emerging leader's consciousness in ways a typical educational programme cannot ever hope to achieve.

To shape the future, we need leaders who can be game-changers. Leaders who can innovate in ways that disrupt current paradigms and create unpredicted shifts in shared consciousness. The future craves leaders who will lay new paths and plant its seeds; the seeds of a future we cannot yet imagine. The pace of change in our already volatile, uncertain, complex and ambiguous world is accelerating. Capabilities shift fast and therefore learning agility is the key. Capabilities that seem important now will be redundant tomorrow. The future doesn't belong to traditional leaders, it belongs to the learners – the game-changers and the game-makers.

As a reminder, game-changers are:

- **Learners**. Game-changers know that learning agility must come first, it's the enabler that allows them to develop the remaining game-changing dimensions effectively. They are constantly open and curious to learning opportunities where others might least expect them.
- **Connected**. Game-changers value people and relationships and move from small talk to deep talk to get the best results from any team, in any situation, anywhere.
- **Informed**. Game-changers look for emerging themes and are amongst the first to recognise their significance.
- **Insightful**. Innovation and creativity are natural extensions of intellect and intuition for game-changers at the cutting edge.
- **Focused**. Game-changers cut through complexity and do the right things well; always with their eyes on the final outcomes.
- **Valuable**. Game-changers commit to making a difference and creating long-term, sustainable value in everything they do.
- **Inclusive**. Game-changers have a global mindset that enables them to connect, influence and deliver across organisational, geographical, historical, political and cultural boundaries.
- **Believable**. Ultimately game-changers are authentic and credible. People choose to follow them regardless of authority.

Game-makers are all of the above and:

- **Hungry**. Game-makers are constantly curious and persistently ask the questions that shift perspective, unearth assumptions and alter the collective consciousness forever. Learning is fundamental to their being and they are internally driven to make big leaps.

- **Playful**. Game-makers enjoy grappling with an issue and learning how to make positive impacts through fun and games. They take play seriously and play with a purpose. Games, experiments and simulations are their go-to activities.

- **Courageous**. Game-makers dare to challenge the established way of operating and the establishment that enshrines and protects it. They question authority and shake the foundations of the status quo. They bravely step beyond to fail fast and fall forward.

- **Integrated**. Game-makers are super-connectors and create fluid networks that adjust and evolve in response to opportunities and threats. When plugged in they contribute fully to the shared hive mind allowing the tribe to swarm as a flock; to think and act as one inclusive and diverse being.

- **Vulnerable.** Game-makers know their strengths and limitations. They are self-aware enough to know when they are out of their depth and to tread carefully but purposefully to test new waters. They open their minds to new information and are willing to change when a different approach is required.

- **Humble**. Game-makers know that magnificent ideas and compelling causes are born of humble beginnings. They see danger in knowing it all and are willing to become novices over and over again. They are apprentices of the future.

- **Dedicated**. Game-makers are dedicated to the cause. Their purpose is pure and simple – to positively change the world one move at a time.

- **Deep**. Game-makers fall in love with the problem and not the answer. They seek to understand the ultimate question of 'life, the universe and everything' and are not distracted by the foretold answer of '42'! Game-makers are most at home deep in the problem they have fallen in love with.

If your role is about numbers, then of course you need to understand the numbers. If your role is focused on engineering or technical design, then it stands to reason that you need to understand the fundamentals of your profession. But to be a leader demands far more and does not depend upon career stage or seniority. Leadership isn't about what position you hold; it's about what you do within the role you perform and how you make a mark beyond its boundaries. Leadership isn't about the important people you may know; it's about how you connect and influence people no matter who they are and where they may be on their own personal journey. Leadership is about being human in a way that takes humanity and the world it inhabits towards a better future.

Here's the thing: leaders don't need to compete. There's always room for more leaders. Inspiring leadership isn't about control and authority, it's rooted in first followership and those who dare to step up, be counted and make the first (or second) move.

We need great leaders everywhere; in every walk of life, every movement and every moment. In fact, let's drop the great and lose the pressure to be loud, proud and well-known. Let's embrace the quiet, unobtrusive leaders who make huge differences to the world sometimes with small actions, modest ideas or seemingly insignificant decisions. They are the true game-changers and the daring game-makers of the future.

We need everyone to feel able to be a leader and confident to become one. If we can encourage everyone to consciously and actively look after their patch, tend their lawn and contribute to their community we can be sure that the next generation will receive a well-cared-for world; a world where leaders focus harder on doing the right thing rather than doing things right. If we think of the organisation as a village, a town or perhaps a city, it becomes abundantly clear that interventions sustainable over the long-term are the only ones that create replicable positive progress. If we cherish our elders and nourish our youngsters, we create a human system to be proud of. A human system where compassion, communication and co-creation are fundamental truths of society. A flexible society that is supple to waves of change. A human system where entropy and disorder no longer break the system or drive conflict but instead become catalysts that raise society to new levels with adequate caution. A supple society that sways with change and creates alternative futures rather than a concrete civilisation that will one day inevitably meet its grisly end.

LEARNING HOW TO BE A LEADER IN THE POST-TRUTH FAST SHOW

Houston, we have a problem – a wicked problem! On a bad day, we seem to have a leadership class that is devoid of leadership capability. If, for example, we take a long hard look at our political systems, they seem riddled with leaders who are in it for themselves. Manifestos built upon outdated and rigid ideologies, competing economic models that have convincingly proven their inability to bring prosperity to all but a few. Machiavellian behaviour and an inability or unwillingness to alter path or make a U-turn, even in the face of undeniable and overwhelming evidence in support of doing so. Petty corruption, prideful intransigence and dogmatically applied ideologies are never a recipe for sustainable success. So committed are our politicians to being seen to be right, many of them seem to now be unable to see the wood for the trees or unwilling to sacrifice ego to do the right thing. Truth and transparency are smothered by spin and sound bites.

There are game-changers and game-makers scattered throughout the political population but the very air they breathe is polluted with apathy and cynicism due to the actions and decisions (or lack of action and reticence to make unpopular decisions) levied by their less authentic colleagues. The leaders we really need are suffocating just when our future depends upon them.

Any social change is complex change. Multiple stakeholders have varied experiences and perspectives and the acts of collaboration, compromise and co-creation are not necessarily the easiest paths to embark upon. Leaders who can only see one way through a situation are not going to arrive safely or, if they do, they will arrive on their own having lost every follower en route. Our leaders must be willing to learn throughout the change journey and willing to change so that the journey can be navigated successfully. The only way to learn these skills is at the heart of a real wicked problem, where cause meets purpose and the various possibilities for progress make themselves known via multiple voices.

The change we need to see in organisations is a shift from political leadership to movement leadership. And for this to be possible we need to ditch all we think we know about leading complex organisations and learn from successful social change movements. Capturing hearts, shifting mindsets, learning through doing and daring to think beyond everything that has come before is what leaders of the future will be known for. If we look back at the greatest leaders of our time it is striking that they too displayed these attributes!

Many of those who changed the world were not elected or formally appointed leaders. They were ordinary people going about their daily lives who suddenly or gradually changed the way they engaged with their environment and the people within it. Their actions were small but daring, quiet but resonating, insignificant but paradigm-shifting all the same. They created a chain reaction that may only be observed with the benefit of hindsight.

Leadership in shapeshifter organisations has more in common with social action and disruptive change than it does with typical political and hierarchical leadership bureaucracy. Everyone in a shapeshifter organisation is a leader of their patch – a hero of their part of the cause! Twenty-first-century leaders aren't born or created – they're unleashed. Shapeshifters believe everyone is a leader and they work hard to unleash the latent potential in everyone in answer to the most wicked problems.

I've worked with many leaders and leadership teams over the years. Without exception, every organisation I have supported has cited a small range of similar issues that prevent their chosen leaders from leading. Regardless of sector, life stage or situation, the same five issues always emerge:

1   How can I get my leadership team to align behind the organisation's strategy and demonstrate 'cabinet responsibility'?
2   How can I generate a greater level of ownership and accountability from my leaders?
3   How can I get my leaders to step up and think more strategically?
4   How can I get my leaders to prioritise robustly and decide effectively and efficiently?
5   How can I be sure I have the right leaders in my leadership team – how can we evaluate this?

For many years I worked hard to design and deliver learning events that would attempt to satisfy all of these requests. It was hard work for me and the leaders, and I resoundingly found that whatever progress we made in the room (and we really did make quite a lot of progress in the room every time) was invariably lost the moment theory hit reality. For a while I thought fault lay with the leaders or their leaders, and then, for an even longer while, I thought the fault lay with me. Eventually the penny dropped – we were attempting to answer the wrong questions! The requests were signposting symptoms of a deeper more complex problem – the organisational problem!

The underlying issues were of a different order and related to the organisation as a whole. The way the organisation approached strategy formulation, culture cultivation, innovation and change told me far more about what was really going on and predicted future success with a far greater degree of accuracy. Of course, leadership capability is entwined with all of these things, but it cannot be viewed in isolation. The organisational system dictates the quality and quantity of leadership at your disposal every time.

More enlightening questions to ask might be:

- Why doesn't my leadership team align? How do we need to redesign or reframe our strategy to allow it to do so?
- Is our strategy based on a meaningful cause that everyone is invested in progressing? How do we really win hearts and minds around here?
- What are the wicked problems that are preventing progress and how can my leadership team better contribute to disruptive thinking, innovation and co-creation?
- What are our competing priorities, where are our ambitions counterproductive and what shared principles form the basis for devolved decision-making?
- Why is leadership invested in so few people? How can we give agency to all and enable everyone to lead?
- What gets rewarded and applauded around here, and why?
- How are we making it difficult for our people to lead, and what can we do about that?

Instead of wasting time fabricating situations where fledgling leaders can stretch and flex their leadership muscles and learn to compete with one another for valuable resources and influential relationships, let's use the real world as a playground for practice so that leadership can emerge where it's really needed rather than in the classroom never to be seen again. Let's use the work of a shapeshifter organisation to provide the machinery through which everyone can find their leadership strengths and moments. Let's use the shapeshifter's magical movement to make some interesting shapes!

Experience has shown me that there are three very effective ways to unleash the leaders we really need.

WICKED: LEADERSHIP IN ACTION USING WICKED PROBLEMS

One sturdy mechanism for leadership development is the very real wicked problems the organisation is grappling with.

Shapeshifter organisations are often built around a wicked problem like a galaxy is formed around a black hole. The magnitude of this wicked problem is often far greater than any one leader or team of leaders can effectively tackle. This presents us with multiple opportunities where people can get involved in a relatively structured way that is guided towards unleashing innate leadership potential and exercising useful capabilities to bring about change in real time in the real world.

Where organisations don't have a clear centre of gravity, there are always random obstacles that pop up along the critical path of any strategy – no matter how well formed. Many of these obstacles involve behaviour, beliefs and attitudes – the stuff of social change. They therefore present equally real and useful vehicles for development to take place in the real world. Presenting issues are often ones of structure, culture and strategy. These provide a fertile environment for leaders to learn about their form of leadership while advancing the organisation's journey through the four moves from strategy to reality.

The benefit of using real issues is that levers for change are not fabricated and outcomes and reactions are genuine. It's not possible to walk away from the learning as it cannot be denounced as 'unreal'. Additionally, organisations are more willing to invest the necessary time where outcomes are related to real situations, people and issues. The time invested in learning can make a material difference to the long-term viability of the organisation or its ability to successfully navigate risks or manifest opportunities.

FUSION: LEADERSHIP IN ACTION USING SUPPLE STRATEGY

A second mechanism is the formulation of strategy itself. In Move One we examined how the process of strategy formulation can become locked into the budgetary planning cycle and how damaging this can be to far-future thinking, scenario planning and the generation of alternative strategic choices. Repurposing elements of the strategic planning cycle has a positive impact both on leadership capability and strategic planning.

Strategies developed behind closed doors are limited in their scope and application. Supple strategy requires inclusive dialogue and sustained loops of feedback and revision. Using these elements as pillars for a structured collective process provides significant benefits to the organisation and the individuals involved.

The very act of working through complex strategic contexts, re-examining the operating model and co-creating potential, plausible and challenging futures (within which the organisation will want to continue to flourish should they come about) requires a level of thinking most are not stretched towards in their everyday operational work. The experience changes thought patterns, shifts perspectives and expands consciousness and capability forever in ways that cannot always be predicted.

Those involved fuse into a shared consciousness that can act as one and make decisions based on the principles and process learning they have absorbed throughout. Shapeshifter organisations create mixed groups to experience the process from which new informal networks can emerge. These networks create new synapses in the hive mind. Less developed organisations can use the same approach within their leadership teams or project teams to create greater alignment and agency which eventually permeates the organisation as a new way of being. Creating fusion around strategy has a tangible and critical impact upon any organisational system and is a great place to start!

QUANTUM: LEADERSHIP IN ACTION USING MAGICAL MOVEMENTS

The third mechanism for leadership capability development in the real world is via the movement itself. The process can use an existing movement where people can learn through finding their place, their voice and their impact, or it can be attached to the creation of a new movement. Both approaches allow people to become amplified versions of themselves that can effect major change through working collaboratively with others in partnership or co-creative activities.

The learning journey is designed to take the learner on a guided tour of themselves, the people around them and the wicked problem at the heart of the movement. It explores the cause it brought about, the positive deviance already in action and the potential for change through leveraging change levers and/or experimenting with disruptive innovation.

Those involved see themselves in greater clarity than ever before and understand how people experience their leadership. Answering the questions 'How do people experience me?' and 'How do people experience themselves when in my presence?' can be quite profound change levers. As a direct result of the experience people grow spiritually, cognitively, emotionally and physically. Being intrinsically involved in the mechanism of a movement can be a life-changing experience with invaluable process learning that just cannot be replicated elsewhere.

Some organisations choose to focus their attention upon one part of the machinery, while others decide to leverage multiple mechanisms. Whichever path is chosen, the result is invariably more leaders, who are all better equipped to work with the future. Additionally, very tangible progress is made within the organisation in terms of strategy formulation, disruptive innovation or approach to change (sometimes all three)! Culture is positively impacted regardless and the invisible barriers between tribes start to evaporate as informal networks create a web of understanding and collaboration.

CHAPTER 18

A SPOONFUL OF SUGAR

I've already mentioned that I'm a firm believer that we make our own luck. In other words, our efforts best place us to take full advantage when luck decides to come to town. The very fact that you're reading this book means that you probably already have more than a passing interest in the future and how to best place you and your organisation to be a successful part of it.

Experience has taught me that the lucky ones are those who take time to work with the future. They seek to see around corners, they make every effort to transcend tribes, they think beyond current paradigms when considering wicked problems and they form magical movements to further meaningful causes.

Amongst the daily hubbub of operational deliverables, logistical challenges, stakeholder demands and financial pressure the lucky ones ensure they have an eye on the future. They know that it can't really be controlled or tamed, but they also understand that it can be examined for clues and influenced and encouraged to behave in certain ways.

Hopefully by now you can see how the four moves that make up the strategy to reality supersystem can deliver true value to your organisation. But what if your colleagues cannot quite see the point of engaging with a future that is, at best, unpredictable and, at worst, entirely uncontrollable while they grapple with the volatility of the present day?

How can you hope to encourage those around you to lift their heads from the fires they are fighting to consider the future for any sensible amount of time? How can we educate the uninitiated, influence potential early adopters, find first followers and eventually convince any doubters and naysayers?

I've found that a range of approaches can work and at times I've deployed all of them at once to wake up a leadership team to the inevitable crisis coming their way if they just keep on doing what they always have done.

FACTS AND FIGURES

Board members and executive leadership teams have a greater tendency than most to rely upon market data and financial information when considering options and making decisions. Decisions at this level carry great consequences and nobody really wants to get caught out having not done their homework. Intuition is often concealed behind a wall of numbers, and mere mention of a gut feeling (no matter how valid the feeling eventually turns out to be) can generate sneers of no confidence. The fascinating thing is that intuition is thought to be generated by our ability to notice a pattern that represents previously experienced patterns. In other words, when your intuition tells you something is either very right or very wrong it's often based on significant data – information gathered over many experiences that builds into a thought pattern. Subsequent reflection often unearths prior experiences where a similar pattern of data and human behaviour was evident and entirely valid to the matter in hand. This process happens so fast that we're blissfully unaware of it at the time.

I know you know that to work with the future is a good idea that will only leave your organisation better placed but, face it, you're going to have to work the numbers. Influencing senior leaders who have not already experienced and benefitted from this kind of approach will demand a set of data that shows the financial benefit of embarking on such activity and the risks and associated costs of not doing so. In short, your business case will need to show such things as evidence of depleting markets in core product areas, demographic shifts that are already impacting the bottom line and anticipated regulatory changes that have the capacity to inject greater risk and/or cost into the operating model. Each of these will need to be costed in terms of potential benefit or loss. In short, to get leaders across the line requires you to have already embarked upon working with the future!

GUERRILLA SCENARIOS

That leads me nicely to the next possible influencing tactic. Sometimes the only way to gain traction is to provide a proof of concept. And, guess what, the only way to generate a proof of concept is to run a trial or a pilot that generates positive, meaningful and potentially valuable results. Working undercover with a coalition of the willing to formulate some relatively straightforward scenarios that already show some promise is a great way to get the interest of those you need to convince. Simple scenarios that have taken little resource to create but deliver early signs of promising ideas, or identify new wicked problems that could become a valid and engaging cause, can shift the most embedded naysayer. It's difficult to argue that a process is superfluous and lacks value when it has already undeniably created value. Sometimes the most effective scenarios are created by relatively junior groups within the organisation attempting to highlight flaws and gaps within an existing strategy but finding that nobody above them in the established hierarchy will listen. Once potentially valuable guerrilla scenarios have been developed and shared, it is usually only a matter of time before at least some key stakeholders will convert initial interest into action.

ONE AT A TIME

Attempting to convince an established group of people with an embedded way of thinking and acting towards new ideas is tough. Presenting to a board or executive leadership team, without sufficient preparation or stakeholder engagement, is potentially a recipe for disaster – a disaster that cannot always be recovered from. When working to influence the opinions of a group it is always good policy to simultaneously influence the individuals within it. These individual conversations allow you to explore the history of the group and identify established allegiances and existing conflicts. It provides context in terms of past experiences that may support or detract from your point of view, and it delivers insight into who may become an ally or supporter. Taking time to engage with individuals to understand their map of the world is the first step towards influencing a group. Group dynamics operate like a typical wicked problem and so the same rules apply – attempt to achieve progress over winning, and bring people with you on the journey of discovery.

STORIES

People learn and relate through storytelling – it's what humans do. A compelling story can shift mindsets and broaden perspectives far more than an intellectual argument or heated debate. Think of organisations that have done what you are hoping to do and have achieved success through having done so. Also, think of those who have not taken the path you have suggested and are suffering as a result. Think of the Kodak moments either enjoyed or suffered by organisations and individuals that are recognisable to and connected with your audience. Find those that best reflect the present situation of your organisation and your leadership team and tell those stories. Make sure you tell the stories with energy, passion and belief. Make the linkages to your suggestions clear and undeniable. Create a compelling narrative that others would be foolish to ignore and embarrassed to later admit they did.

HINDSIGHT

Organisations are like people – they have all had positive and negative learning experiences. Some things we have done and decisions we have taken have turned out well, and others not so good. Leaders and leadership teams are the same; they have good times and bad times. Take a critical look back over the organisation's history and find examples of where things have gone particularly badly or astoundingly well and extrapolate the patterns of thought and behaviour that led to a given outcome. Often this analysis will present irrefutable evidence for the very activity you are seeking to embark upon, or at least that the present course is not one to be celebrated. Be careful how you serve this evidence as it can sting and cause an adverse reaction just when the medicine should be swallowed without further thought. Think hard about how you can best administer hindsight without receiving an unexpected sting from its tail. Choose the medicine wisely and then select the appropriate spoonful of sugar to help it go down.

RIGHT HERE RIGHT NOW

Take a look around you at the present situations your organisation and its leaders are in battle with. Wouldn't it have been great to have seen around the corner or over the horizon to notice their advance and have some pre-prepared strategies up hypothetical sleeves ready for immediate deployment? Notice the patterns that are gathering and already quietly whispering secrets about the next crisis sat just out of sight and already preparing to engulf all. Use the here and now to frame how the four moves of the strategy to reality supersystem could have enabled the organisation to have responded more quickly and appropriately to the current crisis, or how it could have better exploited a fast-emerging opportunity as it galloped over the horizon towards a major competitor.

HUMOUR

If all else fails humour and playfulness can achieve results where other tactics have failed. At one point in my career I worked in the legal sector. One of the partners of the law firm I worked for was habitually late for every meeting. It was a power play. By consistently arriving 20 minutes late for every meeting he was making our difference in authority very clear. Over time I learned to turn up 25 minutes late to his meetings and he gradually warmed to me. My show of confidence, playfulness and lack of reaction to his antics meant that he gradually came to respect me. He was also rather a traditional thinker and would typically refuse to engage with anything he considered to be 'New Age' thinking or a fad (for him this included many things). My refusal to be wrong-footed by his ego-antics gradually led to a situation where he would trust my judgement. I would often say to him 'Just humour me and tell me afterwards if you think it was a waste of time.' He did humour me, and we had great fun exploring all sorts of novel approaches to old problems. Not once did he subsequently tell me an activity had been a waste of time – and believe me he would have done so if he thought it was! Ideas deployed with patience, tact and humour, can sometimes, almost hypnotically, encourage people to experiment in ways they would never have otherwise allowed themselves to!

Perseverance and determination coupled with genuine curiosity and empathy (with a sprinkle of well-placed humour) will often open the toughest mind to at least listen to what you have to say.

CHAPTER 19

THE ONLY WAY IS GROWTH

Yes, I know we can't possibly all hope to just keep growing at the present rate and have a planet left beneath our feet to support our endeavours (or did I just burst your bubble?!). Before you all metaphorically throw a range of soft fruits in my direction, let me just define what I mean by growth.

Growth can mean many things. When used in the context of organisations, growth is often considered to mean an increase in size, an expansion in scale or an increase in monetary value or financial performance. Each of these things, of course, has its place and may be very important to you and your organisation at this stage in its lifecycle. Yet there is a subtler side to growth that has far deeper impact and feeds sustainability more readily than astounding feats of financial performance or speedy escalation to gargantuan size. Any organisation needs to be able to fund its activities and there is some truth in the idea that there's strength in numbers. Money and scale have importance, but focusing on these areas alone will render any growth achieved short-lived and potentially soul-destroying to the culture of the organisation.

Growth of the type that can genuinely fuel long-term ventures, spark disruptive innovation and shape futures beyond our wildest imaginations tends to be of a more spiritual and cultural variety. It involves a widening of awareness, a broadening of perspective and a heightening of shared consciousness. It relies upon collaboration, communication and co-creation with valued and trusted partners. In this sense growth is about the organisation and individuals within it developing physically, cognitively, emotionally and, dare I say it, spiritually.

Growth of this kind expands possibility, advances thinking and ultimately increases value through meaning, invention and progress. Truly valuable growth is the process of learning at all levels of the system and the cultivation of adaptability that leads to evolutionary changes and agile leaps in response to threats and opportunities. The kind of growth we're looking for is that which leaves us forever changed and positively changes the world one move at a time. Growth that augments reality, proliferates great ideas and increases our ability to be a force for good.

Shapeshifters share a desire to grow but know it's all about meaningful growth; the kind of growth that can keep us moving forward and leaves nobody behind.

CONCLUSION

CHANGE YOUR WORLD

Our magical mystery tour is very nearly at an end. On our journey we have met unicorns, imps, giants and dinosaurs and we have examined how shapeshifters are different and why they are so important to our shared future.

The four moves that enable shapeshifters to take strategy to reality in groundbreaking ways are the fundamental elements of a system of systems – the strategy to reality supersystem. A system made up of four moves which are themselves systems of human behaviour and complex psychosocial interaction framed within the structure, processes, technology and culture of organisational systems. While we have taken each move in turn as an independent system, it should now be obvious to all that they are not best approached as a simple linear path. The moves coexist and interweave, a change to one effects change in another and they convincingly show spooky action at a distance.

The organisation is at once a connected whole yet comprised of individual and independent parts and mechanisms that have the ability and authority to impact the overall system. There is an entirely individual and unique pattern to each organisation, but the moves can be a useful framework from which to map our understanding of where an organisation works, and where it works less well; how it manifests symptoms that divulge its deepest problems and where we can best create positive change.

The strategy to reality supersystem is a real-life example of a wicked problem in action. It has a pattern that appears differently depending upon which angle it is viewed from. It is connected to many other systems and supersystems to form a wicked web of interacting wicked problems. Taking the time to fully understand and engage with this wicked problem and the strategy to reality supersystem may just save your organisation. It has inbuilt mechanisms to future-proof strategy and render it supple to disruption, to invent game-changing products and services that meet the future head-on, whichever form that future may take. It gives foundation to the magic of movements that are built around meaningful causes and it enables meta-tribes to emerge that transcend all other tribes. The strategy to reality supersystem is your guide to becoming a shapeshifter. It's the blueprint for an organisation that not only shifts in response to the world around it and the future as it emerges, but an organisation equipped to shape that future and invent the games it wants to play.

Shapeshifters are leading a leadership revolution – leaders are everywhere, and everyone is a leader. In a shapeshifter there's nowhere for potential to hide! Shapeshifters use the machinery of the strategy to reality supersystem to allow their leaders to find a voice and flourish in their favour. Use this book to turn a super storm into a supersystem. Thriving, striving or just about surviving, all organisations need to be able to master the art of working with the future.

DO IT – DO IT NOW!

Look around you – there really is no time to delay! Don't look back and think 'if only', look forward and think 'what if'! The world is changing around you as sure as you live and breathe. The post-truth fast show is getting faster and less predictable by the minute. You can't control the future, but you can work with it so that it has less control over you. You can practise for its many alternative paths and better prepare yourself for its best and its worst realities. You can influence its shape and protect against its impact. Work with others to build strength and change the game. Co-create the novel ideas that will bring the future alive. Combined you can shift paradigms and change the game forever, acting consciously, collectively and creatively to shape the future – being a shapeshifter!

Don't miss your Kodak moment! Make the most of the embryonic creative magical movements bubbling under the surface of your official organisation and spot major shifts in reality long before they take proper hold and change habits forever in ways that were previously unimaginable.

Don't allow your organisation to become a safe refuge for the horsemen of the strategy apocalypse! Step up to the strategic challenges facing your organisation and make a conscious choice to work with the future in a more meaningful way.

Don't find yourself on the wrong side of an event or series of events that change reality! Take the decision to make space for serendipity. Look around corners, transcend tribes, ponder the wickedest problems, think beyond and join together to form magical movements.

Don't be a dinosaur – do it now before it's too late! Giants, imps and would-be unicorns – whether you're thriving, striving or just about surviving, the rules of the game are the same. Step forward to shape your destiny and fully commit to studying the art of working with the future. May the force be with you and the odds forever in your favour.

WELCOME TO OUR META-TRIBE

I set up Gallus in the summer of 2008. Since then, I've been privileged to work alongside my colleagues with many fascinating and ambitious clients (some are profiled in the case studies throughout this book). Most of our clients have negotiated substantial transformations, some have entered into major mergers and acquisitions, and others have navigated IPOs (initial public offerings). We now work with all sorts of organisations – commercial businesses, social enterprises, public bodies and NGOs – large and small, to create strategic success and drive social change.

The concept of a shapeshifter organisation was born of these experiences. The shapeshifter attributes, capabilities and methods you have met throughout this book are those that have been seen to have sustainable and tangible positive impact in those organisations we have partnered with that have achieved remarkable success.

As our clients' needs have shifted so has our operating model. Gallus has reinvented itself continuously over the last decade. Our ambition is to positively change the world one move at a time. Our mission is to co-create the future and to generate sustainable value and growth in an increasingly complex and unpredictable world; a world where novel ideas and bold moves drive longevity.

Our methods spark debate, create shared ambition and co-create practical and enduring solutions. Our approach drives clarity, generates momentum and cultivates the strategic capabilities critical to success. We work with our clients to future-proof their strategy, untangle their wicked problems and capture the pivotal moments for positive change. In a nutshell, we take our clients on a journey from strategy to reality.

If you would like to find out more about who we are, what we do and how we do it, take a look at our website: gallusconsulting.com. You will also find information about the open programmes we run and the causes we deeply care about. You can learn more from other shapeshifters in action by listening to our *shapeshiftertribe* podcast.

We look forward to hearing from you and perhaps working with you one day – welcome to our meta-tribe!

ACKNOWLEDGEMENTS

Thanks to my editor, Julia Kellaway, who has helped me to gather 10 years of thinking into a readable format, and has become the most trusted critical friend throughout the process.

Thanks to Blayney Partnership for their trademark creative genius and beautifully designed cover artwork. Thanks also to the team at Troubador for bringing the book into production and managing its distribution.

A massive thank you to those who have contributed thoughts and encouragement along the way, and of course to the many people and organisations I have the privilege to call clients past and present – without our shared experiences this book would never have been written.

And an enormous thank you to the organisations and leaders that have appeared throughout the book as shapeshifters in action. The UK CAA, CAAi, University of Salford and WorldFirst have added a dimension to this book that shows how the shapeshifter journey is never done and is one of constant discovery. In particular I'd like to thank Ben Alcott, Tim Johnson, Mark Swan, Robert Ritchie, Jonathan Quin and Katie Brownridge for their contributions and support.

Most of all, thank you to Anna Ricchetti, my colleague and friend who has travelled every step of this journey with me, learning as we go!

There are many friends near and far who have provided emotional support, practical advice and much-needed nagging! You know who you are! Thank you!

Thanks to my dad who taught me that there are no real limits, only imagined ones, and to my mum, who, despite her considerable struggles with dementia, has always remained aware of the book, interested in its progress and encouraging to me throughout without any prompting from others – your courage and strength has inspired a cause.

Finally this book would not have seen daylight (and I would not have remained sane) without the unerring support of my husband Andrew (the best-kept secret coach in the world) and my daughter India (who constantly stretches my imagination and whose understanding, creativity and insight surprises and delights me every day).

Last but not least, thank you to Bonnie and Buster (our two rescue dogs) for their patience and cuddles (and amusing distractions from constant mischief)!

ENDNOTES

1   VUCA is an acronym to describe volatility, uncertainty, complexity and ambiguity of a contextual environment or situation. The concept was introduced by the US Army War College in reaction to the end of the Cold War. More recently the term has been widely used in strategic planning by organisations from many sectors.

2   Stanislaw Lem (1921–2006) was a Polish author, best known for his science fiction writing.

3   A unicorn is a privately held start-up company valued at over $1 billion. Venture capitalist Aileen Lee was the first to use the phrase in this context.

4   An Initial Public Offering (IPO) is the initial stock market launch of a company where shares of the company are sold to institutional investors and usually also retail investors. Through this process, the company is transformed into a public company. It is often used to raise capital or monetise the investments of private shareholders.

5   Lao Tzu, otherwise known as Laozi, was a Chinese philosopher and writer of ancient times. He is the reputed author of the *Tao Te Ching* and the founder of Taoism.

6   The larvae of the Ichneumon wasp live as parasites inside caterpillars.

7   Daniel C Dennett, *Intuition Pumps and Other Tools for Thinking* (WW Norton & Company, 2013).

8   A heuristic is an approach to problem-solving that can be used to speed up the process. The term is often used to refer to unconsciously used mental shortcuts.

9   Neurodiversity refers to variations in the human brain regarding sociability, learning, attention, mood and other mental functions. The term was popularised by Australian sociologist Judy Singer and American journalist Harvey Blume.

10 Dr Seuss was the pen name for Theodor Seuss Geisel, an American children's author, cartoonist and animator who wrote and illustrated more than 60 books.

11 Simon Sinek is a British-American author and motivational speaker. He is the author of five books including *Start With Why* (Penguin Books, 2011).

12 A snap general election took place on 8 June 2017. It was called by Prime Minister Theresa May on 18 April 2017 in an attempt to strengthen the Conservative majority in advance of Brexit negotiations. The election returned a minority government and a confidence and supply agreement was struck with the DUP (Democratic Unionist Party) by the Conservative party in order to remain in power.

13 International Business Machines Corporation (IBM) is an American multinational information technology company headquartered in Armonk, New York, with operations in over 170 countries.

14 Nokia is a Finnish, multinational telecommunications, information technology and consumer electronics company.

15 *National Geographic* is the official magazine of the National Geographic Society. It was first published in 1888 and primarily contains articles about science, geography, history and world culture.

16 Aileen Lee is the founder of Cowboy Ventures and is credited with first using the term 'unicorn' in relation to high-value privately owned start-up companies.

17 A wicked problem is a problem that is difficult or impossible to solve. Complex interdependencies, contradictory perspectives, changing requirements and evolving contexts all render the problem socially complex and ongoing. The phrase was initially used in social planning.

18 Groupthink is a phenomenon that occurs within a group of people where the desire for conformity and harmony cause irrational decisions and dysfunctional thinking.

19 Gamification is the application of game design and game principles in a non-game context. It is sometimes used to solve problems or drive engagement.

20 Quantum mechanics (also known as quantum physics, quantum theory or matrix mechanics) is a theory in physics which describes nature at the smallest scales of energy levels of atoms and subatomic particles.

21 Malcolm Gladwell, *Outliers: The Story of Success* (Little, Brown and Company, 2008).

22 Confucius was a Chinese philosopher and politician (551–479 BCE) who brought forth the school of thought known as Confucianism.

23 *Sliding Doors* is a romantic comedy-drama film, written by Peter Howitt and starring Gwyneth Paltrow, first released in 1998. The film alternates between two storylines showing the two paths the main character's life could take as a result of catching or missing a train.

24 Hive mind is a large group of people who share their knowledge or opinions with one another and connect to demonstrate collective intelligence or unified consciousness. Swarm intelligence is the collective behaviour of decentralised, self-organised systems, natural or artificial. The expression was introduces by Gerardo Beni and Jing Wang in 1989 in relation to robotic systems.

25 Douglas Noel Adams (1952–2001) was an English author and scriptwriter. His most notable work is *The Hitchhiker's Guide to the Galaxy* which originated as a BBC radio comedy before being developed into a series of books, a TV series and later a film. Margaret Atwood is a Canadian writer who has written many works of science fiction, historical fiction and dystopian fiction. She is perhaps best known for *The Handmaid's Tale*, first published in 1985 and recently adapted into a TV series. George Orwell (1903–1950) was an English novelist and journalist, best known for 1984, first published in 1949. Ursula K Le Guin (1929–2018) was an American author best known for her works of speculative fiction. Through her works she explored many present-day social issues.

26 SWOT analysis is a strategic planning tool used to help a person or organisation identify strengths, weaknesses, opportunities and threats. Strengths and weaknesses are typically internal, while opportunities and threats are often external in nature.

27 Pestle analysis is a framework used to analyse a range of macro-environmental factors. It is widely used in strategy formulation, market research and risk management.

28 Margaret Atwood, *The Handmaid's Tale* (McClelland and Stewart, 1985).

29 Prime Minister Gordon Brown had repeatedly referenced an end to the cycle of boom and bust – a phrase that came back to haunt him in the autumn of 2008.

30 Peter Senge, *The Fifth Discipline* (Currency, 1990).

31 Target Operating Model (TOM) is a description of the future desired state of the operating model of an organisation, function or business unit.

32 Erwin Schrödinger (1887–1961) was a Nobel-prize-winning Austrian physicist who developed a number of hypotheses in the field of quantum theory.

33 The BP Deepwater Horizon oil spill began on 20 April 2010 in the Gulf of Mexico on the BP-operated Macondo Prospect. It is considered to be the largest oil spill in the history of the petroleum industry.

34 Memetics is the study of information and culture based on an analogy with Darwinian evolution. It attempts to describe how an idea can propagate successfully.

35 Singularity is a point at the centre of a black hole where matter is infinitely dense.

36 Horst Rittel (1930–1990) and Melvin M Webber (1920–2006) were academics who contributed to the definition of wicked problems.

37 Peter Ferdinand Drucker (1909–2005) was an Austrian born American management consultant, educator and author.

38 Richard Pascale, Jerry Sternin, Monique Sternin, *The Power of Positive Deviance: How Unlikely Innovators Solve the World's Toughest Problems* (Harvard Business Review Press, 2010).

39 *The Hitchhiker's Guide to the Galaxy* by Douglas Adams was originally a BBC radio series later adapted into a series of books, a TV show and a film.

40 Steve Paul Jobs (1955–2011) was an American business leader and investor. He was chairman, CEO and co-founder of Apple Inc.

41 *Tomorrow's World* was a long-running BBC TV series on new developments in science and technology first broadcast in July 1965.

42 *Star Trek* started life as a science fiction TV series created by Gene Roddenberry. First broadcast in 1966 the TV series followed the adventures of James T Kirk and the crew of the Starship Enterprise. The original series was the forerunner to many sequels and films.

Printed in Great
Britain
by Amazon